FORTUNE

Molls,.
My whirlins,
healins, & feelins
friend.
Thank you
for beins part
of our life.
Bonne

FORTUNE

Our Deep Dive into the Mysteries of Love, Healing, and Success

Bruce Miller

Miller eMedia
Decatur

Miller eMedia LLC
615 Sycamore Street
Decatur, GA 30030
www.milleremedia.com

Photos: Both cover shots were taken when we were in our twenties. Karen had just met Reshad and was photographed alongside him (cropped out for the cover). Bruce's photo: I was a senior at UCLA when, at Mory's suggestion, we took a self-timer portrait together. Mory is also cropped out for this cover. Back cover portrait by Jill Hendrix Photography.

Contents

1

A hurricane never lasts beyond the morning,
Nor does a rainstorm endure the livelong day.
Yang Hsiung 53 BC – 18 AD

It's 3:00 a.m., full moon, and for the third night in a row, the top of my head buzzes with an energy that makes sleep impossible. This uninvited buzz has bolted me from bed to flesh out *Fortune*, the book that has been floating inside for 30 years.

I didn't know where to start, so I let the words spew out:

"So this is some kind of nirvana?"

And then a 4.1 earthquake hit.

Two quick thoughts: "1) Georgia doesn't have earthquakes, and 2) better keep writing."

And so I am.

My fault line triggered for a good reason. For the last 15 years, I was a partner in Design Coup, a marketing design firm in Atlanta. Two days before Thanksgiving, Matthew, my business partner asked me to go to lunch — nothing out of the usual; we went to lunch most days. As I grabbed my coat, the phone rang. It was my Taoist friend, Corinne.

"Hey, Corinne, what's up?"

"Bruce, I would like to offer you some angels."

Corinne seemed both generous and concerned.

"I was going to offer these angels to Karen," Corinne continued, "but after thinking about it, I've decided to offer them to you."

Great, my very own set of angels – invisible ones. My business was falling apart, my wife Karen was falling apart, and now Corinne called to offer me Gabriel, Michael, Raphael, Uriel, and Metatron.

Who the hell is Metatron?

To receive my angels, I would need to follow elaborate instructions. But rather than kicking the angels to the curb, I shocked myself when I uttered, without hesitation or consideration, "I'll take them." And off to lunch we went.

Matthew and I sat in our favorite corner of the Corner Pub. I love to order off the menu, so I ordered my regular – half Cuban and half veggie Cuban, what I called the Fusion Cuban. Our brand development business excelled at naming things — products, start-ups, Web domains, tag lines — so, I never understood why the Corner Pub didn't realize the brilliance of "Fusion Cuban" and put it on the menu.

Matthew didn't bite into his sandwich. He sat quietly and then casually unloaded:

"I've decided to leave the business."

Matthew's calm masked his discomfort.

"I'm going to work for Thrive Farmers."

Thrive Farmers was a coffee brand we developed from scratch and nurtured (without much payment) until it hit the jackpot. We developed the pitch to Chick-fil-A who adopted Thrive Farmers as their official coffee brand. It was a brand coup that came to fruition after only 18 months from the seed idea. Like Fusion Cuban, Thrive was one of my name babies. Our business dream was to build a startup client into a national brand, then charge full agency rates — something that always eluded Design Coup. Thrive Farmers was our success story, and now Matthew was leaving to become an employee and take Thrive Farmers with him.

"When are you leaving?" I asked.

"In a month."

Matthew was oblivious to the emotional and financial havoc his decision would unleash. But for now, I was thoughtful and stoic.

"Hmm. Okay," I said.

Rather than saying "fuck you" for collapsing our 15-year-old creative business without making an effort to map out a transition plan, my inner scriptwriter saw all the plot pieces falling into place. I hate it when shitty events reflect divine perfection.

Matthew and I made an impossible marriage. He was a right-wing control freak, and I'm way on the left. I'm okay letting things unfold. Talking politics was a disaster. My world view wants to embrace the whole, while Matthew would arm himself with talking points from Fox News. I likened our creative partnership to The Beatles. We were like Paul and John, pop musician and radical thinker. The Beatles made world-changing music, but they lasted all of six years on the American scene. Design Coup's creative act outlasted the Fab Four with a fifteen-year run. But all creative streaks end in a rut. The energetic structure of the musical octave guarantees it – but I'll get into that later.

Matthew expected me to buy out his half of the business. It made sense on paper, but John would never buy The Beatles from Paul. That would be like buying half a poodle — minus the best client.

My emotional freak-out came later that night — and night after night. An alarm clock of dread would wake me every night at 4:00 a.m. You see, I'm at the age where you no longer look for a job. I didn't realize the degree to which Design Coup cushioned my brain from the fragility of existence.

Fearful of my future, I fell to my knees each night in a mix of prayer and despair. When Corinne's angels arrived like a set of imaginary friends, I was thrilled to have signed up. The good Fortune of having a five-day supply of angels was proof that I still had an ace in the hole to play in life's game. They offered hope that the structural dissolution of my livelihood would portend something better.

The angels came with elaborate directions — imagine Ikea angels packed with an annoying instruction sheet. I had to procure a five-day glass votive candle, a fresh white flower, an apple, three written wishes, and follow very specific instructions for their arrival, stay, and departure.

As a procrastinator around emotional pain, I waited until 5 p.m. on angel day to start the project. I drove to what our neighborhood referred to as "the little Kroger" and quickly realized that I had not thought this out. Working parents swarmed the store desperate for dinner. I headed to the flower bin and found tired bouquets of fake-colored mums. Next, I went to the candle aisle — no glass votives. I dialed Corinne in a panic.

"Corinne, I am struggling here," I pleaded. "Where are you?"

"I'm at the Big Kroger, getting ready to check out," Corinne replied.

I clung to this small shred of Fortune like a miracle. Corinne kindly left her place in line and headed to the candle section.

"I can get you Jesus on the Cross," Corinne offered. "Seems a little heavy. How about the Immaculate Conception or Our Lady of Guadalupe."

"None of those are really my scene," I snarked.

My genetic sense of irony was helping me feel myself again. Jesus suffering the sins of the world freaked me as a child, and Mary's fate did not end so well from a mother's point of view. I opted for the Lady from Guadalupe. As a supernatural vision, she seemed more receptive to good Fortune.

With the candle scored, I raced to the Dekalb Farmer's Market, a one-acre building jammed with shoppers and employees from around the world. By now it was raining. I sprinted to the flower section and grabbed a white lily.

"This is insane," I thought while dripping in the checkout line. "These angels are pushing me to the edge, and THEY'RE NOT EVEN REAL!"

That evening, I followed the instructions to the letter. I put my three wishes into an envelope – one for Mother Earth, one for my family, and one for me. The last wish — for me— was the hardest. Was I hoping for my emotional discomfort to go away? Or, did I seek for some vaguely-defined future providence to come into my life? I decided to get more specific. *Fortune.* I want some good old fashioned Fortune. Yes, it's okay to ask. It's been a bummer year, and it's time to open the door to Fortune.

At the appointed hour and minute of 11 p.m., I opened the door and invited the cold December night into our home. Hopefully, the angels would slip in, too. As per printed instructions, I recited:

> "Hallo and Welcome Archangels to my home. You were sent to me from Corinne. I am very grateful to each of you for purifying and bringing peace to this place and to beings that live in it. I am very grateful to you for bringing harmony, joy, and serenity to all of us. I am very grateful to you for fulfilling my wishes."

For the next five days, Karen and I huddled in our small study whenever our spirits needed boosting. Quietly, we bathed in the flickering glow of our angels. The candle, apple, white flower and three wishes felt like random symbols, but we were deeply comforted by having the angels in our home.

Years ago, Reshad Feild, my Sufi teacher, explained that angels are not pudgy little babes with wings. Technically, they are "harmonics." Pluck a guitar string and natural frequencies vibrate. Angels represent our higher vibrations — the finer sensibilities of our being. These subtle sensations routinely get squelched by the daily onslaught of living. The instructions told me what to expect:

> From that moment on, the archangels make things happen. It is recommended to regard the five days as a special time to give room for the vibration of higher energies to re-align many things. For some, this may mean you want to ask questions, or you may only be able to find a quiet moment in your busy day. But remember, there is no limitation, TRUST.

Yeah, trust. In today's world, it's criminal to trust. Trust destroys logic, the scientific method, and consensus reality. My wife, Karen often tells me to trust, but doing so would defy my emotional instincts and my adult sense of responsibility. But, sometimes trust is all you get.

The culmination of the angel visit happened to be on my birthday — two weeks after Matthew dropped the bomb. To celebrate, I cooked Coq au Vin and apple pie for ten guests. Dinner parties have always served as a measuring stick for the quality of my life, and this one unfolded as a rich orchestration of passion and personalities. As we sat down to eat, something lifted from my heart. Thank- you angels for performing your magic.

Afterward, with the house sweetly quiet, Karen and I snuggled in our angel sanctuary. As is our custom, we measure the "afterglow" of each party. Feeling a heart-warming gratitude, we scored the "glow" a ten. For a brief moment, the angels had lifted my fear and heaviness.

As per the instructions, I burnt the paper with my three wishes, ate the apple, and sent the angels off on their missions. At that moment, Glinda, the Good Witch could have appeared explaining that there were never any angels, not one, let alone five. The angels were inside me all the time, blah, blah, blah. But, it wouldn't have mattered; the afterglow was real.

2

Belly Brain

*The lotus flower sends forth pure white blossoms
from roots sunk deep in muddy water.*

Daisaku Ikeda

The afterglow was short-lived.

It's New Year's Eve, early afternoon. I'm at the bank. Just me and two bank tellers who want to go home. I return the expensive check scanning machine that worked two times, close out the feeble checking account, pay off the $30,000 line of credit with my retirement savings, and pull the plug on the business. I sense a weird feeling — like the sinking atmosphere that proceeds a tornado.

"Shit, it's noon," I realize calculating my timing. "If I get home by 12:15, that leaves five minutes for lunch before Karen's doctor appointment."

I'm impeccable (or maybe anal) when it comes to time. If I can master time (or so I pretend), I can master myself. Science acknowledges that time is something perceived, a perception. Our sense of time changes with boredom, excitement, aging, meditation, sex, and the endless summers of childhood. If time is a malleable perception and not an absolute, then the "perceiver" of time must be able to stand outside of time, observe time, and even shape time.

For this reason, I like to play with time. I like to goose the time gods to deliver a timely arrival despite bad traffic or whip up a three-course meal in an hour. Today, I was pushing it. Karen had a 1:00 p.m. doctor's appointment across town. Feeling the pressure, I called Karen.

"Karen, can you make me a sandwich? I'll be there in twelve or thirteen minutes."

"Okay, I love you; be safe," she replied.

Karen sounded fragile, but I visualized her packed and ready to go. I turned onto the freeway and switched to action mode.

"Maybe I can gain a minute for lunch," I muttered.

Bargaining with the traffic gods, I penetrated the atoms of time that stood between me and the cars ahead. I visualized the five-minute drill: Eat with one hand, scoop up Karen's things, fill a cup of water for the road, and take my convoluted back-route across town to Buckhead.

I exited the freeway, got two free green lights (woohoo) and stole a minute.

I raced up the driveway and jumped out of the car. Still in action mode, I whipped into the kitchen.

And then… whoa, something's not right. My inner clock froze. The scene shifted to slo-mo.

Karen stood at the counter fiddling with sandwich parts. She looked out of sorts — in a wholly different time zone. I down-shifted further as she looked up. Our eyes lingered briefly in the void.

"I wanted to make you a sandwich," Karen offered sweetly, but sounding more like pleading.

I scanned the scene. A four-dollar box of fancy lettuce littered the floor.

"I wanted to make you a sandwich," Karen repeated.

I could see through her eyes. The sandwich was to consummate our love, but bigger forces conspired against it.

"What happened?" I asked.

My heart changed gears; my time game crashed to a stop.

"I don't know. I really wanted to make you a sandwich — for you."

The extra punctuation — for you — underscored the Herculean love task, unfulfilled. I grabbed a broom, swept the lettuce, glopped mayo onto bread, plopped some turkey, and squeezed the kid-like sandwich into a one-handed meal.

"Let's get in the car," I said.

We were in week six of what we now refer to Biblically as "The Six Weeks."

Six weeks ago, Karen passed a grueling, three-year journey to attain professional certification in Clinical Pastoral Education or CPE. This achievement lets her train ministers and seminary students to deepen their pastoral skills. These students pop out of school with deeply-felt but often naive ideas about God and ministry. Karen leads them through a life-changing journey of self-reflection, embodiment, and presence so that they can be useful as hospital chaplains in a crisis.

The Six Weeks began when Karen passed what is known around here as The Committee — similar to a dissertation and oral defense. The challenge was to remain bright, outgoing, and collegial while you and your work are grilled by a panel of five. If you fail to pass, it's "sorry, see you next year," and you start all over again.

So, six weeks ago, Karen finally passed attempt Number Three by surmounting the waves of anxiety that sunk her previous attempts. I can't overstate the accomplishment. Each attempt summoned the spiritual, mental, and emotional strength of the entire family — and earned me lifetime spouse points. Most importantly, by passing, Karen made peace with her childhood history and self-esteem.

Committee denials Number One and Number Two were devastating.

For her first try, Karen got the thumbs-down in Washington DC and then was unable to return to Atlanta to tend to our son who needed emergency surgery.

Committee failure Number Two ended famously with Karen using the "f" word.

This takes us to Committee Three, but first, let's turn back the clock a few months.

Karen and I were hanging out at our little cabin on a lake in Turtletown, Tennessee. I hadn't brought anything to read because I planned to sit and notice things. If you choose to become a student of Fortune, it's all about "noticing" — noticing how little things add up to something important. I've come to understand that I'm powerless to affect the flow of little things, but I can respond to their promptings, and this requires noticing. Little by little, noticing becomes the only game in town, the only tool to carve out a meaningful Fortunate life.

With nothing to read, I turned to interrupt Karen, but she was quicker on the draw.

"Here, read this," she muttered tossing a magazine.

The cover caught my eye: *Out of Our Heads: Philip Shepherd On The Brain In Our Belly.*

"I think you'll like it," she said, returning to her book.

I took this as a wifely dig at my in-head-ness, but something clicked when I read the blurb:

"Scientists recognize that the web of neurons lining the gastrointestinal tract act as an independent brain — and a new field of medicine, neurogastroenterology, has been created to study it."[1]

Wow, an independent brain? I could use one.

The article interviewed Canadian author and actor, Philip Shepherd, who spent a lifetime exploring what he calls the "belly brain." For the last five thousand years or so, according to Shepherd, our culture has fixated on a head-centered, thinking-brain approach to organizing life. Philip described an equally vibrant neurological center in the gut — the enteric nervous system or "belly brain." This other brain knows things intuitively, connects us to each other, serves as the seat of pure feeling, and engages our experience of the world.

Philip's inciting incident occurred when, as a seventeen-year-old,

1. Amnon, Buchbinder. 2013. "Out Of Our Heads: Philip Shepherd On The Brain In Our Belly." Sun Magazine, April.

he had the idea to bicycle from England to Japan. Peddling around the planet must have seemed totally plausible to a teenager, so he acted on it. He slept in olive groves in Greece, worked on an Arab cargo boat in the Mediterranean, bedded under the stars in the Great Syrian Desert, spent a night in an Iraqi police station, toured with an Indian theater troupe, and eventually made it to Japan.

In Japan, the young Philip encountered *Noh,* the world's oldest ongoing theater art. This highly ritualized, medieval form of drama uses masks, chanting and movement rather than personality conflict to *embody* the drama. The experience awakened Philip's inner question and propelled his life journey to explore body-centered ways of knowing.

I was transfixed by the prospect of a whole new body part — the belly brain, so I called my angel-supplier, Corinne.

"Corinne, what do you know about the belly brain?"

"I would imagine it's similar to the lower *dan tien* in Tai Chi and Qi gong," Corinne replied.

I proposed that we co-lead a six-week study class on this other brain, that my knowledge of transformation and Corinne's understanding of Taoism and movements would mesh. It was more a mash-up than a mesh, but our belly brain class was a success.

A few weeks after the belly brain class, Karen and I returned to our little lake dock to savor the tranquility of the waning summer. In the distance, I could hear "splish-splash, ka-plish, ka-splash." I looked up; a lady was swimming with her dog, headed our way.

Five yards from the dock, I could see that it was Terri, a yoga teacher I knew from our little town of Decatur, Georgia. Avery, her big black Lab swam dutifully at her side. Terri had the nautical decorum to tread water without invading our sanctuary.

Terri, is that you?" I called out.

"Hi Bruce," Terri huffed back. "How's it going?"

"Great… and permission to come aboard," I replied.

Terri and Avery climbed onto the dock. With one big shake, Avery destroyed my tranquility.

"So, what are you up to?" I asked.

"I just came back from a seminar in Toronto. It was on this really neat island with no cars."

"That's funny," I said. "I read an article about an actor who lived on a car-free island in Toronto. His name was Philip Shepherd."

"That's the guy!" Terri exclaimed. "The seminar was with Philip Shepherd!"

Terri had journeyed to Toronto after reading the same article. She made a strong connection and considered inviting Philip to Decatur. I was mind-blown by the synchronicity, but with so much coming up, I knew to avoid getting too involved. I would be leading my annual course in the turn of the Whirling Dervishes and Karen would be in super-stress mode preparing for Committee Number Three.

I didn't completely blow off the idea of Philip coming to Decatur, because if you study Fortune like I do, you follow life like breadcrumbs in the forest. The thing about crumbs is that birds eat them and if they're pumpernickel, the caraway seeds might re-sprout in another time and place. In this way, Fortune doesn't follow a linear sense of time and causality. Like a well-crafted screenplay, seeds get planted early in the story to reemerge in act III.

At this point, Philip Shepherd had sprouted twice in my life, and now I began to suspect that he would pop up later. Rumi describes this mish-mashed sense of causality:

> Were he not impelled by desire of fruit,
> The gardener would never have planted the tree.
> Therefore in reality the tree is born from the fruit,
> Though seemingly the fruit is born from the tree.
> — Rumi

From a cause and effect point of view, trees make fruit. But from Fortune's point of view, fruit is the cause of the tree — the tree's purpose. In a similar manner, our life's fruit drives our story. When we discover our purpose, we realize that our destination has propelled the narrative. The fruit is the driving force. In this way, Fortune unfolds from necessity and reveals itself as the future flowing into the present.

Several weeks after Terri and Avery splashed onto my dock, I spotted Terri selling charity tickets from a small table in front of a store in downtown Decatur.

"Hey, Terri," I said. "How's that Philip visit coming?"

"Funny you should ask," Terri replied. "He's coming in seven days, and I'm still struggling to find a place for him to stay. He may be sleeping on a cot in my basement."

"That's a bummer," I said, keeping my generosity in check.

That night, I shared the Philip news with Karen. She looked up from her Committee documents and replied matter-of-factly, "I think we should invite him."

"Karen, we can't always be taking care of the universe," I stammered. "We can't have some Canadian actor in our house on the day of your Committee!"

§

Seven days later, I glanced at my watch and mentally calculated: Plane landed at 3:30 p.m., 20 minutes for baggage, 35 minutes on the freeway, 60-minute lunch — make that 75 minutes. Should be here now.

Just then, a car pulled up to our back door. (Quick mental note: Fortune always sneaks in through the back door.)

Out stepped a bright and supercharged Philip Shepherd running at 220 volts.

"HOW ARE YOU? WHAT A JOY TO BE HERE!" Philip regaled with his unbridled tenor.

We hugged like the longest of friends.

"THANK YOU SO MUCH FOR INVITING ME TO YOUR HOME!" Philip announced with overflowing Shakespearean gratitude.

My keyboard can't express the *voce profonda* that Philip's fully-awakened belly projected.

As I lay in bed that night, I contemplated the chain of events — one moment Karen tosses a magazine and the next moment Mr. Belly Brain himself is sharing our upstairs bathroom.

After 29 years of marriage, I've learned to begrudgingly accept Karen's intuitive instincts — particularly when it's off the wall. The truth is, I secretly wanted Philip to stay with us. My own belly brain is prone to be tight and timid. My hard-wired patterns were formed in a cerebral Jewish family from Chicago. My brilliant engineer dad and my outgoing narcissistic mom didn't converse through feelings, and this probably stunted my own *voce profonda*. So, when Karen reasoned that Philip might give her the belly boost needed to surmount her anxiety, I didn't resist. I could already feel Philip's vibrational resonance awakening my dormant underworld.

Philip was the perfect guest. All he required were copious cups of British tea. I tended to his needs while Karen worked with a newly-arrived Committee Report — a packet detailing how the Committee planned to test her mettle.

The next morning, Karen and I walked to the local hotel where the Committee would take place. It was a stroke of Fortune that the national ACPE Committee was being held a few blocks from our house.

"Hold my hand," Karen instructed as we walked. "That's too fast."
So I slowed.

"Stop, I want to take a breath."

Like an executioner's walk, Karen measured each step. Between our house and the hotel, we stopped maybe 20 times. We finally entered the hotel where she was warmly received by her peers. I knew she was in good hands and that the Committee gods would be kind today.

I headed to Philip's seminar to invert my thinking brain.

"If you look at human history," Philip explained to the class, "we used to experience our center of thinking in the belly and that seems bizarre today. With the Neolithic revolution, we began to take control of the world around us, and our thinking center began to migrate up. Our allegiance turned from the goddess of the Earth to the gods in the sky."

I wasn't so sure about this. I know people whose feelings hijack their thinking, and it's not always a good thing. But rather than resist, I stayed with it.

"Locate the perineum," Philip instructed, "that little muscle at the pelvic floor, and then imagine a hollow column running up through your body like an elevator shaft. You can follow this shaft from the pelvic floor to the top of the scalp."

We all closed our eyes and sensed our bodies.

"Locate the center of your awareness in your head. If you can find it at the top of the shaft, you can move it slowly down the shaft. Feel that center of awareness descend like a pearl dropped into a vat of olive oil until it finally comes to rest at the perineum."

This part wasn't so easy. Compared to my head, this lower place of awareness felt fuzzy and blocked.

"Understand that when you arrive at the perineum, you are in a place of pure feeling. You're in a place that doesn't require supervision or comment or judgment. So give yourself permission to allow that to fall away."

For the next few hours, we squatted and moved and touched and growled and groaned — all to build awareness of this lower center. Like Orpheus, Philip was leading us to the Underworld to reclaim our long lost Eurydice.

The seminar culminated with the Mirror Exercise. Philip explained that the exercise would expose the fundamental human schism — the conflict between body and brain — and how we think independently from being.

It was my turn to face the mirror. Philip asked me to recite a simple verse while mirroring his movements. It sounded easy. I recited the verse as Philip lunged left and I followed. Soon, the exercise grew intense. Philip squatted lower and lower. My legs and thighs began to burn. Philip would not allow me to recite "once upon a time" in a mousy voice. He challenged me to seize the body energy — the thigh burn — and transmute that burn with heroic exhortations: "O N C E U P O N A T I M E!!!"

I squatted eye-to-eye with Philip and let it rip. I broached my cathartic edges. The glacial ice shielding my netherworld cracked and groaned. What was this visceral feeling? The group applauded my emotional daring. I switched to a Hebrew prayer: "B A R U C H A T A H A D O N A I." My inner nerd exploded like a thundering Moses on the mountain.

Shaking from newfound energy, I sat down to regain my composure. Then my phone beeped. All eyes turned to me as I took the call. It was Karen.

"Bruce, I passed, I passed." Karen reveled in wonderment as if waking from a fairy tale. "Bruce, it was the most amazing moment. Right before I started they said, 'We want to certify you today.' I couldn't believe it; my anxiety left; I got into this place; I was in command; I was engaged the whole time. Oh, Bruce, I am so happy."

By now, we were both crying. Three slogging long years: Committee One and setback, Committee Two and the "f" word. Finally, Committee Three and success. In theory, it's possible to pull free from one's karmic gravity — your emotional escape velocity — but I was never convinced, until now.

That night, the four walls of our kitchen burst with love and celebration. Food and friends appeared, wine poured freely, toasts were made, music throbbed, and we danced. Karen's hero's journey was palpable — the ordeal, the reward, the resurrection and now, the elixir. Thanks to Philip, our underworld had been unlocked; Eurydice ascended her throne of Light at last.

I raised my glass, kissed my beloved wife, and felt complete.

As the party wound down, Susan, the seminar organizer, approached with her clipboard. "Philip may have two slots open tomorrow. Would you and Karen like them?"

3

Waking Dragons

Don't worry that your life is turning upside down.
How do you know that the side you are used to
is better than the one to come?

Rumi

"We have this hour," Philip said. "What would you like to do?
Where would you like to go?"

Susan offered us complimentary private sessions with Philip if they
remained unsold. As Fortune would have it, two slots remained. By
instinct I would decline such an offer — I'm not sure I wanted to dive
any deeper into my underworld — but since we had grown close to
our house guest, protocol alone demanded that we accept.

Karen went first. When she came out of her session, she appeared
to be in an altered state — vulnerable, profoundly open and sensitive,
and different from anything I had witnessed before. I embraced
Karen's fragile being.

"Are you okay?" I asked.

She nodded and hugged me again. Now it was my turn.

"So, where would you like to go with this?" Philip asked.

"There's a deep place in me, in my voice, where I've always felt blocked. I had a taste with the Mirror Exercise, but now I want to go deeper."

Philip looked me over as if he was divining unseen forces to guide the session. Or, perhaps like most great artists, he was going to make it up as he went along.

"We don't have time for voice work," Philip said, changing course. "Just start moving. Give yourself permission to move. Go wherever it takes you."

That wasn't much to go on, so I gently swayed. My movements grew into bigger postures and silly contortions. Before long, my inner Isadora let loose, pushing my boundaries, spinning and jerking and jumping. It didn't look pretty, but I gave myself permission to let go. Finally, having exhausted my bag of tricks, I laid on my back, knees up, and made a little scoot with my butt.

"Hmm, a scoot." I pushed my feet again. Another scoot. Soon I was scooting around the room, back to the floor, like a baby. Bizarre. My cerebral Memorex activated, I was nine months old again. Was this time capsule of babyhood buried in my recesses? Is this now or is this then?

I had a similar experience of defrosted memory when my friend Eleanor was training to become a polarity therapist. Once a month, Eleanor gently moved the energy in my body via the expert placement of her hands. Little by little, the sheaths of my energetic armor fell away. A few sessions into this, she touched my hip flexor.

"Whoa, what the hell is that?" I wondered. "Grief in my hip flexor?" "I" wasn't grieving, but the emotional residue of some ancient grief bubbled to the surface — an awakened zombie of feeling, an inconvenient piece of emotional shrapnel carried in my body.

My pelvic grief forced me to look at the human experience as an iceberg. The tip of the iceberg, the "me experience," is a small piece of the story. Beneath the surface lies a mountain of buried impressions going back years and maybe generations. Safely sealed, our subterranean memory longs to see the light. This is the stuff of myth. Think *Iron John* in the lake, *The Creature from the Black Lagoon, Orpheus in the Underworld*, and Smaug, the *Hobbit* dragon who awakens after two centuries of buried slumber to wreak total havoc. Maybe Philip came into my life to awaken my dragons from slumber.

Mirroring Philip, I growled and groaned from my belly, imagining my little dragon belching wisps of smoke. Not sure what to do about it. Not sure I was ready for a fully-awakened belly brain, but the REALLY DEEP NOISES AND MOVEMENTS were having an effect.

Sound awakens memories. Years ago, Karen and I attended an Imago Couples Therapy weekend. Karen and I huddled in a corner with lights dimmed. We were instructed, via our memories, to walk into our childhood home and listen to the sounds. We both closed our eyes and stepped into our childhood soundscapes.

I heard the telltale slap of the kitchen screen door. Whap, whap, whap. All summer long, children ran in and out. I heard my mother and father talking. I heard everyone in the house talking *at* each other, but no one listening, no one feeling. My childhood sounds were not feeding my emotionally-starved feeling body.

Philip used sound to awaken these crystallized patterns of frozen time. If you trust, the waking dragon is friendly. If not, the experience can be threatening.

Sound does this. Think of soldiers breaking step when they march across a bridge. In 1850, 226 soldiers marched in step across a suspension bridge in France. The oscillations from their cadence collapsed the cement and steel cables killing them all. My cement and steel were cracking from the vibrations.

"Give yourself permission," Philip guided. "Go with it!"

More sounds, more groans, and then, beep-beep-beep. How inconvenient. Not wanting to break the magic, I ignored my phone's ringing. A moment later the beeping started again. Sensing urgency, I picked it up.

"Hello?" I wasn't sure I should have broken the spell. It was Karen.

"Bruce, I hit a car!" Karen screamed, shattering the spell.

"Are you all right? Where are you?"

On the alarm scale, Karen was at a 10, maybe 12. Karen grew more frantic.

"I don't know where I am," she cried in terror. "I don't know what's going on!"

The desperate exchange continued.

"Are you pulled over? Are you hurt?"

I bolted from the session, hopped on my bike and peddled frantically through dark, rush hour traffic. Trying to make sense of the situation, I was now in the control tower instructing a terrified passenger how to land the plane.

Karen screamed again, "Oh my god, oh my god, oh my god!"

I felt powerless. I heard the drama but had no idea what was going on.

I ran to my son's room. "Jake, get in the car immediately; you drive. No questions; your mother is in trouble."

Another shrieking scream blared in my ear.

"Oh my God, Bruce. I think I hit another car! Oh, Bruce, I can't see. I can't see." And then a little later, "I can't move the car. I'm on a ramp. People are honking. I don't know what to do!"

Jake drove at my side unaware of the crisis playing in my ear.

"Where are you?"

"I don't know. I don't know," Karen cried. "I have no idea where I am!"

"Can you read a sign, any sign, anywhere."

Karen struggled to form words out of the visual gibberish she was seeing. On the outside, I was cool and collected. Inside, my heart felt jacked to the roof:"WHAT THE FUCK IS GOING ON?"

My ever-sinking phone battery was the only lifeline to my wife, and the line was in danger. Karen was out there, somewhere in the night, lost amid a million people on Atlanta's insane freeways. I grabbed my son's phone; now two phones were in play, one in each ear. I was supposed to lead my Whirling Dervish class in 30 minutes, so I had to sort out additional complications in the other ear. The class was locked out; they had no idea where I was; the key to the dance studio was in the house; Jake had locked the door; Corinne had a spare; I tried to reach her. It was a split screen disaster playing out on two phones.

A full hour in the control tower, I began to doubt that this episode of "Lost in Hell" would end on a good note. My heart raced, but I didn't lose a breath. Karen managed to get off the freeway. Thank God. She flagged a passerby who got on her phone.

"My name is Ben. Your wife seems to be lost. She is at 5246 Oakbrook Parkway in Norcross."

I thanked the man profusely. He had no idea he was the front-page hero in my terrified mind.

Jake and I quickly reversed course. We had followed our instincts, pieced together the clues, and now realized we had gone the wrong direction, wrong freeway, and to the wrong city. So much for instinct. As we pulled into the industrial park and saw a single lone sedan in the darkened lot, my heart swelled. Houston, we had a problem, but now, just 48 hours after The Committee, after the celebration, and after the triumph of sipping the hero's elixir, our Fortune was strangely turning — for better or worse, I didn't know. But at least Karen was safe and heading home.

Thus began the Six Weeks. Yes, it was Biblical, not in the sense of Job and his misfortunes, but in the blowtorch intensity of change that was entering our lives. We chalked this incident up to a perfect storm: The Committee, Karen's three-year push, Philip melting our frozen time, emotional breakthroughs, and now breakdowns.

Oh, those buried dragons. For now, it was one big bump in the road. We were used to Things that Go Bump in Your Life. We knew that there were no straight lines in nature. Rivers meander; they take you into rapids and rocks and then dump you into gentle pools. You have to know when to lay back and go with the ride and when to paddle like hell.

§

A week after this incident, a gentle pool beckoned. All was well. Karen interviewed for her dream job: CPE Director for St. Luke's, a venerated Episcopal church that trained chaplains to work with the homeless.

Ten days later, Corinne invited Karen and me to a housewarming. It was a Sunday morning.

"Bruce, you go to Corinne's," Karen offered. "I'm going to St. Luke's for the service. I just feel it would be good to go."

I couldn't believe Karen would miss Corinne's gathering and since when did she start going to church? And why St. Luke's? Karen had never gone there before. But, we went our separate ways.

As I nibbled at Corinne's, my thoughts were ever-present with Karen. When she returned, her intuition proved prescient. The service was not led by the regular priest. It was led by Marianne, the Executive Director who had interviewed Karen ten days earlier.

"It was the strangest thing," Karen explained. "I got there, and Marianne was at the pulpit. I took communion from her."

"You took communion from your potential new boss?" I asked.

And then, a muffled ring. Karen dug and dug through her impossible purse and pulled out the beeping phone. On the spot, the battery chose to die. Holy shit. Charger now in the wall, Karen redialed.

"Hello, who's this. Did you just call? This is Karen."

I watched her eyes grow wide. A thumb went up. Her smile widened. She put the phone down.

"Bruce, it was Marianne. She was planning to call me on Monday, but since I was at the service, she wanted to let me know right now. I got the job."

"For real?"

"Yes, MY DREAM JOB!"

With that, Karen started to cry. I threw my arms around her and cried too. Soon, we were both on the kitchen floor crying, bawling. Not from sadness, not from happiness, but from pure cathartic release.

So much effort, so much failure, and now this little echo of vindication came into our life. Karen's dream job. She got it.

I don't have the emotional energy to play the full Six Weeks blow by blow, but if you're trying to follow this thing on a calendar, our joyous Marianne moment was followed, THE VERY NEXT DAY, by my career-ending lunch with Michael, followed by my foray into the world of angels. I served birthday Coq Au Vin a few days after that, which was the night the angels left. My annual Rumi event with the turn of the Whirling Dervishes followed seven days later. While I hung lights and prepared the space, Karen suffered another anxiety attack. But, with a hundred people arriving, the show went on.

On Christmas, we gathered buoyantly around our forlorn Christmas tree — the ornaments still in their boxes. The Six weeks culminated on New Year's Eve, closing the business at the bank while Karen spilled the lettuce.

Looking back at the emotional seismograph of the Six Weeks, the needle swung wildly — from one extreme to another, exultation to catastrophe — on an almost daily basis.

This puts the Six Weeks in context as I raced from the bank to pick up Karen before heading to the doctor. The drumbeats of crisis were building, so I felt relieved that Karen had an appointment with Dr. Jacobs, her naturopath. He had been treating Karen for years and kindly offered to see her on New Year's Eve.

Karen and I arrived at the medical building. She looked shaky after the lettuce episode, so I pulled up to the lobby and helped her out.

"Just sit here while I park the car."

"Okay," Karen replied.

She seemed childlike as if a big stone of buried experience was loosening.

I returned to the lobby and noticed a Most Stunning Woman waiting at the elevator. I couldn't not notice. I wondered what it would be like to have a hair stylist, make-up artist, fitness coach, and wardrobe consultant all working full time to make me a Most

Stunning Guy. I couldn't go there, but I felt a weird karmic pull, that she was somehow in our script. More importantly, that slo-mo feeling returned as the aging elevator groaned up the floors.

Signaling a premonition, the elevator thumped twice. The doors creaked open, and I let the Most Stunning go first. Before her high heels could take a step— and here is where perceived time morphed into jarring freeze frames — Karen completely collapsed, full weight, into my arms, right as I expected to step out. I braced my legs and held Karen tightly with a desperate grip.

"Is she alright? Can I do something?" The Most Stunning asked.

The Most Stunning was now the Most Helpful. Score this in the Fortune column if you're keeping track of our ups and downs.

"Go get the doctor, Doctor Jacobs, down the hall," I commanded.

I maneuvered Karen out of the elevator. It took forever with all that slo-mo for Dr. Jacobs and his assistant to reach the scene.

"Karen went completely limp in the elevator," I explained.

My adrenaline kicked in. Is this a medical drama? Where are the cameras?

"I'm really not feeling well," Karen added tenderly.

Even in a full blown emergency, Karen's sweet nature didn't miss a beat — just deeper surrender to the ever-changing moment.

"Go directly to Piedmont Hospital," Dr. Jacobs ordered. "This is not a time for herbs and muscle-testing. They have the best team for this."

With that, we muscled Karen onto an old rolling office chair and with three guys wrangling it, we scooted Karen into the elevator. I ran to the car, again feeling WHAT THE FUCK IS GOING ON?

Cue the dramatic strings, close-up on our clasped hands.

"I'm not going to let you go," I thought as we drove the 3.1 miles down Peachtree Street feeling utterly vulnerable, like two baby bunnies who had stumbled into the asphalt world.

If you've been to the ER, you know the drill; you know the wait. But, the ER was strangely empty. Being New Year's Eve, everyone was postponing their visit until after midnight. We were seen immediately.

The nurses asked all the wrong questions — they had not been privy to the Six Weeks. We settled into a little ER room opposite the nurses' station, just the two of us, waiting and waiting. Unbeknown to us, Dr. Jacobs had followed us to the ER and drilled "neurological event" into their triage brain. They got the message. Karen was wheeled away for a CT scan while I sat alone. Should I start making phone calls or just take it all in? I chose to feel the full effect of Fortune's capricious nature. One moment I'm closing bank accounts, and the next moment I'm in the hospital. My wife, the ultimate Miss Healthy had collapsed.

Karen was wheeled back, and a short time later an ER doctor gave the report:

"You're wife has a significant lesion on her left occipital lobe. It will take further testing to determine the full extent of what is going on."

"Lesion?" I thought, "What's that, fancy language for an owie, a big boo-boo?" It seemed clear that there was a tumor in her brain, but medicine is all about naming things. At this moment, it was still a lesion. Tomorrow, who knows?

The ER gave Karen steroids to relieve the inflammation pressing against her brain. Almost instantly, the Six-Week roller coaster of symptoms disappeared — the extreme anxiety, cognition, dizzy spells, memory, vision, verbalization problems — all gone.

"Wow, here we are," I thought. "We're celebrating New Year's Eve in our own little ER room at Piedmont Hospital like nothing ever happened."

I let the outside world know about our medical saga with a group text:

Karen has a significant lesion on her brain. She will be admitted to ICU for closer observation. I feel like I was deep into one movie and then have the channel abruptly change. The good news is that Our great love affair will continue.

That message is still on my phone. Two things jump out. First, we never left the ER for the promised ICU. And two, my phone's idiosyncratic auto-correct insisted that "Our great love affair" receive a capital "O." The implication: Not *our* matrimonial love, but a message to the tribe: We're all in this together.

That night, an ever-changing cast of friends, food, and flowers flooded into the ER. Carrie, one of Karen's co-workers, famously left another New Year's party (she sensed we had the better bash) and got things started with her no-dread-allowed instinct for merry-making. Even though Karen was hard-wired to a bevy of beeping monitors, Carrie kept the room pumping. It felt radically brash, almost morally illegal, to have a happy bash. But for one moment, we looked the scary diagnosis in the eye and said, "Fuck off. We are living and loving. Our collective heart will remain buoyant in this storm. Take that, C-word!"

Using our party metrics, the great Brain Lesion Party made our all-time list of New Year's Eves. Afterglow — check.

Another metric is the Unexpected Guest. In the tradition of the prophet Elijah, Khidr the Green Man, John the Baptist, and even Johnny Appleseed, the Unexpected Guest plays a paramount role in the mechanics of Fortune. The Unexpected Guest's role is to upend the status quo and open the door to the creative force.

In business change management, I use this metric all the time: Is this organization open to the Unexpected Guest, and open to change coming in from the outside? Can the creative force to sneak past the corporate politics, through the fear buffers, and subvert the organizational defenses, or do structural impediments prevent change?

Years ago, Karen and I faced a sad celebration when no guests showed up for our annual Rumi event. At the last moment, a car pulled up. The door opened, one leg stepped out, then another. Hunched over and grabbing the car door for support, our Unexpected Guest took a tentative step. He hobbled up the walkway, bent nearly ninety degrees at the waist. It was an old Sufi friend,

Akbar. He had been bed-ridden from a back ailment for weeks and had made it his do-or-die mission to join us as the Unexpected Guest.

On election night 2008, over 100 people, almost all of them Unexpected, showed up at our house. I felt Fortune's magic when one Unexpected Guest pulled up with a full keg of beer purloined from another party.

Our little New Year's party in the ER was winding down. Where's the Unexpected Guest? Karen's phone rang. It was Miriam, an old therapist friend.

"I'm leaving a party in the area," Miriam said. "Can I come by?"

Miriam was Unexpected in so many ways. Years ago, we were the closest of friends sharing nightlife, conversation, and esoteric study. Something soured our friendship, and Miriam disappeared from our lives. By an unknown chain of events, Miriam got the message about Karen in the ER. And with that, the Unexpected knocked at the door.

"Can I come in?" Miriam asked.

Like an unexpected angel, Miriam's knowing nature lifted our fears. Decades earlier, she faced an inoperable, terminal, and potentially disfiguring cancer — the Roger Ebert disease.[1] With few medical options, Miriam sought out another path. She redefined her cancer, not as an invasive disease, but an energetic disturbance, something ingrained, and a forced opportunity to inquire into her sense of self.

"How's it going, Sweetie?" Miriam asked.

"I've had better days." Karen grinned. "What a treat to see you."

"So, what's going on?" Miriam asked. "Is it okay to do a little work, some visualization?"

"Yes, please," Karen replied.

Miriam had an attuned sense of boundaries and always asked permission.

"Close your eyes and just be with yourself," Miriam guided.

1. Stöppler, MD, Melissa Conrad. 2013. "Roger Ebert and Thyroid Cancer."MedicineNet.com. 4–9.http://www.medicinenet.com/script/main/art.asp?articlekey=169088.

Karen closed her eyes as Miriam gently placed her Reiki-trained hands.

"Sense what's there. Find this old, energetic pattern that has taken root in your brain tissue, in your cells. These are cells that are not doing their job. There's no blame, but they are not you, not who you are. They don't know any better. They are still young, immature, undifferentiated. They didn't grow into their rightful role, into their adult job as functional tissue with clear boundaries."

Karen closed her eyes and let the stillness unfold.

"Be in that deep place where you can see them, talk to them, guide them to do their job," Miriam guided.

I watched Karen descend into a deep cellular consciousness. The beeping monitors traced their own picture of what was going on, but I sensed that Karen was reorganizing her very identity as if Karen 2.0 was getting ready to launch.

Outside the door, New Year's Eve in the ER was heating up, but inside, we sat in silence and maintained a sacred sanctuary.

Miriam pulled out a book. "It's getting late. Can I read you a bedtime story?"

A day earlier, a used book caught Miriam's eye in a store. She paid three bucks and put it into her purse.

"It's from *Beauty: The Invisible Embrace*, by John O'Donohue."

With perfect timing, Miriam pulled it out and began to read:

"All through your life your soul takes care of you. Despite its best brightness, your mind can never illuminate what your life is doing. You are always in a state of knowing, but that knowing, while often lucid and deep, is more often faltering and shadowed. At times you feel immensely present in your life, rooted in what is happening to you, utterly there. At other times you are only vaguely in your life; things are blurred, confusion or distraction owns your days… Yet through all these times, your soul is alive and awakened, gathering, sheltering and guiding your ways and days in the world. In effect, your soul is your secret shelter."

As Miriam read, I felt safe knowing that my soul, mostly-ignored but ever-constant, had not forgotten me. Miriam continued.

> "Without ever surfacing or becoming explicit, your soul takes care of you. Never once while you are here does your soul lose touch with the eternal. Your soul makes sure that God's dream for you is always edging towards fulfillment even when at times the opposite seems to be the case. At times of immense suffering or the most ecstatic joy, your life breaks through the shadowing and you come to sense that something else is minding and guiding you. This is the nature of the consolation and infinitely tender embrace your soul always provides for you."[2]

Miriam put the book down and held Karen's hand. We all lingered in the softness of Karen's soul. For that moment, I felt safe that my soul had not lost touch with the eternal, that it was guiding me.

"Thank you, Miriam," Karen whispered.

With a burst of static, the PA system announced:

"Attention all, attention all. It's the New Year."

Outside the door, the world continued to unload its celebratory carnage. But here in our little room, frozen time was melting. Buried dragons were emerging from slumber to see the light.

---

2. O'Donohue, John. 2005. Beauty: The Invisible Embrace. Reprint edition. New York: Harper Perennial.

4

The Big Plan

The moment you accept
what trouble you've been given,
the door will open.
Rumi.

If you're grumbling about buying a book about Fortune that's already riddled with so much misfortune, I'm with you. I didn't plan, choose, or want the cozy structure of my world to collapse.

My original book plotted years ago was much more theoretical. It explored the Law of Octaves — how simple progress in our lives is governed by the natural tendency of vibrations (just like musical vibrations) to behave a certain way. I wanted to show how the challenge of personal progress is to ride these waves of vibration, but this is only possible if we surmount our structural resistance to change and allow ourselves to be changed in the process. As it has turned out, rather than write about the Octave, I've been forced to hang on with a desperate grip, while the Octave demolishes my structural resistance.

Just so you know, this book is being written in real time. If there's going to be a big, happy Fortune-filled ending, you'll learn about it when I do. I'm currently unemployed, and a For Sale sign stands in front of my office. To put it into context, at this point in my life, I was expecting a big fat Fortune to give proof-of-concept credibility to this book: "Brand strategist reveals secret to his success."

Three years ago, Matthew and I joined forces with Jeff, a former client who had intimate knowledge of the retail sector. Together we created a unique car-selling product. We invested big dollars in Web development and got our product into Lowe's. Next, we used that little coup to catch a more lucrative fish — AutoTrader.com. We partnered with the billion-dollar car-selling giant and got our newly-branded AutoTrader.com product into Lowe's, AutoZone, Advance Auto, O'Reilly's and True Value. In addition to selling retail products, our deal included a cut from upgrade sales on the AutoTrader.com Web site. Matthew and Jeff got giddy looking at the six-figure spreadsheets. Being older, I was more hesitant when it came to premature giddiness. But people who know the retail industry marveled at our fast-track ability to get our product on the shelves. It was an unparalleled exercise in timing, bluster, and creativity.

Our product replaced the ubiquitous Car For Sale sign with a clever vinyl sign that stuck to the vehicle's side and rear windows. A free AutoTrader.com online ad ($20 value!) was included. Did you get that? FREE! And there's more. Buyers could zap the sign with their phone, instantly see the online ad, and click to email or call the seller. Sweet! What could go wrong?

As we found out later, there was one little problem. People who buy For Sale signs don't use the Internet all that much.

For this reason, Fortune and misfortune have been inextricably fused in my head. It started many years ago when a small ad in the back of Rolling Stone caught my eye: "Woodstock Music & Art Fair presents an Aquarian Exposition in Wallkill, NY." My high school buddies and I latched onto this adventure, but had no idea what to expect. Rock festivals hadn't been invented yet. All that mattered was that every important band in the universe, from Hendrix to The

Who, was slated to play for seven bucks a day. A mighty Big Plan — what could go wrong?

Well for starters, the Wallkill Zoning Board of Appeals officially banned the concert. This unexpected misfortune created a swell of fortuitous publicity.

As our boyhood adventure carried us ever closer to the substitute venue near Bethel, New York, we quickly realized that we weren't the only ones following this lark. Scratchy local AM radio stations blared, "Turn back, turn back. The New York Thruway is closed! The area is shut down. Go away."

The organizer's original plan envisioned 50,000 concert-goers communing in a suitable location, but by now a full million people were heading to the new location: Max Yasgur's dairy farm. Ultimately, half of that number would make it. Roads were blocked; cars littered the landscape. People camped with tents in the highway median. Every piece of planning failed to anticipate that half of the nation's youth would simultaneously act on the same tribal impulse — and this was before the Internet.

We heeded the appeals and turned around; at least we were moving again. But then, my buddy Rob stopped the car.

"We drove this far," Rob reasoned. "What's the worst that can happen? Let's just go for it."

Since we were driving from Chicago, we had half a chance compared to the flood of migrating youth driving up from New York, Philadelphia, and DC. We abandoned our maps and took random back roads, side roads, gravel roads — anything that could keep the car moving eastward. Ten miles from our destination, forward progress came to a final, utter stop. The road was now a river of freaks. We abandoned the car and started to walk.

By every logistical measure, Woodstock was an utter failure (score one for misfortune). The last-minute venue change (no time to build fences) forced the concert to become free. There was insufficient food, security, sanitation, medical help, and transportation. Summer thunderstorms turned the site into a sea of mud, urine, and orange peels. Wavy Gravy, the event's announcer and clown impresario, took to the stage after a late-night rainstorm tested everyone's resolve.

"The Governor just declared this a disaster area," Wavy Gravy grinned with his goofy hoarseness. "You know what I always say? There's always a little bit of heaven in a disaster area."

Wavy Gravy's declaration struck me then and has guided my dance with Fortune ever since. That bit of heaven in a sea of disaster has become my pole star, my inner Yoda, and my source of buoyancy in an emotional wipeout.

My grandfather fled the pogroms of Eastern Europe as a teen by stowing away in a barrel on a ship. He headed toward a family connection in Chicago, but the meager money in his pocket took him only as far as Cincinnati. So he got a night shift job, studied to become a doctor by day, and ultimately created the Cincinnati family that produced me. This unflappable core that's not afraid to dance in a disaster area is the inner secret to Fortune.

The Chinese understand the yin-yang way that Fortune plays your cards. If you look at the symbol, there's a white dot of yin — a little bit of heaven — amid the big chunk of yang. It's the seed of renewal inherent in failure. Flip the dots and heaven hosts the seed of its own destruction. Good times carry the ingredient of eventual collapse.

So, when Karen's brain tissue and my crumbling career collided on New Year's Eve, I struggled to find a little bit of heaven. Maybe Fortune made a bad flip of the coins. Shit happens, so stop freaking out. My Sufi teacher used to say, "There is no such thing as a problem, only an unattended situation."

I could see the unattended: I let my business stagnate. Karen let stress get the better of her. But there was more going on. Every step of our disaster seemed choreographed. I could feel John O'Donohue's wisdom. My soul was directing traffic on this one.

After our New Year's guests had left the ER, Karen and I were alone again. There were no cots or recliners in the ER, so I arranged three hard plastic chairs, stole some pillows and constructed my little bit of heaven. As I struggled to find comfort, late-night paramedics continued to wheel in a growing wave of medical misfortune. I couldn't judge; I was spending New Year's Eve with them.

While Karen tried to sleep, my bony body kept slipping off the plastic chairs. So, I left the ER, crossed the icy parking lot, and found one unclaimed couch in the lobby. My solace was temporary as a chorus of snores rose like bullfrogs in the night. Defeated, I headed back to the ER and surveyed my wired wife in her too-small-for-two gurney.

"Glad you're back," Karen whispered. "I couldn't sleep without you."

"This is so crazy," I muttered.

"I have a feeling that everything is going to be okay," Karen offered with her characteristic optimism.

Squeezing in delicately, lest some important piece of data became unplugged, I tuned out the noise and savored the familiar warmth of Karen's body. Cuddling, I could feel that everything was still right in the universe.

In the world of crisis, the wee hours usher in the freak-out time. At 4:00 a.m., when the hovering soul intermingles with the dreams and fears from the underworld, I tried to take comfort by forming a Big Plan — a mental road map to create the illusion of stability and to keep hope alive. I ignored the fact that this kind of thinking, known as "expectation," forms the fundamental lie of causality. But, it was my Big Plan, and I was hanging on to it.

Expectation is an "*If I do X, Y will happen*" form of thinking. We are trained to see the world this way from infancy onward. And yes, there is a world of causality, but it doesn't govern Fortune. That's because the fruit is the *cause* of the tree. The only people honest about expectation are hobos and graduating high school seniors. When asked about life plans, they shrug. For them, life is a stream of unfolding possibility.

My Big Plan was to create a new business from the ashes of the old — Miller eMedia. I created a detailed business plan, filed papers, opened an account, created a logo, secured a domain name, proposed rent, calculated income from our fast food client, prepared a transition plan for our employees and shared it all with Matthew. I was already pitching new business via Webex presentations to get the ball rolling. Even though the Six Weeks had pushed me to the edge, my responsible nature needed a Big Plan.

The cornerstone of the Plan was Karen's new job, her dream job, which was set to start on Monday — OMG! How do you start your dream job three days after brain surgery? Karen couldn't manage a cell phone let alone direct an educational program. We decided to wait until after an official diagnosis before telling her new boss what was going on — not for Marianne's sake, but for ours. Our capacity for managing freakout had tapped out.

The day after New Year's, Dr. Dunbar, our neuro-oncologist came to visit our new digs — an actual hospital room. Dr. Dunbar and Dr. Chandler, the neurosurgeon, had created a dream-team brain tumor practice. Score a point for Fortune; Dr. Chandler was one of only two surgeons in the city who specialized solely in brain tumors. And, if there was a good cop/bad cop, Dr. Dunbar played the heavier role. She wheeled her PowerPoint into our room and took us through a weirdly upbeat, clinical presentation of our worst-case scenario — incurable glioma.

Sobered by the grim news, I left the hospital and drove across town to Design Coup. Our CPA advised me to wait until after the New Year's Eve dissolution date to inform and terminate the employees. My plan was to fire them, obtain signatures, hand them severance checks, and then offer the opportunity to continue working with me as a team. Seinfeld could have found dark humor in my back-to-back meetings — jumping from the wife-with-incurable-brain-cancer meeting to the fire-my-loyal-employees meeting — but I was too crazed to appreciate the double scoop of gloom.

All eyes were strangely vacant as we gathered around the conference table. I announced the dissolution, handed out severance checks, then quickly backpedaled to paint a promising vision. My grand idea was to restructure our focus — less on design (since we were losing Matthew) and more on making the sales process a brand-driven experience.

"Any questions?" I asked at the end of my presentation.

George, David, and Haley looked at me like a chump, thanked me for the checks, and went back to work. Feeling something ominous in the air, I confronted George, our most-veteran designer.

"Did you just come back from meeting with Wing Zone?" I asked.

"I think we need to meet offline," George said diplomatically.

George explained that while I was receiving the grim news about Karen, he and Matthew met with our client. Wing Zone agreed to work with Matthew and the former Design Coup designers at the full retainer rate, minus me. I looked at George and saw my Big soufflé of a Plan collapse.

"It's just about business," George explained rationally. "Matthew offered a better deal."

I stared into the abyss, feeling the betrayal, the suddenness of events, and the hardness of hearts. Matthew now had our two cash-cow clients — one in a salaried position as Chief Marketing Officer and the other to run as an entrepreneurial venture on the side.

Everyone continued to work like nothing had happened. Head sunk, I leaned over the railing of the work area. George and David sat at their stations; Matthew sat immediately behind me.

"You fucked me! You fucked me over," I vented. My heart was ravaged. "You all have your nice new jobs. I have nothing to turn to, but a WIFE WITH FUCKING INCURABLE BRAIN CANCER!"

David, a just-out-of-school twenty-something, had not been prepped for this kind of event at design school, so he buried his head into his monitor. I couldn't blame him. It wasn't pretty.

There's a certain point in Moby Dick where Ahab's war with the whale becomes his war with God. As I drove from the office, I felt the universe closing in on me. My clever mind was no match for my whale. God held all the cards. And, if God were going for a straight flush, our AutoTrader.com business would be the final ace.

I met with Jeff after the collapse of my Big Plan. He explained that Matthew's dad agreed to take on the business debt for our struggling AutoTrader.com venture if I relinquished my stake. If there was an upside at that moment, I discovered an unexpected lightness as I pushed all my chips away and left the game.

My friend Brigitte, who had lost a child and two marriages, wisely explained the Fortune of double misfortune.

"It's better this way," she explained. "Since Karen is going through hell and needs your full-time attention, double misfortune relieves you from focusing solely on your own misery."

The logic felt like one of those double negatives that make sense in math but still feels rotten.

I went home after firing the employees to take a shower. If there was going to be a moment to fully savor my half of the misfortune, this was it. I know how to ride the ups and downs of life, but this was something bigger. I could see all the pieces on the board expertly positioned to trap my king. In the movies, when the hero gets in a jam, there's always an enemy weakness to exploit, a file in the cake, a hackable error in the code, or a *deus ex machina* introduced to move the plot forward. But, I had none of that.

As I lay on Karen's side of our marital bed feeling her absence, I could see only one way out of this Grand Trap — up, as in upshift, upgrade, a whole new operating system: Bruce 2.0. This would require processing my luckless load in one cathartic swoop.

If I uttered a prayer, it went something like this: "Okay Lord, your Perfect Storm has ravaged my Perfect Plan."

I looked at the Six Weeks and saw how every note fit together like a perfect score. Even if the score played like a dance of destruction, there were too many harmonics to ignore.

My prayer continued: "Like a sea of pixels resetting to white, I will allow my future to take form without judgment or expectation. I open my heart to the world of possibility, to Fortune."

Feeling is a vibration. Pain is a vibration. Pain is a sound that hits your heart with a certain sinking frequency. It's also a sound that can be transformed by raising one's energetic pitch and expanding the resonant space.

In the spirit of John O'Donohue, I sensed my soul watching over me. Or maybe Corinne's angels had returned for a house call. Or maybe it was just me — at that moment I let the higher vibration embrace my pain.

Somewhere, my emotional lodestone had lost its course in the world of business. It was my mother's world — she was a groundbreaking woman in the field of public relations. She pushed me into business, and I followed. The parallels with my father's world didn't escape me. He was an engineering genius who brought stereo high fidelity to the world (yes, the stereo signal coming through your radio was his creation) and then he died penniless because creative types are usually driven by something other than money.

Healing is a process that touches several generations. Something new was birthing for Karen and me. Maybe, this was just a scene change between acts. The curtain comes down, and the stagehands quickly move the set pieces away. Unfortunately, I didn't have a program to see if in my life story, Act III was a tragedy.

Birth is a messy, painful process, and since my Big Plan was kaput, I had no other choice but to trust.

5

Reyes of Creation

Because God is pure imagination and the only creator,
if you imagine a state and bring it to pass,
you have found Him.
Neville Goddard

My '65 Volkswagen bus struggled up the unpaved excuse for a road toward Reyes Peak, near Ojai, California. I wasn't concerned that the road's sheer drop-offs were not well-suited to my playful VW steering, or that my funky brakes might be problematic on the way back down, or that my air-cooled 40 horsepower engine was no match for the steep grade. No, my anticipation centered on the rite of passage that loomed at the top, a journey cooked up by the grinning 15-year old kid sitting next to me.

It's 1973. I'm shifting to back story because the "inciting incident" of my Fortune journey sheds light on my current predicament.

Ryan, the 15-year old at my side was the barefoot sadhu of Las Flores Mesa, my parents' Malibu neighborhood. In 1973, Malibu wasn't yet dripping with money and celebrities. Neighbor kids would head to the beach for a bit of surfing with the same ease that today's kids plug in a video game. Ryan was the exception. His greasy complexion never got near the sea. He roamed the neighborhood in a continuous state of pilgrimage, a bag of rotting fruit in one hand and a well-worn copy of Vivekananda's *Raja Yoga* in the other.

"Ryan, I'm not so sure about this," I said swerving to avoid a rock.

"It's totally organic," Ryan assured with teenage conviction. "Aldous Huxley took organic mescaline when he wrote *Doors of Perception.*"

I had never touched psychedelics. Risk-averse by nature, I preferred to stay grounded and responsible when I hung out with my "tripping" college friends. Like most campuses during the Vietnam War, the University of Illinois was an epicenter for cultural change. Campus riots, sit-ins, teach-ins, the first Earth Day, the Vietnam Moratorium, and the Grateful Dead formed the backdrop for my coming of age. Even though I was a psychedelic virgin, I was in-tune with the acid landscape. My trippy film about a bored student's subconscious took first place in the campus film festival. The prize also earned me a ticket to UCLA Film School. My parents had already left the cold winters of Illinois behind for California, so I joined them in Malibu to go to film school.

I didn't anticipate that campus life at UCLA would end up being commuter life, so I quickly fell into an existential funk. Living at home, the bumper-to-bumper grind of Pacific Coast Highway, and my unexpected loneliness hit me hard. Rather than seeking out new friends, my journey turned inward.

One night, as I laid in bed, sealed into my enormous Koss headphones, I tuned in Elliot Mintz, L.A.'s legendary underground DJ. Mintz was interviewing Richard Alpert, a former Harvard professor and consciousness researcher who had just come back from India as Ram Dass.

"Are you asking people to run off to India in search of gurus and give up the 9-to-5?" Mintz asked.

Ram Dass spoke directly into the center of my brain:

"This is a trip you can take right here, right now," Ram Dass explained. "There's nowhere to go, nothing to do. It's about learning to watch your drama unfold. It is important to expect nothing, to take every experience, including the negative ones, as mere steps on the path, and to proceed."

The words "learn to watch your drama unfold" propelled me into unexpected territory. My drama, my head trip, my melodrama, my little story suddenly became palpable. I had been looking at life as an absurd form of theater for some time. During the campus riots, I found myself removed from the passion of the crowd and watched both sides, protesters and police, define one other like a modern day Bhagavad Gita. And now Ram Dass was challenging me to observe my drama without taking sides.

A few months later, my old Illinois friends and I planned a spring break road trip up the coast to Big Sur and ending in the Bay Area. What could better lift my doldrums?

I counted every day until spring break arrived. But, I had not anticipated a tectonic shift in my being. When my friends arrived, I was pursuing big soul questions while they wanted to party. When we got to Berkeley, I ditched my friends to sneak into Shambhala Books.

"You got anything by this guy, Ram Dass?" I asked.

A stack of *Be Here Now* sat on the counter. In 1973, this hand-lettered guide to the inner life had become the must-have owner's manual to consciousness.

I built a sadhu loft in my parent's garage and read the book from cover to cover, flipping it over to start again. With each reading, the words spoke differently. Weird, I wasn't the same person from when I started.

While the neighbor kids were out surfing, Ryan would amble up to my little puja loft in the garage to make mystical small-talk.

"I'm living on papaya this week," Ryan would explain with his spaced-out grin. "From a macrobiotic perspective, it's the LSD of fruit."

Ryan was my spiritual partner in crime. I can't say that he totally put me up to the mescaline idea. I had long been curious. And as the drug literature makes clear, "Set and setting are vital in determining the direction of a mescaline trip." So, wanting the perfect experiment, Ryan and I took off to Reyes Peak.

At an altitude of 7500 feet, the views were spectacular and the setting remote. In one direction, the Channel Islands glistened in the Pacific and in the other, a striking tableau of mountains rippled toward the eastern horizon.

Ryan and I fasted for both spiritual preparation and because cactus psychedelics can make you violently sick. With no dinner to clean, we settled early into sleep atop the mountain.

Throughout the night, an ominous wind wailed through the pines, beckoning from the natural world. I had no idea what to expect, but I already sensed the shore of my familiar world receding.

At daybreak, we swallowed our capsules — they looked and tasted like brown dirt — and that was that. Reyes Peak was a mile from camp, so we started up the trail.

"I can handle this," I reasoned enjoying the views.

I should add that at the time I was taking an experimental course at UCLA led by Chuck Rusch, an education visionary. Titled "Creative Problem Solving," the goal of the class was to discover how we deal with internal road blocks. Little did I know that this class and my journey up the mountain would launch my life question about Fortune.

I wrote a paper for the class which I still preserve like a talisman in its scruffy old envelope. The scribbled report begins with a note to the professor:

> Chuck, I wanted to write a theoretical academic paper, but then I had the very profound experience described in this paper. It was necessary to write about it to understand the importance of what happened.

"Fair enough," Chuck replied. And my paper begins:

> Ryan and I began the hike, and the drug came on full, exactly at the peak. I had no real interest in the visual hallucinations as I was troubled with anxieties that were blocking me from letting go with the flow.

I was in a precarious place where I could attach to the anxieties, become scared, and flip out. I could see that everywhere there was anxiety, there was Bruce. Everywhere that there was harmonious flow, there was no Bruce.

I laid on my back and silently inhaled, "Let" and exhaled, "Go." "Let go, let go." I saw the mind, disassociated myself from it and fused with the earth. My mind was near to clear consciousness, and my body was warm glowing energy.

As I fused into the ground, there were still the most subtle ripples of anxiety. "Let go, let go." The ripples became still, and I merged into nothingness. Ahhh.

I went through a field of white light that merged into a golden tunnel of kinetic patterns and left ego-Bruce behind.

A very long time ensued. I found myself laying outside of space and time in a fetal position suspended in a sea of infinite consciousness. The feeling was, as Ram Dass loves to put it, "Well, here we are."

Reading this now, the paper clearly misses the existential quicksand I faced riding the edge of freakout while melting into light. On the flip side, it was here, atop Reyes Peak that I discovered Fortune — Fortune as the unfolding flow of a dramatic universe. In other words, God (through us) is making it up as He or She goes along.

To put this into perspective, my trip was not about "me" having an experience. It was the annihilation of self. I was just a young guy without any preparation for this particular pickle. When my notes read: "outside of space and time," please understand that eternity is a very long time — like really, really long. Somehow, I summoned the courage needed to live in eternity, because outside of time, there's no down time, just eternal vigil.

More notes from Reyes Peak:

Instantly or years later, we were back at my van which I had to drive to L.A.

Yes, the VW bus with the loose steering and funky brakes. Fortunately, as it turned out, Ryan chose to be the designated still-in-body companion and never took the drug. Unfortunately, Ryan didn't know how to drive. Not sure what to do, I willed the vehicle back into existence and off we went.

Every action involved with driving required complete consciousness.

Yes, because if I didn't consciously create my VW bus, it would dissolve into a sea of electrons.

Every aspect of driving had to be relearned for the first time. The entire universe existed in the key inserting into the ignition. Even though every action and decision were carried through with complete consciousness, I was unattached to any of it. The driving happened on its own accord.

This last bit, "The driving happened on its own accord," was Fortune revealing its secret. But, it would take another forty years (and another 15 chapters) to understand it.

So, down the mountain, we went. The curly-headed guy sat in the driver's seat and the spaced-out fruit eater rode shotgun. There was also a "third person" witnessing the whole thing from outside of time. Amazingly, the curly guy knew to keep the vehicle on the road and not steer toward the colorful waves of cascading energy flowing down the hillsides.

I was relieved when the drug left my system and my normal occluded self returned. It was clear that what happened was a once-off. I now wanted to experience the self directly — no buffers, additives, adjusters, or mood enhancers. Factory-installed awareness is the only tool supplied for discerning the meaning of life, so best to not muck it up.

According to my screenwriting guru, Robert McKee, the inciting incident is "an event that radically upsets the balance of forces in the protagonist's life."[1] Reyes Peak set my inciting incident into motion. I could no longer look at life on Earth the same way. I could not pretend that this brief lifting of life's curtain hadn't taken place.

1. McKee, Robert. 1997. Story: Substance, Structure, Style and the Principles of Screenwriting. 1 edition. New York: ReganBooks.

By the time we reached Malibu, the veils had crashed back down, shrouding my brief view behind the curtain. In Sufi language, I had been given a "taste." My savor of certainty had receded, but in its place, a question emerged that would guide my life:

What is this dance masquerading as life? Do personal efforts drive the story, or is there a God directing the show? And, if so, what is my role as a human being?

Wishful thinking would not open the hood to see Fortune's mechanics. I would need real knowledge from real teachers. I decided to throw myself into Fortune's embrace and let life inform me.

6

Mory

I believe the purpose of death is the release of love.
Laurie Anderson

A handwritten sign caught my eye: "Festival of Light, Noon, Janss Steps, UCLA."

I changed route from my film class, and instead, headed down the famous steps to join the "festival."At this point we're talking about a couple of guys playing flute and tambourine. Endeared by their awkward lack of festivity, I stayed to watch. Sam, the flute guy in his twenties, stopped to make an announcement.

"Mr. Mory Berman is here today," Sam announced to wholly uninterested students climbing the steps. "Mr. Berman is looking for people interested in cosmic consciousness. He would be happy to talk to you."

With Reyes Peak still fresh in my mind, I approached Sam.

"Maybe, I'm interested in cosmic consciousness. What's the deal?"

Sam guided me to an older Jewish gentleman seated on a bench. His shock of gray hair and pensive eyes gave him an Einstein air. Sam introduced me.

"Mory, this is…" Sam started.

"…Bruce," I interjected. Mory leaped to his feet.

"Bahh-ruce!" Mory exclaimed. His open-arm familiarity was off-putting, yet strangely comforting. "Come, sit down; let's talk." He gestured to the bench.

"Uh, I'm actually on my way to class."

At this point, Sam was scribbling on a piece of paper. "Mory likes Thursday afternoons," Sam chimed in seemingly in on the plot. "Can you do Thursday at four?"

"What is this about?" I asked.

"This is very important," Mory reassured. "You are a racehorse, a thoroughbred. That's who I am looking for."

Sam handed me the address. Sam and Mory both seemed pleased, but since I was late for an important screening, I moved on. The legendary director, Fritz Lang, in his last years, would be wheeled in to present *Metropolis* to our film school. And with that, I went from festival of light to Lang's dark dystopian world. Somehow they fit together.

On Thursday, Mory's invitation continued to gnaw at me, so I drove to his Santa Monica apartment, waited at the door until 4:00 p.m., then knocked.

"Come in, come in," Mory welcomed with his Yiddishy Russian accent. "I have made you a special stew. Rutabaga, parsnips, prunes. Lots of prunes."

There was no gracious escape, so I sat down to a bowl of Mory's Famous Laxative Stew.

"I was not getting anywhere with Sam," Mory explained. "And, he's got trouble with his parents. But you, my friend. You are the racehorse."

That was the closest to an explanation I ever got for our arrangement. Mory never mentioned being a teacher or what I was supposed to do. For the next several months, every Thursday, I arrived promptly at 4:00 p.m. Mory would share random thoughts and recollections and if things went particularly well, he'd announce after an hour, "Let's celebrate. Let's have some coffee."

With this, he'd grab a jar of Nescafe, mix a spoonful for each, and serve in a glass. On most Thursdays, I would drive Mory to the bank, to the drugstore, or to the Safeway where I would watch him squeeze all the peaches.

"It's okay," Mory protested sensing my disapproval. "It's self-service!"

Mory knew his fruit. He worked in wholesale fruit when he was younger. Together, we would drive to the wholesale market and buy papayas by the case. With stealth, we would swap the prettiest papayas from one case to another. And, since fruit was all Mory ate, he selected the best.

"Your undergarments smell sweet, like fruit," he exclaimed, proving his fruitarian point by sniffing under his arm.

It became apparent that Mory was some type of realized being, but what type, wasn't clear. It was not something he mentioned. I intuited this from things he said like, "I spoke to you in your dreams last night." Or. "Bruce, I see you with a beautiful wife and child."

One afternoon, I brought Ryan with me. Ever the eager sadhu, Ryan wanted to meet my mysterious guru. Mory greeted us both, gave Ryan a look, then shrugged and whispered to me, "He's just in kindergarten."

And with that, Ryan's incessant grin sank below his knees.

On one occasion, I drove Mory to Malibu so he could see where I lived. I played a vinyl recording of Ram Dass. Mory's response caught me off guard.

"That's me," he said listening to Ram Dass. "That's me talking."

As I set up my camera to take a portrait together, Mory became thoughtful.

"So, vhat do you want to do with your life?"

I took him to my garage and showed him my darkroom, animation stand, optical printer and other tools for experimental cinema. In the 60's and early 70s, these abstract, non-narrative films broke ground for what would later evolve to become today's music videos and commercials. Rather than going into a big explanation, I replied, "I want to be a cinema artist."

Mory became quiet, then looked baffled, and then disturbed.

"Ar-tist?" he asked puzzled. "AHR-teest! Vy do you vant to be an AR-TEEEST?" he challenged. "You just end up in the cuckoo house!"

The two words "cuckoo house" reverberated in my head for several miles as we drove toward Ojai, the next stop on the learn-about-Bruce tour. I wasn't thinking right when I picked up two young hitchhikers, a common practice in Malibu in those days. A few miles later, I let them out.

"Why did you do that?" Mory glared. "You don't understand. They take all my energy."

So far, the trip was not going well. We reached Ojai, and I parked the VW bus. Before we got out, Mory turned toward me.

"So, why are we here?" Mory asked.

He looked stern. I was uncomfortable.

"I don't know," I said. "Just to fart around."

Mory looked at me and through me.

"You don't know who I am. I have very lee-til time, very lee-til. We turn around now."

We drove for the next 90 minutes without exchanging a word.

Mory left Lithuania in 1912, a time when thousands of Jews were fleeing anti-Semitism, famine, and strife. In America, Mory quickly found himself fighting in the labor movements "for the little guy." Somewhere along the way, Mory underwent a spiritual transformation, possibly from spending time alone in the desert. He reemerged as a self-styled writer modeled after his spiritual mentor, Khalil Gibran.

"Here, take this," Mory offered shyly. "It's just a little offering."

I studied the title: *Autumn Leaves, A Collection of Essays*. Full confession, I never read it. As a twenty-year-old, I dismissed it as the simplistic, stumbling rants from an old man. Being older now, I realize that Mory was on to something. One line stands out:

The height of rascality is sinking low enough to try teaching that which no man can grasp, measure, analyze or describe. That is the Creator and the creative force.

I hope I don't stand accused of rascality in trying to explain the Creator and the creative force (and disguising it as Fortune).

Opening the book at random, more of Mory emerges:

> I wanted reality, at any price, and I paid for it dearly. I went right down through the length and breadth of the abyss. There is nothing but pain down there, yet I am glad that I had that kind of courage and enough strength to come up — scarred, yes, but still clean, still warm, a bit singed, but now I float a lot. I rest that way and go farther. Also, I sing more often a joyous song, a soulful hymn to life. Never do I trouble the Master with special requests. And you, whoever or wherever you are, my friend, do not envy me. We must all pay the price. There is no other road to peace of mind. I did not look for shortcuts, nor did I travel on God-forsaken trails on which pleasure-seekers wander. All of them find sorrow, but no serenity. Also, what I found down there was that the roots of reality may not appear beautiful, but without the roots, there would be no trees, no grass, not even weeds.[1]

There was no quid pro quo with Mory. No promise, expectation, or reason for my Thursday meetings. Years later, I came to the conclusion that Mory was teaching me the path of service. I eventually abandoned this explanation, too. As Karen wisely explained, "Sometimes we do things for no reason at all."

One afternoon, I parked my VW bus in the familiar spot and walked to Mory's apartment. I had just graduated from UCLA, and my life was hovering. Like the expectant void between in-breath and out, I didn't know what path to take. So, like any other Thursday, I knocked at 4:00 p.m.

Knock-knock. No answer. I raced over to the corner drug store looking for Mory. An enormous sensation hit, that the storyline of my life was preparing to shift. I turned around, sprinted back,

1. Berman, Mory. 1961. Autumn Leaves: A Collection of Essays. Exposition Press Inc.

ran up the apartment stairs and knocked on the door of the Russian landlady.

"Mr. Berman, number three," I panted. "Something's not right!"

"Vhat… vhat are you saying?" The landlady and I headed down the stairs.

"Mr. Berman. I'm concerned. He might be dead."

"Dayd? DAYD?"

An alarmed pitch rose in the landlady's voice. She turned the key and disappeared.

I went inside and found everything neat and serene. If there was one small problem, it was Mory. He was stretched out on the carpet in perfect savasana pose, very much a corpse.

Not knowing what to do, I didn't do anything. I sat for the longest time, cross-legged, breathing. I guess Mory knew I was coming and wanted to pass on today's teaching, that we are not the body. His presence lingered and "we" felt totally at peace. My thinking intervened. Shouldn't I be alarmed? Be sad? Be upset? Or grieve? What should I be feeling? I felt none of those things, so I sat in peace.

Eventually, I covered Mory with a sheet and dialed his old rotary phone. I called the police, then found an address book and called a long-lost sister in Van Nuys. What started like a transcendent passage from Siddhartha devolved into a macabre scene as the police looked for foul play and ka-womped the room with blasts of photographic flash.

The relatives soon arrived and poked at the furniture (a rickety card table, two metal folding chairs, a single bed). They shook their heads at Mory's pauper status. And who was I? Student? Friend? Passer-by? By default, I became the authority on all-things-Mory, so I stayed until the black-suited Jewish funeral directors took him away in a Cadillac.

As I drove away, an energetic presence filled my soul. Mory often said, "I am just a stepping stone, a pebble compared to the great ones." Maybe, I had stepped across the creek and was ready to join the river. But, why did I feel this elation? Maybe Mory was still riding shotgun with me, overjoyed to escape the grim scene in the apartment and follow his next adventure.

Considering all the ways people die, Mory had done it right. Find a young protege to hand your life work to, lay down, and slip out of your body. An inner instinct caused me to pull over. In the spirit of pilfering papayas, I had wisely taken Mory's treasured collection of Khalil Gibran books from his apartment. I pulled *The Prophet* from the stack and flipped to the end:

> "We would ask now of Death." And he said: You would know the secret of death. But how shall you find it unless you seek it in the heart of life? … For what is it to die but to stand naked in the wind and to melt into the sun? And what is to cease breathing, but to free the breath from its restless tides, that it may rise and expand and seek God unencumbered? Only when you drink from the river of silence shall you indeed sing.[2]

I wanted to sing, but not end up singing in the "cuckoo house." So, when I got home, I packed up my cinema gear to be sold.

2. Gibran, Kahlil. 1923. The Prophet. Alfred A. Knopf.

7

The Octave

The law of octaves explains why there are no straight lines in nature...
In order to understand the meaning of this law it is necessary
to regard the universe as consisting of vibrations.
P. D. Ouspensky

Muhammad said, "Seek ye knowledge, even unto China," and that was my plan. And while there are quiet, stable, reliable people with spiritual knowledge, they don't become spiritual teachers — they become nurses' aides.

So, let's just get it out of the way. For 25 years, from Watergate to the World Trade Center, I had a "spiritual teacher." I'm not sure if people have spiritual teachers anymore or if it's even a good idea. As Mory said, "The height of rascality is sinking low enough to try teaching that which no man can grasp."

Yes, my spiritual teacher was a rascal. But, I think it takes a rascal to keep you sufficiently off balance to finally let go.

I was at another "Festival of Light" a few months after Mory's passing. Amid the spiritual hucksters and dreamers on the line-up, a balding and bearded Englishman wearing a leather fur-lined vest caught my eye. He stood in the hallway, away from the main stage, demonstrating a mysterious power to a young woman. I watched as his tightly-gripped dowsing rod curled up to his chest like a psychic erection.

"Look, I'm not doing anything," he boasted.

I wasn't sure what he was trying to prove.

The dowsing rod guy took the stage, and my curiosity grew. He was introduced as Reshad Feild, born Tim Feild, a British aristocrat, former singer with Dusty Springfield, esoteric healer, new age author, antique dealer, mentor to Ellen Burstyn, and of course, a dowser. Reshad skipped the spiritual pablum and went straight to the point:

"I am here today to offer you the possibility of working in a real school," Reshad announced. "A real school arises where and when it's needed. It may last four to six months. When the school has fulfilled its aim, it will disband, disappear and reappear in a different form somewhere else if it is needed."

I liked the hit-and-run quality of what Reshad offered.

"The purpose of this school is to provide the best possible conditions for people to learn to work with energies," Reshad continued. "We are preparing the groundwork for what is called the Second Cycle of Mankind. This change can come about through the transformation of consciousness that is needed at this time. We are starting this school so that we can learn to fulfill our obligation in being born man and woman. And this means to come to know who and what you are. Only then can you be of real service to the reciprocal maintenance of the planet."

Wow. Planetary consciousness. Awakened by Reshad's mellifluous voice, I could feel an epochal shift stirring inside me.

"I can come back to Los Angeles to lead the school," Reshad offered, "but you have to do all the work."

And with that, I scribbled my name to the list.

Fate and my signature enlisted me into a hapless crew. We met at a drug rehab center, sectioned off the city, and started to look for the "school" guided by a "Field of Dreams" type of thinking.

I was skeptical, but a month later, Eureka… a vacant 15-room mansion appeared in a tired section of the Wilshire District. We inked the deal and almost immediately people began to arrive from the East Coast and West, England, Canada, Mexico and more. There was Joan the stripper, Lisa the biker chick, George the Communist, Suzanne the clairvoyant, Donna the cellist, Christopher the genius, Hassan the Afghan drummer, and so on. I was Bruce the impresario. Thirty-six people signed up to maintain the planetary grid of consciousness.

On move-in day, Reshad looked at me: "So, Bruce are you moving in?"

I could see Reshad's grand design — a boiling pot for three dozen uncooked egos. I had watched the enterprise unfold with apprehension, but since my quest had led me here…

"Yes, I'm in."

And with that, I left Malibu and joined what would become the Institute for Conscious Life.

The Institute had its roots in G.I. Gurdjieff's Institute for the Harmonious Development of Man, an intensive school founded outside of Paris in 1922. Gurdjieff was possibly the most original esoteric thinker of the twentieth century. As a younger man, he sought out remote sources of esoteric knowledge, then synthesized his findings into a practical teaching that embraced the totality of the cosmos.

"Man is asleep," Gurdjieff proclaimed. "He has no real consciousness or will. He is not free. To him, everything 'happens.' He can become conscious and find his true place as a human being in the creation, but this requires a profound transformation."[1]

Gurdjieff felt that people could awaken from their "sleep-like" state by bringing heightened attention to the subtle impressions of ordinary life. Gurdjieff called this wakefulness "self-remembering." As he stated, "There are moments when you become aware not only of what you are doing but also of yourself doing it."[2]

---

1. "G.I. Gurdjieff." n.d. The Gurdjieff Society.http://www.gurdjieff.com/about.php.

Gurdjieff used the friction of different personalities in his Institute to create heat for the boiling pot — the heat needed to awaken the sleeping self.

Reshad's school was unique in that it fused elements of Gurdjieff's work with elements of Sufism and particularly Rumi, the 13th-century poet and pole of mystical love. Friction and love provided the ingredients for the Institute for Conscious Life.

The idea was that spiritual seekers from all walks of life and backgrounds would come together for forty days, receive a spiritual transfusion, then go off into the world to live meaningful lives.

A steady stream of students and visitors passed through the doors including Governor Jerry Brown, his girlfriend Linda Ronstadt, singer Dusty Springfield, Sufi leader Pir Vilayat Khan, and Bhante Dharmawara, a Cambodian monk who lived to be 110 years old.

Life in the Institute was hardly glamorous. Since few people had jobs or income, meals were meager, and the work was non-stop. The day began at 4:30 a.m. with wake-up. Competition for the bathroom was intense.

"I can't believe I'm doing this," I grumbled.

I staggered out of my Army surplus metal bunk, splashed water, then descended into the basement vault where Hassan, the Afghan drummer sat wrapped in a blanket. The flickering candlelight gave his blunt words an ominous tone.

"This is no joke," Hassan warned. "This is serious stuff. If you aren't sure, get out now."

And with that, we linked arms and started chanting, "Allah-Allah."

I had been hanging with this crowd for a couple of weeks, and now for the first time, it dawned on me: "Holy shit (Allah-Allah). This path has something to do with (Allah-Allah) ISLAM!"

Being a good Jewish boy, I was in a muddle (Allah-Allah). I decided to go with the flow and engage but not identify.

2. Gurdjieff, Georges Ivanovitch. 1973. Views From the Real World: Early Talks of Gurdjieff as Recollected by His Pupils. 1st edition. New York: Dutton.

"Don't get caught in the drama," I resolved to myself. "Don't get attracted or repelled by what is going on."

For the next 25 years, this was my strategy: "I'm not following Reshad, not following Rumi, not following Gurdjieff or Muhammad. I am, hopefully, following myself."

My lofty goal, of course, was impossible. The purpose of the school was to create sufficient internal friction for transformation. By definition, friction creates emotional identification, so there was no escaping the fact that everyone's buttons were being pushed all the time.

Late one night, Reshad started losing it. I don't know if it was too many gin and tonics or because he was frustrated that the energy wasn't "going through" — not going through us "idiots" as he fondly called his pupils.

"I'm not going to bed until you can love one other," Reshad declared.

It was close to midnight, and we were bone-pleading tired. If exhaustion makes you pliable, our primordial clay was ready to be shaped.

"I want you to love one another," Reshad ordered again.

"Yes sir, coming right up," I grumbled.

A few people made awkward attempts with hugs, staring into eyes, and forced bliss. Fifteen minutes into this, Reshad threatened again.

"I remain true to my word. I will not go to sleep until you can love one another. Bring me my mattress!"

And with that, two men went up the stairs and returned, wrestling Reshad's queen size mattress down the stairs. Denise, Reshad's pregnant young wife quickly followed, furious to have been evicted from her bed.

I'm not convinced we succeeded in loving one another, but the energy eventually "went through" and we went to bed.

My plan was not to identify with the drama, so I made it my practice to "notice." I observed how the play unfolded, how the emotional friction created heat, and how heat was energy. Like lightning seeking ground, the energy must go through. And when it didn't, tension and trouble ensued.

At night, screams of emotional release awakened the neighbors. "The energy must go through," I thought.

I also watched the girth of several women expand over the course of a few days. No mere weight gain, I surmised that the energy was not going through; it certainly wasn't the food. Round-the-clock work, prayer, exercises, and study unleashed a powerful force, a kind of spiritual lightning. This energy had a job to do — it needed to go through. One moment we would be whirling like dervishes, then Vipassana Buddhist meditation, then Arica exercises, then brain-burning Ibn Arabi studies, maybe a fling with Scientology, a little map-dowsing, singing vowel sounds with movements, vortex meditations, green meditation; it never ended. We were young; we had the energy, but we didn't have the emotional ballast to live at this pitch. Our only solace was the Astro Cafe — a late night Greek burger joint on Western Avenue where we could bitch and complain outside the boiling pot, blowing off the precious spiritual energy through a greasy relief valve.

One day, the three-ring circus finally made sense. A workshop titled "An Introduction to the Law of Seven" revealed the grand plan. Each hour of the seminar was based on a note of the musical octave. We set our intention on the note *Do*, performed movements on *Re*, talked about the illusion of self on *Mi* (rhymes with "me"), had lunch on *Fa*, and so on. The screenwriter in me was intrigued by the dramatic flow of events in our school, and now Reshad had revealed the musical score.

A brainy guy named Doug was scheduled to present the Law of Seven at 2:00 p.m. — on the note *Sol*. He had studied with British mathematician, scientist, and philosopher, John G. Bennett. Mr. Bennett had worked with Gurdjieff in his younger years and then made it his mission to transmit this knowledge to the next generation of young people before he died.

Doug introduced Gurdjieff's two fundamental laws of the universe:

The Law of Three and the Law of Seven —also known as the Octave. Today, what we know of these laws comes from a 1912 lecture given by Gurdjieff to a group of students in St. Petersburg, Russia. One of the students, scholar P.D. Ouspensky, turned the talks into the seminal book, *In Search of the Miraculous.*[3]

Ouspensky's recollections — of Gurdjieff speaking non-natively in Russian to a group of students who were not allowed to take notes and which were translated into English thirty years later — represent the source material for Gurdjieff's two fundamental laws of the universe.

Mr. Gurdjieff felt that the most complex mechanisms of life can ultimately be explained by simple principles observed in everyday events. The first of these is The Law of Three or Law of Three Forces. According to Gurdjieff, every phenomenon in the universe is the result of three forces: Positive, Negative, and Neutralizing. They can be observed in the makeup of atoms (protons, electrons, and neutrons), electricity (positive, negative, and ground), natural phenomena like the forces of weather (high pressure, low pressure, and precipitation) as well as actions, events, and human affairs.

In everyday activities, the Three Forces manifest as Active, Passive, and Reconciling, or in human affairs: Affirming, Denying and Mediating. If two countries are locked in opposition, a third country acts as mediator. In marriage, the birth of the child represents the Third Force as she brings a meaningful purpose to the relationship. In Christianity, it's the Father, Son, and Holy Spirit. In Taoism, it's Yin, Yang, and the Tao. In physics, it's space, time, and the continuum. In a sitcom, there's the setup, the complications, and the resolution.

Even a simple yoga stretch draws from three forces: the *active* effort to touch toes, the *resistant* force of stiff muscles and the inner *release* when you breathe (Third Force) into the tension. Knowing how and when to invoke the Third Force is the key to healing, diplomacy, relationships, child rearing, creating art, and telling a good joke.

3. Ouspensky, P. D. 2004. In Search of the Miraculous: London: Paul H. Crompton Ltd.

The Third Force manifests as an outside force that changes the course of events. The Third Force enters through the grace that follows a prayer, the unexpected guest who enlivens the party or appears in the ER, the guy named Johnny who arrives unexpectedly to plant apple trees, or even the creative insight that pops in from out of the blue when you run out of ideas. Third Force sneaks in when you confront the inevitable, accept your fate and let go of the fear of change.

The Law of Three made sense to me, but the Law of Seven, known as the Octave, was more perplexing. If the Law of Three Forces is about reconciling opposing forces, the Law of Seven describes growth, process, and unfoldment — basically, how things happen.

If I plant a seed, the Octave describes how the plant will sprout and branch out. If I start a term paper, the Octave maps the struggle toward completion. When we make our wedding vows, the Octave predicts the swing from bliss to blame — what Harville Hendrix describes as the natural transition in marriage from the *Romance* stage to *Power Struggle*.[4] In this way, marital love faces vibrational ups and downs. Consider Marilyn Monroe colliding into Tom Ewell's marriage at the crucial octave interval: *The Seven Year Itch.*

When we go on a diet, the Octave delivers a tempting cheesecake on day three. If we seek fame and fortune, the Octave explains how our efforts become thwarted. The Octave reveals itself through seven visible colors, seven notes in the musical scale, seven visible planets, seven days in a week, seven groups of elements in the periodic table, and seven chapters to get to this point in the book.

You know the Octave is real because you can feel it.

Close your eyes and hum the musical scale: *Do-Re-Mi-Fa-So-La-Si-Do.* The feeling of completion and satisfaction when you sound the culminating *Do* is undeniable because from *Do* to *Do*, the vibrational rate gets doubled. If the first *Do* vibrates at 220 cycles per second, the second *Do* reaches 440 cycles per second. Put another

4. Hendrix, H. (2001). *Getting the Love You Want.* Holt Paperbacks.

way, if you pluck a 6-inch string to sound the first note, plucking a 3-inch string creates a feeling of satisfaction and completion. We sense this feeling of completion going up the scale. It's the same feeling when you complete a task, when a drama climaxes, a song ends, when aggrieved parties reconcile, when a child reaches a major milestone like walking, graduation or marriage, or when we recline into *savasana* after a grueling yoga class. All of these are octaves.

When you pluck a string, other frequencies vibrate in sympathy — those angels. These harmonic overtones are expressed in whole numbers — a third, a fourth, a fifth. Before you know it, a pleasing musical scale is derived from these tones. When you tune your instrument, the tuning feels right when the vibrations harmonize.

Going up the musical scale, each note, each vibration has a rightful place based on whole numbers. The most pleasing sounds have simple ratios, one note to the other, compared to the starting point: 2:1, 3:2, 4:3, 5:3, 5:4 and so on.

Here's the interesting part. If you look at a piano, the major notes (the white keys) don't progress uniformly up the scale. Black keys are inserted at regular intervals. There are two places on the keyboard where a black key (a semitone or half step) is missing. Between *Mi* and *Fa* and between *Si* and *Do* there are no black keys. The piano layout was not designed for aesthetics. The groupings of keys conform to how vibrations occur in physics and nature. The vibrations don't increase uniformly. They slow down slightly at the *Mi-Fa* and *Si-Do* — the intervals are smaller, so the black keys are missing.

If the piano keyboard were a set of stairs, the building inspector would not approve. Imagine if the stairway to your second floor had eight steps. And suppose the clumsy carpenter set a smaller rise on two of the steps. Sober or not, you would stumble every time you hit those steps. Vibrationally, this is what happens at the *Mi-Fa* and *Si–Do* intervals. In human events like a business meeting, an entrepreneurial enterprise, a marriage, an election campaign, an exercise regimen, and especially efforts in pursuit of Fortune, these intervals predict stumbling points — places where the original intention gets diverted, chaos can enter, or unexpected outside forces change the stakes.

Another way to look at it: Imagine climbing to cruising altitude on an airline flight while you lean back to enjoy your tunes. The steady push from the jet engines delivers a consistent rate of climb, a comfortable 1800 feet per minute. We all know this familiar feeling of ascent. You barely notice it. Now imagine if the pilot were to jerk the throttle back just a bit — whoops, the plane dips — then he pushes it forward again. Whoa, not a happy stomach.

This dipsy-doo represents the "discontinuity of vibrations." This natural retardation in the rate of increase between *Mi* and *Fa* and between *Si* and *Do* results in the missing black notes on the piano. If you construct a scale that is most pleasing to the ear (with a perfect fifth and a doubling of the octave), these retardations result. More than a tuning problem, they reflect the physics of vibration in the natural world. The Golden Ratio and the Fibonacci series — the harmonic basis for beauty and growth in the natural world — are derived from the Octave.

Why does the knowledge of the Octave matter to Fortune seekers? While the physics of vibration creates beauty and harmony in the natural world, in human affairs, these good vibrations can place roadblocks against mental pursuits and even upset the status quo. Here's how:

The human mind seeks a kind of binary experience. If I do A, I expect B. It is a world of expectation and causation, straight-line thinking, and comparison. If I apply myself, I will succeed. If I get a product into Lowe's, I will become rich.

But the vibrating, living universe is not arithmetic; it's harmonic. There are no straight lines in nature, but instead, curves, spirals, ellipses, undulations, twists and waves. The physics of vibration shapes our world. Plants grow in spiral patterns, as does the nautilus shell, and the human ear. Manufacturing jobs disappear in one part of the world and expand in another. NASA has gone so far as to listen to the internal vibrations of thousands of stars to determine if any are supporting planets.[5]

The human soul longs to go through octaves — hence the appeal of music, theater, films, and literature. Since the time of Aristotle's *The Poetics,* dramatic structure — the Octave — has been used to drive a cathartic experience. When the audience arrives feeling foul or distracted, the performer works to consciously lift the energy to an emotional plateau. The performer is taking the audience on a journey through the Octave.

Reshad was a master of energy vibration and knew how to move the energy in a room. As an author, healer, teacher and above all, a performer, Reshad inserted shocks with precision to disrupt emotional complacency and move the energy through the Octave.

I became Reshad's Octave student and watched his mastery of the moment. My movie background fueled my fascination. When a movie begins, the world of the story is in balance. But soon, something kicks the character's life out of kilter. An inciting incident creates an unexpected problem or a burning desire. This dramatic event ups the stakes and pushes the character into a mission. Halfway into the story, a midpoint loss forces the character to face his soul. The original crisis spawns a confrontation which requires the character to reach deeply into his heroic capacity. The conflict catapults the story forward, toward a climax, and finally a heroic realization. In this way, the Octave drags the initially reluctant protagonist through the transforming events of the story.

Here's the kicker. Just like the stairway with the funky steps, energies don't proceed up the scale uniformly. At the *Mi-Fa* interval, the original intention often deviates, enthusiasm wanes, distractions sway, or chaos can enter. According to Mr. Gurdjieff, the *Mi-Fa* and *Si-Do* intervals invite an outside shock. This shock, the entry of the Third Force, appears to be disruptive but ultimately proves to be transformative. In this way, the Third Force enters to challenge the

5. Overbye, Dennis. "Listening to the Stars." *The New York Times.* N.p., n.d. Web. 30 Jan. 2011.

status quo, kick complacency into higher gear, increase the vibratory rate, advance the plot, and open the heart.

Octaves are multi-dimensional. Like Russian nesting dolls, the seven steps of one octave serve as a single step in a larger octave. Octaves also intersect and branch out. My journey and your journey intersect to open an opportunity. Your note *Do,* (your first day as an armored car driver), collides at my *Mi-Fa* crisis (kidnappers have just demanded a ransom payment, so I frantically decide to rob a Brinks truck).

There are also qualities associated with the notes to the Octave: *Do* – Intention, *Re* – Rhythm, *Mi* – Identification, *Fa* – Expansion of the Heart, *Sol* – Facing one's soul, *La* – Reaffirmation of intention, *Si* – Acceptance in gratitude. These are not carved in stone, but rather, how I experience them.

I began to watch how the transformation process at the Institute invoked a daily drama. A series of small "crises" would disrupt the normal flow of events: an impromptu wedding, a home birth involving Reshad's wife, the visit of an NBC News crew, a Cambodian monk requesting that the walls be draped in green fabric — by tonight! — and any number of spiritual celebrities dropping in. With each crisis, we would drop everything and be forced to stop thinking about oneself and throw ourselves into the need of the moment.

If there weren't a convenient crisis, Reshad would create one. During one evening talk, we listened intently as Reshad guided us into a state of deep receptivity. As the hour dragged on (as predicted by the Octave), people began to fatigue and lose concentration. The energy started to feel thick. One by one, eyes drooped, heads dropped. At a remarkably timed moment, an unexpected guest came to the door. Thirty sets of sleepy eyes turned to see who it was, and Reshad roared:

"LISTEN!!! I NEED YOU TO LISTEN!" he bellowed. "JUST BECAUSE SOMEONE COMES TO THE DOOR DOESN'T MEAN YOU CAN LOSE ATTENTION. WE ONLY HAVE

THIS TIME. THERE IS NO OTHER TIME THAN NOW, SO LISTEN!!!"

These kinds of shocks were frequent. There was also something called the Stop Exercise. In the typical social setting, there is a kind of chatter or hubbub that grows and grows like a room full of bleating sheep (think cocktail party where everyone talks about themselves). According to the Octave, in most social settings the energy is not going through. It gets stuck in identification, at *Mi*, bleating about "me." When this happened in the Institute, the person in charge had the responsibility to yell, "S T O P !" The rule was to completely freeze, without a sound or motion, until the command, "continue" was given. It seemed harsh, but if you sensed the energy, you could feel it move through. The "play" would continue.

Bottled-up energy defines everyday life. We get stuck in a mental "hubbub." Instead of *Do-Re-Mi-Fa-Sol-La-Si-Do*, we live in *Do-Re-Mi—Do-Re-Mi—Do-Re-Mi*. It's the world of habit, comfort, conformity, and commuting. Stuck-in-a-rut describes Gurdjieff's "man the machine." Everything in the machine resists change until a crisis intervenes. The machine resists the new being born because the old must die. And like a machine, the battery runs down. The natural curiosity of youth becomes tired. Bodies hunch, muscles droop, ideas become fixed. It's the dissipation of energy predicted by the Second Law of Thermodynamics.

Going through the Octave releases energy. Imagine raking leaves for an hour and feeling exhausted. Conversely, why do you feel invigorated at the end of a strenuous one-hour yoga class? Going through an Octave makes the difference. We have all been in meetings that get stuck. People doze off; the conversation loses direction; thoughts become redundant, and the Octave piles up like a log jam. Finally, someone mercifully remembers the original intention and pushes the meeting to culmination.

This is how to move through the Octave: Like an energetic juggler, you learn to keep three balls of awareness *simultaneously* aloft: 1) remembering your original intention, 2) remembering your destination, and 3) maintaining awareness of the quality of the present moment. Have we become stuck? Distracted? Have we started down a different track? Inevitably, tension builds at the *Mi-Fa* and the balls begin to drop. Self-awareness keeps them aloft.

I became fascinated watching the energies of the Octave at the Institute. After Doug delivered his presentation, Donna played the octave on her cello. The qualities of each note spoke to me, inviting me to raise my vibrational rate. Listening to the scale also prompted the question: "If this school is an octave, are we getting stuck? Have we deviated from our original intention? What is the next big plot point?"

Four days later, we received an outside shock — a stern letter from the City of Los Angeles:

"You are operating a school on property zoned for single-family use. You are ordered to cease operations and vacate the premises."

Four months after the school's launch (and eighty days after ignoring our original 40-day intention), the Institute for Conscious Life was forced to abandon its epochal mission. I remembered Reshad's original promise:

"When the school has fulfilled its aims, it will disband, disappear and reappear in a different form somewhere else if it is needed."

8

Rumi Comes to America

If you pray from your heart,
you don't even need to make a sound or say a word.
God accepts it, and prefers it that way.
Suleyman Dede

"Maybe, God appears in the form of zoning enforcement," I mused to George the Communist as we watched the swirl of guests stream out of the Institute for Conscious Life. "This is might be too much energy for one little boiling pot."

We had been staging three public events per week — a study night, an open house, and a worship service. Like an esoteric version of Saturday Night Live, we were pressed to develop new material each Thursday with story, song, film, movements and a talk.

I crumpled the useless flyer announcing the now-canceled events. I would never learn what August 14, *Aligning with the Esoteric Geometry of High-Velocity Inner Space* was about. Tonight we staged our finale, "*Mysterium Conjunctum, The Alchemical Marriage.*" And yes, it was still a mysterium.

"So, what's your take on this God business?" George asked.

I said something stupid about it all being energy. I didn't pick up on George's real question. He saw life through the lens of social justice and was disturbed by Reshad's prima donna way of mixing God with personal drama.

But now it was time for the Institute for Conscious Life to pull up stakes. George and his Berkeley contingent moved into half of a duplex in Silverlake. Their goal was to live a communal, socially-conscious life in a working class neighborhood — and as far from Reshad as possible. Reshad, his wife, and infant moved to a guest house one block from the Whisky a Go Go on the Sunset Strip. Everyone else scattered around town.

For the next couple of months, our little group was in a holding pattern, waiting for Fortune to turn — and it did when the second half of George's Silverlake duplex suddenly became vacant. Reshad, wife, and baby took that as a "sign" and settled into the other half of George's duplex. Others followed to the neighborhood. Just like that, the Institute for Conscious Life 2.0 was born.

Each evening we gathered in the duplex to hear Reshad read typewritten pages from *The Invisible Way*, his follow-up to *The Last Barrier*, his spiritual best-seller about his Sufi journey to Turkey. Reshad put the freshly-typed manuscript down and seized the pregnant pause.

"I've been deeply contemplating the next step in our work," Reshad announced. "I've been in contact with Suleyman Dede."

Everyone ooh'd and ahh'd, but I had no clue who Suleyman Dede was.

"If you're willing," Reshad added, waiting for the pause to impregnate, "we can invite Dede to Los Angeles."

After more oohs and ahhs, Reshad explained that Dede was the Sheikh of the Whirling Dervishes in Konya, Turkey and the head of the line of the mystical poet Rumi.

"Sure," I thought, "why not invite the Pope while we're at it?"

"You'll have to raise the money, find a translator… and understand, he's not glamorous. He was a humble cook who fed the poor," Reshad explained. "He's never been to America."

And just like that, the Octave shifted, and the mission changed.

To understand how this giant 700-year turn of the Octave delivered Rumi to America, you must follow the history — but I'll try to keep it short.

In 1970s America, Rumi was hardly a household name. Nobody heard of the guy. Maybe, one or two Rumi books were available, not the thousands of titles that currently pop up on Amazon.com.

Today, Rumi is America's bestselling poet, not Maya Angelou, Robert Frost or even Shakespeare. He's the interest of celebrities like Madonna, Martin Sheen, Demi Moore, and Deepak Chopra. I've even seen Rumi's poetry scroll by on the in-flight monitor of a Delta flight.

It's ironic that in post-9/11 America, a classically trained Muslim theologian who taught Sharia law in an Anatolian madrassa nearly 800 years ago would become the nation's infatuation. Like a new age Forrest Gump, I would soon find myself at ground zero for Rumi's Western invasion.

Mevlana Jalaluddin Rumi was born in 1207 in present-day Tajikistan (or possibly Afghanistan). His father was a noted theologian. When the Mongols invaded Central Asia sometime between 1215 and 1220 (the disruptive outside Third Force), Rumi's family began a several-year journey westward, passing through Baghdad, Mecca, and Damascus. Along the way, Rumi met many of the great philosophers and scholars of the age and likely encountered the brigands, wanderers, Sufis and impostors who populate so many of his stories.[1]

At the invitation of the Sultan of the Seljuks, Rumi's family finally settled in Konya, Turkey where he and his father established a madrassa. Rumi grew to become a prodigious religious scholar with an adoring crowd of students.

Fortune came knocking one day when a wandering dervish — The Unexpected Guest — came to Konya in search of Rumi.

In one version of the story, Rumi was on a donkey, riding past the

1. Lewis, Franklin. 2000. Rumi Past and Present, East and West. Oxford; Boston: Oneworld.

sugar merchants' stalls when a man dressed as a beggar reached out from a doorway and grabbed the reins. It was Shams of Tabriz.

Shams challenged the startled Rumi, "Who was greater, Beyazid Bastami or the Prophet Muhammad?" Rumi answered that the Prophet was greater, but Shams pressed further: "Didn't the Prophet say, 'We have not known Thee as Thou ought to be known,' whereas Bastami said, 'Glory be to me; how great is my majesty.'"

This challenge may seem arcane, but like a heretical wrench thrown into the gears of Rumi's scholarly mind, Shams threw Rumi into soul-shaking perplexity. Rumi dropped everything to follow Shams. The two began a months-long *sohbet*, an illuminating communion of words and silence.

Shams upended Rumi's world like a bolt of lightning — or rather, an outside shock. You could think of Shams as a vector of Third Force energy, releasing Rumi from his scholarly life and transforming him into the mystical poet of love.

According to Rumi's eldest son, Sultan Valed, "When Rumi saw Shams' face, the secrets opened up for him. He saw unseen things and heard things that he never heard from anyone. It was almost as if Rumi's shadow disappeared in Shams' holy light."[2]

Rumi dropped everything to follow Shams, leaving students, school, and family behind. His students were not pleased. Shams disappeared once or twice, and then finally, was never found again, presumably murdered out of jealousy. His heart rent with despair, Rumi searched far and wide for Shams. Rumi's longing was answered with the realization:

Why should I seek? I am the same as He. His essence speaks through me. I have been looking for myself![3]

One day after Shams' disappearance, the grieving Rumi passed through the metalsmiths' bazaar when suddenly, the tap-tap-tap of

2. Can, Şefik, Zeki Saritoprak, and M. Fethullah Gulen. 2004. Fundamentals of Rumi's Thought: A Mevlevi Sufi Perspective. Tughra Books.
3. Nicholson, R. (2001). *Selected Poems from the Divan-e Shams-e Tabrizi*. IBEX .

their hammers opened his heart. Round-and-round, he whirled. The rhythmic tapping sounded like zikr, the repetition of God's name. From this, the whirling tradition was born.

From this point on, Rumi's poetry poured out from his heart — a sea of creation written down by his loyal disciple, Husameddin. This poetic outpouring ultimately became Rumi's magnificent opus, the Masnavi. With six volumes and 50,000 lines, the Masnavi is a multi-layered weaving of mystical fables, Koranic references, spiritual commentary, and bawdy tales.

When Rumi died in 1273, worshipers from all religions traveled to Konya to pay their respects — Muslims, Christians, Jews, Arabs, Persians, Turks, and Romans. They understood what Rumi meant when he said:

I am neither from the East nor the West. No boundaries exist in my heart.

Soon after, Rumi's son, Sultan Valed, started the Mevlevi Order of dervishes to venerate Rumi's work. For the next 650 years, the Mevlevi dervishes performed a far-reaching role in Turkish society, touching every aspect of civic life — politics, the arts, academics, and spirituality.

The Mevlevi's influence reached its zenith in 1925 when, in a move to modernize Turkey, the founder of the Republic, Mustafa Kemal Atatürk waged an aggressive campaign to secularize the country to a European model. Before 1925, the Ottoman Empire was an Islamic state in which the political leader, the Sultan, was also the spiritual leader, the Caliph. Atatürk felt the caliphate system was backward and corrupt compared to modern civics in the West.

Atatürk decreed in his "Law for the Maintenance of Public Order," that all dervish tekkes (communal lodges), tombs, and schools must close, including five Mevlevi tekkes in Istanbul alone. Dervish practices, clothing and books were forbidden. The Mevlevi tekke (the focal point of dervish practices and the site of Rumi's crypt) became a museum.[4] Around this time, the Soviet Union was also suppressing religion, but unlike modern Russia, traditional Sufi brotherhoods are still officially illegal in Turkey. Yes, in today's Turkey, where the Whirling Dervish stands as the national icon and the draw for millions of tourists annually, Sufi brotherhoods are illegal and the whirling ceremonies exist mainly as cultural displays.

Atatürk reportedly stated to the Çelebi, the head of the Mevlevi dervishes, "You, the Mevlevis have made a great difference in combating ignorance and religious fundamentalism for centuries, as well as making contributions to science and the arts. However, we are obliged not to make any exceptions and must include Mevlevi tekkes [in the ban]. Nonetheless, the ideas and teaching of Rumi will not only exist forever, but they will emerge even more powerfully in the future."[5]

For the next 50 years, the sacred practice of whirling went underground. In 1953, the authorities relented and sanctioned a modest whirling presentation in a theater, ultimately becoming an annual tourist event in a Konya gymnasium, albeit with police scrutiny to suppress any overt spirituality.

When Reshad suggested that we raise money to invite Suleyman Dede, I knew nothing of this history. I couldn't see how our Sunset Boulevard rummage sales would release Rumi from modern bondage, or how by roaming the streets looking for restorable furniture, we might restore what Atatürk had banned.

We were young spiritual hippies riding the wave. We spotted a couch on the curb, put it up for sale and made some cash. We doubled our money when we spotted the same couch on the curb a day later. This wheeling and dealing raised $2500 in two weekends — $15,000 in today's earning power — and allowed us to bring the head of the Whirling Dervishes, the Sheikh of Konya, to America.

Suleyman Dede, or Dede, as we affectionately called him, was

4. Friedlander, Shems. 1992. The Whirling Dervishes: Being an Account of the Sufi Order Known As the Mevlevis and Its Founder the Poet and Mystic Mevlana Jalalu'Ddin Rumi. Albany, NY: State Univ of New York Pr.
5. "Mevlevi Order & Sema." n.d. International Mevlana Foundation. http://mevlanafoundation.com/mevlevi_order_en.html.

twenty-one years old when Atatürk's law turned the spiritual tekkes into soup kitchens. As the last sheikh to have lived the traditional Mevlevi way of life before it was banned, this humble cook was likely the last living link from the spiritual line of Rumi before Atatürk.

As we prepared the house from top to bottom, I pictured Dede, prayer beads in hand, kneeling in his airline seat during his eleven-hour flight to Los Angeles. I wondered what he was thinking. He experienced Rumi's full flourish as a young man, and now as an old man, he had been invited halfway around the globe to hand Rumi's legacy to some well-meaning young Americans. Maybe Dede realized that Atatürk was right: Rumi would emerge stronger again, but in Los Angeles, and in our living room.

When Dede pulled up to the house, I didn't really know what to expect — hardly a diminutive Turkish gentleman wearing a striped three-piece suit, pocket watch, fedora hat and sly twinkle.

Dede's words were deceptively simple. Even through the translator, they carried a deliciously heretical truth:

"God is in your heart already, no matter what religion you have," Dede told us as we huddled around. "All you have to do is to open your heart and listen to it, and you will find God."

At this point in my life, I was already curious about Fortune's capricious nature, so my ears perked up when Dede underscored the prophetic nature of his mission:

"Rumi wrote the Mesnavi 715 years ago," Dede declared. "At that time, Rumi prophesized that the world of Islam would forget him, but he felt that years and years and centuries later, the Western world would appreciate him and understand him better. This came true today."

Later that afternoon, in a touching ceremony, Dede initiated Reshad as a Sheikh of the Mevlevi. He wrapped a traditional wool hat, placed it on Reshad's head, performed prayers, and signed a Mevlevi document, the *silsila* or chain of official permission.

That evening we were summoned to our garage meditation room. Dede gestured to stand here, cross your arms, bow, turn, now do this, now do that. He was initiating us into the whirling ceremony, or *sema*. While this initiation was moving, I was intrigued by something politically more significant the next morning.

At breakfast, the cooks served Reshad an all-American meal of eggs, toast, bacon, coffee and orange juice. In a flurry of Turkish, Dede pointed at Reshad's bacon, gesturing that something was wrong. In deference to his Muslim faith, the cooks had served Dede's plate bacon-free. A flurry of words through the translator ensued.

"Tell Dede that I humbly apologize about the bacon," Reshad offered sheepishly. "I'm sorry if it offends him and I will remove it from my plate."

More translation and more shaking of Dede's head.

"Dede explains that he would like bacon, too," came the translation.

And so it happened that Dede ate bacon in Los Angeles. More than a gracious accommodation, Dede demonstrated Rumi's point that religion should adapt to the time and place.

"I come to Los Angeles to plant a seed," he explained. "I come to plant Mevlana's message of universal love in this soil. The way of Mevlana, of Rumi, will grow here in the West in its own way."

That afternoon, I lugged cases of lighting equipment up the grand stairway of the magnificent neo-gothic Elks Hall. As I strung cables and hung spotlights, I sensed that something meaningful was about to happen.

When the lights came on, five young American dervishes unfolded their arms, lifted their hearts, and whirled to the ritual cadence of Mevlevi music. For the first time in history, men and women performed the sacred rite together. Was this the *Mysterium Conjunctum* Reshad promised — the Alchemical Marriage, the reconciling of opposites?

Afterward, someone asked Lisa, one of the *semazens* (whirlers) if the energy went through. She coyly answered, "Maybe, my lunch went through." But she knew; we all knew: This was the precise moment that Rumi took root in America.

The next day, Dede joined us at the park for a picnic. As Reshad strummed the intro bars from an old Ewan MacColl song, Dede got up from his seat. Reshad began to sing:

"I met my love by the gas works wall
Dreamed a dream by the old canal…"

Dede gently grasped his lapel and began the sacred turn of the dervish, ever so slowly, round and round on the grass."

"I kissed my girl by the factory wall
Dirty old town
Dirty old town"

And with that, I was freed from religious form. Yes, kissing one's girl in a dirty old town can be an act of prayer. Thank you, Dede.

Within days, Rumi's seed began to sprout. The first tendril appeared two weeks later in the form of Coleman Barks, a young University of Georgia English professor who was attending a conference with Robert Bly on the other side of the continent in Maine.

"The conference was about poetry, music and mythology and just whatever Robert had been reading lately," Coleman explained. "At that point, Bly had been reading translations of Rumi, and he had a stack of these that he gave to me. In his Lutheran Minnesota accent, Bly said, 'These poems need to be released from their cages.' And so I began doing that, just on my own for seven years."[6]

Until that moment in 1976, Coleman had never even heard of Rumi. But it was done. Fortune released Rumi from his scholarly cage a second time — first with Shams challenging Rumi in the marketplace and now with Robert Bly challenging a young Coleman Barks 700 years later. Rumi's octave was complete.

Dede's visit to America began what I called the "Mevlevi Spring,"

6. "Coleman Barks, Foremost Rumi Translator, Talks about the Persian Mystic's Timeless Appeal and His Own Spiritual Life." n.d. SF Gate. http://www.sfgate.com/living/article/Coleman-Barks-foremost-Rumi-translator-talks-2537796.php.

a Rumi love bubble that lasted two and a half years — maybe seven — starting at the same time Coleman began his creative magic, turning Persian couplets into contemporary free verse.

"Every afternoon, after I finished teaching," Coleman recounted, "I'd go into a restaurant and work on poems — have some tea and work on those. From 1977 to 1984, there are seven years when I wasn't even thinking about publishing. So that was a kind of practice I did."[7]

To celebrate December 17, the traditional observance of Rumi's passing, we rented a baroque former movie palace on Melrose Avenue in Los Angeles to stage our first full performance of the Whirling Dervishes. The young dervishes huddled around me, chanting in prayer, as I hot-wired the breaker panel to run our stage lighting — a trick I learned at film school.

At that same moment, Jonathan, a twenty-two-year-old aspiring dervish living in Boulder, Colorado had a vision — not of me being electrocuted, but of Rumi. Following an inner prompting, Jonathan started to paint Rumi's likeness on a bed sheet as we turned. Jonathan took this omen to encourage his Sufi group to invite Reshad to Boulder. Soon after, the group offered us a magnificent house in downtown Boulder to turn into a Mevlevi tekke.

We accepted the invitation, packed a U-Haul truck, loaded up children, a newborn, and a caravan of cars and headed across the desert toward Boulder.

Thus began the Mevlana Foundation. Fifty years after Atatürk, a tekke was born in the West. Two years later, Suleyman Dede returned to consecrate the space. People arrived from various parts of the world — all seeking contact with Dede, our living link to Rumi.

My friends reminisced:

"I remember my first encounter with Dede in Boulder. My heart burst open, and I seemed to melt into thin air. The powerful effect of love made me speechless for days. What an amazing experience. What an

7. "Interview with Robert Bly and Coleman Barks." 2002. C/Oasis: Writing for the Connected World. http://www.sunoasis.com/blyinterview2.html.

incredible time in my life."
Barbara

"I was pregnant. Dede placed his hand on my head and said a prayer. I felt such silence through my body. Then he said that this child was a boy, and the next one will be a girl. I had NO plans to have any more children, but, he proved to be correct — my next child was Alisha."
— Judith

"I was cooking a pilaf for about a hundred visitors by myself. Dede passed by the kitchen with his interpreter. He stood there for a moment watching me. Then he said, 'May you never recover.' Only now do I know what he meant."
— Jonathan

"He kissed both of us on the forehead, told us to sit down and listen. We did as we were told. He took both our hands and proceeded to talk to us about love and understanding and forgiveness... We walked out of the room radiating love for all.... We were in awe of him and his incredible love and wisdom. May he rest in peace."
— Lima

At the end of the visit, Dede headed down the walk, reached the gate and turned to face us proclaiming, "Even though I leave you now, know that Mevlana is in your heart."

And with that, the Mevlevi Spring ended. The wave of love that had washed up to our shore would quickly pull back with a dramatic undertow. Within a year, the Mevlevi authorities in Turkey stripped Reshad of his title, official permission, and privileges. Was it because Reshad wasn't a Muslim, or his excessive drinking, his rocky marital life, or because he was too much of a loose cannon to represent the legacy? No one really knows. But Reshad took pride in being a loose cannon, explaining, "A true Sufi is the son of the moment."

Dede had initiated several young Americans as Mevlevi sheikhs — titles that were also annulled. In fact, Suleyman Dede's legacy role seems expunged as well. There's no mention of him on any official Rumi Web site in Turkey.

The end of the Mevlevi Spring also marked the beginning of Islamic world's long descent into turmoil. Within a month of Dede's departure, troops implementing martial law for the U.S.-backed Shah of Iran fired into crowds of worshipers, marking the point of no return for the Iranian revolution, the Ayatollah, the hostage crisis, and the emergence of radical Islam.

And just like that, poof, it was gone.

A few years ago, a friend of mine visited Konya and was told in no uncertain terms, "That story about Dede and the bacon, it never happened."

9

A Decaying Orbit

Life is a process of becoming,
a combination of states we have to go through.
Where people fail is that they wish to
elect a state and remain in it.
This is a kind of death.
Anaïs Nin

The Octave predicts that every enterprise — every line of vibration — will decay on its own until that vibration bears no resemblance to the original impulse. Gurdjieff describes this tendency in everyday activities:

"After a certain period of energetic activity… a reaction comes, work becomes tedious and tiring… becomes mechanical; feeling becomes weaker and weaker, descends to the level of the common events of the day; thought becomes dogmatic, literal."[1]

We express these energy dips matter-of-factly: "I'm feeling tired; I'd

---

1. Ouspensky, P. D. 2004. In Search of the Miraculous: London: Paul H. Crompton Ltd.

rather stay home; I'm too tired to cook; I'm in a foul mood; Maybe, I'm getting sick."

Yesterday, my friend Lisa noticed a dip. She posted on Facebook:

Putting this out there. i'm in an ebb...not a flow. i feel backwards...or at the very least, stuck. i'm sad, down with little upbeat joyous moments peppered in...admiring the pretty weather but secretly wishing it would be rainy and stormy so I can stay inside and retreat to my bat cave without feeling like i'm missing out on anything.

Science observes this as entropy, the tendency of energy to dissipate and for systems to gravitate toward disorder. While this is an unalterable law, strangely, the world has not collapsed into a chaotic heap. Machines eventually break down, but they can also be rebuilt. In the same manner, Gurdjieff sees man as a machine:

The "man-machine" is in the power of accident. His activities may fall by accident into some sort of channel... giving the illusion that aims of some kind are being attained... The attainment of aims in small things creates the conviction that he is able to attain any aim... to arrange the whole of his life.

This is the illusion of moving through the Octave while, all the while, the "machine" is losing energy. The vibrations slow down, complacency settles in, until additional shocks enter where needed:

Octaves can develop consecutively and continuously in the desired direction if "additional shocks" enter at the moment when vibrations slow down. If "additional shocks" do not enter at the necessary moments, octaves change their direction.[2]

Every time we abandon intentions, or even break away from work to surf the Web, the Octave changes direction. Recently, while on an Ayurvedic cleanse, at a critical juncture, I became convinced I needed some protein. Before long, I was devouring chicken. Just like that, the Octave changed direction.

2. (Ouspensky 2004)

If we can stay engaged with the twists and turns, and inherent suffering, the Octave drives the narrative arcs of aspiration, transformation, and the Hero's Journey. The heroic Octave goes against lethargy, against nature, and against the tendency of a perfect garden to become a bed of weeds. This anti-entropic impulse expresses itself through evolution, biological complexity, and the aspirations of living beings that feed off the sun — the sun being a higher energy.

Evolution takes its anti-entropic leaps through natural selection — the collision of environmental shocks and genetic chance. On the gaming table, you don't get to carry your cards from one round to the next. When the dealer shuffles the deck, the landscape changes, reopening the door of possibility. The Octave predicts the reshuffling — the opportunities to shift gears, reinvent oneself, pick up the pieces and renew the mission. These opportunities present themselves at the intervals (the missing black keys on the piano). Importantly, they are jump-started by an "outside shock."

In this way, the shock of sudden illness, discovering infidelity, a job loss, an accident, career change, having a baby, going back to school, an unexpected kiss, meeting your Shams of Tabriz — anything that shatters complacency and upends the established order — renews the creative process.

The world of economics observes a similar phenomenon — *creative destruction.* The term is often used to morally justify the actions of hedge funds buying and destroying companies. It can also be observed when disruptive technology "destroys" entire industries while allowing new ones to blossom.

Today, traditional newspapers are struggling while *The Huffington Post* blooms. Kodak went bankrupt, amazingly, amid an explosion of picture-taking. Nature has cooked up many evolutionary dead ends — birds with teeth, giant horses, and the dinosaurs. But, as I discovered with my own business, things don't always work out. The challenge is to catch the next wave on your soul journey.

Hinduism recognizes the cosmic role of creation and destruction represented by the dance of the god Shiva. Shiva stands perfectly balanced as the pendulum swings from creation to destruction. According to the Vedas, Shiva destroys the universe at the end of each 4 billion-year cycle which allows a new Creation to appear. Not a Big Bang, but a bang-bang-bang to Shiva's cosmic drumbeat.

Why a particular line of force evolves or devolves is the mystery that plays in front of our eyes. We see it at track events when the front runner loses steam and the skinny Ethiopian lurking in the back sprints to the finish line. We see it in the sagging nature of the aging process. We watch the promise of political change crumble when a candidate's soaring vision must conform to the politics of expediency. Even more alarming, we see it today as America's 240-year-run with democracy seems at peril. When life becomes mechanical, the creative opportunities die with it.

Entropy is insidious. One moment we're healthy; the next moment we're sick. We miss the little turns where our emotions take a dip.

Gurdjieff explains how the vibrational rate loses force and deviates from its original intention and how these turns, if unchecked, ultimately descend "in a diametrically opposite direction, still preserving its former name." He presents the history of Christianity as an example:

> Think how many turns the line of development of forces must have taken to come from the Gospel preaching love to the Inquisition.[3]

In this way, inspired religious movements descend into dogma. When rigid forms become unsustainable, an outside shock may enter, forcing a renewal. In this way, Shams of Tabriz upended the theocratic world of Rumi's madrassa and allowed the creative force of mystical love to enter.

Consider how the Inquisition put Galileo under house arrest. This shock was intended to suppress creative thought, yet Galileo's

3. (Ouspensky 2004)

incarceration spawned one of the founding documents of physics and nature: *Discourses Concerning Two New Sciences.*

Atatürk was also a creator-destroyer. You can follow the improbable line of force that connected Atatürk's 1925 decree, to Dede serving in the soup kitchen, to Dede meeting Reshad, coming to America, the Mevlevi Spring, and to the book in your hands. Atatürk was an agent of transformation. By crushing a traditional religious culture that had presumably become corrupted by political power, Atatürk created the conditions for Rumi's mystical knowledge to re-emerge at another place and time. By crushing the rose, he released the scent.

Other cultures have endured similar destructive/creative shocks. One could argue that the Communist Chinese were agents of change. By violently displacing ancient Tibet, the formerly remote and inaccessible Tibetan Buddhist tradition now plays a much larger role on the world stage with a globe-trotting Dalai Lama and a big Western following advancing the cause.

The Octave helped me recognize that our Mevlevi Spring had begun to fade. After Suleyman Dede left Boulder in 1978, the descent kicked in. We had persevered long and hard to launch Rumi in the West, yet overnight our work began to lose altitude. I wasn't aware that the Mevlevi Spring was coming to an end, just that things were settling into a mechanical routine. That is the cunning nature of the Octave and the identified mind. The Octave can take many little dips before you sense the descent — before the conviction of faith imprisons your free-thinking Galileo.

After Dede had left, and Reshad with him, we fell into an ebb — not a flow. Reshad moved back to England where his marriage quickly fell apart. With Reshad gone, the shock came: The Colorado Sufi group that provided our stately home for the Mevlevi tekke sued us for breach of contract. Our octave was over, and now they wanted the house back. We spent the next twelve months, not advancing Rumi's message of unconditional love, but dealing with lawyers and depositions.

Around this time, NASA engineers noticed that the orbit of Skylab, America's first space station, was decaying faster than anticipated.

Take this as a parable about the Octave. When Skylab launched into orbit in 1973, one of the solar arrays that converted light into energy was damaged. Instead of nine years of space research — Skylab's intended full octave — the spacecraft didn't have the energy to go the distance. In classic bureaucratic fashion, NASA failed to build control mechanisms to bring the 77-ton space station safely back to earth. Doing so would "cost too much," NASA said at the time. The hope was that the Space Shuttle — the next octave — would be ready in time to push the no-longer-needed space station into higher orbit. With no Plan B, NASA now had a crisis: Skylab would soon crash spectacularly to earth.[4] The parallels with my decaying Mevlevi orbit did not escape me.

"I need to get out of here," I thought. "It's time to leave the circus and start a real life."

I should add that I was 28 years old — the critical life juncture (and octave multiple of 7×4) called Saturn's return. While I contemplated my Saturnian funk, a worldwide Skylab frenzy began to grow. People hosted Skylab parties and wore silly protective hats. The San Francisco Examiner famously offered $10,000 to the first person to deliver Skylab debris to its office.[5]

On July 11, 1979, with Skylab rapidly descending, engineers fired the station's booster rockets, hoping that by sending the crippled space station into a tumble it would crash into the Indian Ocean. Well, almost. The bulk of the craft crashed into the outback in Western Australia. Kaboom, the Skylab story was over.

But a short time later, I received a phone call from my mother, Nann Miller. My mom, recognized as the "P.T. Barnum of the public relations world," famously staged enormous publicity stunts that earned her place in the Guinness Book of World Records,

4. Hanes, Elizabeth. 2012. "The Day Skylab Crashed to Earth: Facts About the First U.S. Space Station's Re-Entry." History.com. July 11. http://www.history.com/news/the-day-skylab-crashed-to-earth-facts-about-the-first-u-s-space-stations-re-entry.
5. (Hanes 2012)

including the world's largest group photo (L.A. Olympics), world's largest ice cream sundae (Knudsen Dairy), world's largest root beer float (Hires Root Beer), and the world's largest ribbon cutting (Long Beach Harbor) and others.

"Bruce, I just received the most amazing phone call," my mom said. "Some Australian guys found Skylab in the Outback and approached Hill & Knowlton in Sydney. They want me to handle the PR, and I need your help."

Things bump into our lives all the time. Like little meteors, most flame out without effect. Others advance the story. If a tree crashes into your house, that's terrible news, but it's a great opportunity for the young guy starting a tree business. These intersecting octaves open windows of opportunity. Like the branching points of a magnificent tree, the branching points of the Octave grow a richly-lived life.

I returned to Los Angeles and met the two eager Aussies from Perth who laid claim to the Skylab rubble. I tried to temper their get-rich enthusiasm, but Fortune's allure had blinded their judgment.

Two weeks later, a shipping van pulled up to our Malibu house. With hammer and crowbar, I pried the panels off a closet-sized crate. With one final pull, I braced myself to culminate the worldwide Skylab frenzy. Maybe, the "Wild Man from Borneo" would jump out with a bone in his nose. As I pulled the last nail free, no wild man — just damaged insulation wrapped around a burnt oxygen tank.

Today, if you visit the U.S. Space & Rocket Center in Huntsville, the shredded tank that landed in my driveway sits forlorn in a glass museum case. The Aussie guys didn't understand that *hazard* drove the Skylab story — the *risk* of it crashing into your house. After its dramatic front-page descent, Skylab landed in the scrap bin of history.

The Aussie's lost their shirts, but like intersecting octaves, their loss was my gain. I built exhibits to showcase the space junk which toured carnivals, state fairs, shopping centers — anywhere they could earn a few nickels.

Like a gigantic toss of a 77-ton coin, the NASA engineers put Skylab into an uncontrolled spin. The fact that Skylab crashed into Esperance, Australia was an act of chance. It could have just as easily plunked into the ocean or landed in some country without a Hill & Knowlton office. Like an open point on the backgammon board of my Saturn return, Skylab opened an opportunity to move my next piece.

10

How I Met Your Mother

The universe as a Being is trying to reveal its software
through its hardware… and we're not listening.
Pir Vilayat Inayat Khan

For even the most hard-hearted skeptic, Fortune reveals her game through the marvelous serendipity of "How I met your mother." Is it chance? Is it destiny? Do romantic match-ups result from wanting or woo-woo? What sort of "software" orchestrates the dance of two people coming together? Seeking the answer, I went to Yahoo! Answers:

- "I was on a plane to Frankfurt. A gorgeous tall European man sat next to me, and since he was so tall, I offered to switch seats with him."

- "I was a driving instructor. She was one of the few students that scared the crap out of me."

- "I asked him to be my lab partner because he seemed friendly."

- "He set up his telescope in the backyard, and I went out to look through it."

- "We met on top of the Eiffel Tower."

- "In an atheists' chat room."
- "I was running to school, and I literally crashed into her."
- "I met my loving husband on Xbox Live while playing *Call of Duty*."
- "I was sitting on a bar stool at a club. He asked for a hug, and I said yes. So he lifted me to stand on the bar stool and hugged me. He's a big guy."
- "We met on the plane to Paris!"
- "She was hitchhiking, and I gave her a ride — on my Harley!"
- "My son introduced me to her at a little league baseball game. She was his 6th-grade math teacher."
- "I was calling into dispatch and heard a voice in the background, 'Xerox Service, this is Robyn. How may I help you?' And right then and there I knew that I had found her."
- "I happened to see a snapshot of a co-worker's family. Something about his sister intrigued me."
- "I was working the Gay Straight Alliance's Welcome Week booth. I saw him, and we exchanged numbers."
- "I was standing in line at Starbucks with my white lab coat, and he spilled coffee on me. He offered to dry clean my coat and the rest is history."
- "We met in his bed the next morning. Couldn't remember the night before."[1]

The Universe loves games of chance. This explains why dating advice books suggest joining a ski club, coed softball league, or a cooking class — to increase the odds. But, increasing the odds also raises the question: If you bump into Mr./Ms. Right while learning to make risotto, is the cooking class the *cause* or the context? Is it the *source* of good Fortune or just the setting?

1. "How Did You Meet Your Significant Other?" n.d. Yahoo! Answers. https://answers.yahoo.com/search/search_result?p=How+did+you+meet+your+significant+other%3F&fr=uh3_answers_web_gs.

When I told my friends about this chapter, everyone wanted to add their stories. From Nancy:

Bruce, you gotta put my story in. I was working on Wall Street and on this particular Friday afternoon, I snuck out of the office early — around lunch time. Even though I was lugged down with all my stuff, I decided to buy an Ansel Adams print on my way home. It was the Vatican Cherub. For some reason, I had to buy it that day.

I took the train to Yonkers with the print and hailed a cab when I arrived. Another guy and I piled into the same back seat. That's how it worked. A couple of people would pile in and Ruthie, the cabbie, would take us to our individual places.

The first thing the guy says is, "It's funny that that print is so popular after all these years."

I acted pretty snotty and retorted, "Oh, like you know something about art?" I insulted him, but he went for it.

"As a matter of fact," he replied, "I'm an art historian…"

"Oh Really?," I replied.

"…and the Director of the Hudson River Museum."

And I fell for him. To this day, Ruthie tells everyone that she facilitated our marriage.

Chance or destiny? In the mechanical world, every fortuitous event can be charted in a string of chance encounters. On a whim, Nancy left work early, bought a print, flagged a random cab, and bumped into a museum director. That's the mechanical world. But there is also a causal world, the larger imperative from which one's life story unfolds — like the tree's destiny to bear fruit — where encounters appear accidental, but carry purpose.

As a child, I remember my mother backing the car out of a train station parking lot in the midst of a Chicago blizzard. "Is the coast clear kids?" she asked. "Yes, Mom." BAM! And that's how we started a decades-long friendship with the other driver's family.

Was that an accident? According to the police report, yes. But in the world of Fortune, maybe not. How people come together is a function of the wave you are riding. Whether something is an "accident" is a question of the "world" you live in — your vibrational state.

For a couple of months last summer, we employed Tommy, a marginal character who came up our walkway with just a hint of a stagger.

"I kin paint your house," Tommy seduced with his sweet toothless drawl.

Tommy's visible qualifications consisted of his splattered white pants and painter's cap. Seeking a deal, I hired him. Later, I discovered that he couldn't work for more than a couple of hours without sneaking off for a swig, but he was a meticulous painter and not very expensive — that is if you didn't mind paying his hourly rate while he drank.

Every morning, Tommy would tell tales of his evening life which got me thinking about living in different worlds. We live in a sweet little town filled with pubs, coffee bars, and frozen yogurt shops. It's the kind of place where people say hello, smile, and ask to pet your dog with a politically-correct offer to sniff their hand.

When Tommy walked down the same tree-lined street, he'd get his backpack stolen, get into a fight, get hassled by the cops, or get hauled off to the drunk tank. For Tommy, our sweet street was a mean street. It dawned on me that Tommy and I lived in different worlds — different energetic worlds that may look similar, but only partially interpenetrate and are governed by different laws.

Tommy's world was governed by mechanical forces — the world of accident and reaction. Imagine living on the surface of a pinball game where steel balls careen around in a dangerous world of flippers, bumpers, switches, relays, and chutes. This cause-and-effect world is the Flatland. People living in a two-dimensional world cannot conceive of a third dimension to life. Metaphorically, if they look at a sphere, they can only see a circle. J.G. Bennett uses the idea of Flatland to describe different worlds:[2]

2. Abbott, Edwin A. 1992. Flatland: A Romance of Many Dimensions. Unabridged edition. New York: Dover Publications.

The ordinary state of man is like flatland… He has no real experience of height and depth, only an illusory experience coming from his emotions and the interaction between his different functions.[3]

If we use the analogy of dimensions to describe these worlds, a person living in two-dimensional Flatland lives in reaction. Like a two-dimensional animal, the Flatlander's over-taxed nervous system reacts continuously and mechanically to internal sensations. Like pinball flippers, the Thinking, Feeling, and Instinctual centers ricochet from one stimulus to another. With no third dimension, events that can't be understood through cause and effect can only be explained as "miracles."

The third dimension opens through self-awareness. If Flatlanders live on a two-dimensional plane, extending a point above the plane adds a third dimension — the still point that witnesses life in action. We call this "being present."

Self-awareness is a uniquely human characteristic. Self-awareness emerges from a fundamental trust in life's embrace. We experience the third dimension through subtle feelings. It is the product of knowing you are loved.

Ouspensky described a fourth dimension connected to the mysteries of consciousness and time.[4] The fourth dimension guides Fortune. Like migrating birds drawn by invisible currents, our subtle senses guide us through the fourth dimension. In this way, Fortune leads to chance romance in a cab or serendipitous encounters with long-lost friends. We ascribe these encounters to intuition, dumb luck, psychic powers, and synchronicity.

Fortune signals its presence through synchronicity, defined as: *"The simultaneous occurrence of events that appear significantly related but have no discernible causal connection."*

The key word is *discernible*. Just because we can't discern a causal

3. Bennett, John G. 1977. Material Objects. The Sherborne Theme Talks Series 3. Coombe Springs Press.
4. Ouspensky, P. D., and P. D. Uspenskii. 2005. Tertium Organum. Translated by Claude Fayette Bragdon. New York: Cosimo Classics.

connection doesn't mean there isn't one. Imagine waves coming ashore on a peaceful day. Just because we can't see violent storms generating waves thousands of miles away doesn't mean they don't exist. What we see in this world is the echo of unseen forces and events.

For example, yesterday, I went sailing. I typically head to the car after I dock the boat. Instead, I decided to sit for five minutes and cool off with a drink. At the five minute mark, I looked up. There was Ann, an old sailing friend I hadn't seen since we sailed together in Greece. When I got home, I told Karen, "Guess who I bumped into today."

We treat these serendipitous moments as pleasant, but random events rather than evidence of an intelligent, interconnected universe.

When we notice the hand of Fortune, the fourth dimension kicks in. In the fourth dimension, time not only moves forward from the past, but also in reverse, from the future into the present — the fruit being the cause of the tree. We experience forward time as if we were climbing a mountain trail toward the peak. Reverse time is like meeting a descending hiker who warns you of a rock slide ahead.

In this way, there are two simultaneous octaves: ascending and descending. In reverse time, the world of possibility comes into manifestation from the future into the present. Eventually, the rock slide emerges, and we must *integrate* the obstruction — the octave coming in — into our present moment. Similarly, watching the storm waves roll in, we face our hero's journey. Our job is to remain open to the flow of this descending octave — but it's not easy because thought blocks the flow. In theory, opening to the flow should be effortless, but you have to become comfortable living with uncertainty. In the realized state, a balance point exists, outside of time, where the mind is still, the play unfolds, and the moment is complete in itself.

A couple of weeks ago, I was walking my dog when I "bumped" into my neighbor, Steven, who was raking leaves.

"Hey Steven, how's it going?" I asked. "Is Julia coming home for the holidays?" Julia was Steven's 25-year old daughter.

"I hope so," Steven replied. "She's been in Prague for the last nine months."

"Wow. Like the real Prague, not Prague, Oklahoma?"

"Yes," Steven replied with pride. "Czechoslovakia — I guess it's now the Czech Republic."

"How did Julia get to Prague?"

As Steven told Julia's story, I could sense the invisible wiring of the universe revealing itself.

"Julia and her boyfriend, Peter, had been living in New Hampshire," Steven recounted. "She moved there with Peter so he could get his master's degree."

"Wasn't she in California?" I asked.

"Yes, but the actual sequence went like this. Julia left Atlanta to go to school in New York City. She met Peter and followed him to Los Angeles. After a couple of years, they pulled up stakes, and she followed him to New Hampshire."

"That's a lot of boy-following," I said.

"Yeah, but she also grew increasingly mature and independent," Steven continued. "She enrolled in school in Santa Monica, then got a job selling Mercedes in New Hampshire and then got some modeling jobs in the city. She could set up her life pretty quick."

"Good for her," I added, "but how did she get to Prague?"

"One day, her boyfriend, Peter, announced that he wanted to go back to California. Peter's a surfer at heart. Julia was not thrilled at the idea of uprooting a second, or I guess a third time, so, she asked him, 'Peter, before I follow you again, I need to know one thing. Do you see marriage down the road?'"

"That's a reasonable question," I agreed.

"Peter said, 'buh-buh-buh' and couldn't give a straight answer, so Julia left him. Sayonara, just like that."

"Wow, five years and she pulled the plug," I said. "That's a long time when you're twenty-five."

"Yeah, she was hurt pretty bad."

I sensed Fortune entering the story. Steven continued.

"So, Julia left Peter and moved to Boston. Two days later she was walking down a street in Summerville when, completely out of the blue, right there on the sidewalk, she bumped into her best friend's sister from Atlanta. Her name was Pam. It was one of those inexplicable chance encounters."

"She bumped into her best friend's sister in the middle of Boston?"

"That's right," Steven explained.

"I'm writing a book about this bumping business. So what happened next?"

"Pam invited Julia to a party. Julia arrived and in the corner was this Canadian guy, Daniel — a young entrepreneur who puts businesses together. They hit it off from the start. You need to talk to Julia for the full story."

And so I did. A few weeks later, Julia and Daniel arrived from Prague, and we talked:

"Julia, I spoke with your dad, how you split from your boyfriend. What happened?"

"I wasn't ready to move again, back to California," Julia explained. "Peter just expected I would. But, he didn't want to take the relationship to the next level. He was happy with our life the way it was."

"What happened after you left?"

"My mom came up to help me move to Boston," Julia explained. "The day we arrived, we decided to walk to dinner. And we're walking down the street, and I see this girl, Pam, the sister of my best friend from high school. And Pam's like, 'Julia, wow, this is so weird. How are you? You're moving here?'"

Julia paused at the improbability, then continued.

"And so Pam was really excited. She said, 'I have this friend from Prague. He just moved to Boston, too. And he's going to come over on Saturday, and I don't know what your type is or if you're looking, but he's great. You should come and hang out with us on Saturday.' And I said, okay."

"So what happened when you walked into the party?" I asked.

"I saw the guy, Daniel and thought, wow, this is a person I can really see myself with. And that's super surprising because he is not someone I would have seen coming into my world in a million years. So, two days later, it was my birthday, and Pam threw a party for us. Then two days after that we went out on a date. Soon we were dating seriously. Daniel had just brought his company to Boston and then left the company to spend the summer in Prague. So, he asked me, 'Would you like to come to Prague for the summer?'"

"What were you feeling?" I asked.

I was nervous, because once again, I'm leaving. I left New York, then I left L.A., then I left New Hampshire, and now I'm leaving Boston. But I was excited because it was a new opportunity."

A few weeks later, I met Julia and Daniel after they returned from Costa Rica. The first thing I noticed was the engagement ring on her finger — and her big smile. I asked her the crucial question:

"Julia, so many people struggle, and are lonely. So many people walk down that same street in Summerville without bumping into Fortune. Why did this work out so well for you?"

Julia thought for a moment.

"Number one is that neither of us was looking for a serious relationship," Julia explained. "Daniel had just been in a relationship and was out. And I had just been in a relationship and was out. When people are really looking for something, it's never there."

Julia paused to consider the swirl of events, then continued.

"The weirdest thing was the randomness of the connection. That's what was strange. I never hung out with this girl, Pam, in high school. She was much older than me. Next thing, she's inviting me to her house, and I'm meeting her friends and she – she didn't know Daniel that well either. He had just moved to Boston. It was all so random."

"But somehow this happened to you," I pressed. "It doesn't happen to everyone."

Julia paused and considered.

"It's about the choices you make," she explained, "but I don't know why you make those choices. That's the weird thing. Why do you make a choice? It's because of the state you are in, and how open you are to a scenario. And then there are all the coincidences that lead to these choices. It's strange, and it's unexplainable."

In that little statement, Julia hit all of Fortune's themes: Raising your vibrational rate ("the state that you're in"), being open to reverse time ("how open you are to a scenario"), and the synchronicity of Fortune ("the coincidences that lead to these choices.") But, the big enchilada ("I don't know why you make those choices") remained a mystery. The most elusive mystery of Fortune is the illusion of choice.

I loved Julia's nonchalance about it all. Like this happened, then that, and like life kept happening. "How I Met Your Mother" stories work this way. They give us a glimpse of living in the fourth dimension where Fortune unfolds from the world to come.

I pondered Julia's story. If there is a world of possibility from which opportunities emerge; is there a way of living where opportunities increase? And conversely, when we're in a rut, do possibilities diminish? If the world of Fortune opens like a door, is that door always waiting to open? By shutting one door decisively, did Julia open another? Or did her Fortune flow from personal destiny, a preordained future coming into the present? If God holds the Big Script, is Julia supposed to make babies with Daniel and not with Peter? Or is it all chance? Clearly, she walked down a random street, random city, at a random time.

> We have arrived at the heart of a paradox: each time a door closes, the rest of the world opens up.
> — Parker Palmer[5]

5. Palmer, P. J. (2000). Let your life speak: Listening for the voice of vocation. San Francisco: Jossey-Bass.

Recently, another old friend, Lynden, a theater director, was in town. Lynden added a vignette of her own as we talked over dinner:

"My friend Kathy and I were walking to a performance on the UNC campus in Chapel Hill," Lynden said. "We were talking about our search for romantic partners. Kathy was a widow. She had recently spoken to an intuitive who said, 'Kathy, you're not meant to be alone for the rest of your life.'"

"Intuitive? Like a fortune teller?" I asked.

"Yes, sort of. When Kathy shared this, I stopped right in the middle of the street. I stamped my foot, saying, 'That's not good enough. I want someone now. RIGHT NOW!'"

"That's a bold request," I laughed.

"I just said it. So, when Kathy and I entered the performance hall, and I looked up toward the stage, there strumming a guitar was Rick — my future husband. I looked at him and said to Kathy, 'I want to sit on that man's lap.'"

I shared Lynden's story with my friend, Sarah, who immediately interjected, "I've got a story."

"I was at one of your famous New Year's Eve parties when you asked us to write what we wished for in the coming year," Sarah recounted. "I had gotten divorced in June, so I wrote on my list that I would like a man with the following characteristics to come into my life: I wanted someone who could talk about and express feelings and was willing to go deep — deep with me — and could look deeply within himself. I also wanted someone who enjoyed dancing and liked to hike. And enjoyed children."

"You were meant to be writing a resolution, not a partner shopping list" I quipped.

"I was very resolved," Sarah bantered back. "I was intent on finding a partner who was willing to grow, to share my journey of personal growth."

Karen jumped in, "What about sex? Was that on your list?"

"Oh, for sure. I wanted someone who loved sex and was a good lover," Sarah twinkled. "It was a long list. And, there were things that I didn't put on the list which I wished I had!"

Karen and I laughed.

"More than anything, I was seeking someone who liked to do the same things I like to do," Sarah continued. "I wanted someone who was thoughtful, who enjoyed reading, and had a spiritual path."

"So, what did you do with your list?" I asked.

"At the stroke of midnight, I put it into the fire — releasing my request to the universe."

"What happened next?"

"Three weeks later, at a contra dance in Sarasota, I went out by the water to be quiet and meditate. Joe walked by and asked if he could sit down. I said yes and we shared that quiet space together. Fifteen years later, we're still together."

"And the moral of the story?"

"Be careful what you ask for. You might get it."

There's a common theme with all of these pairings: the forces of Fortune pull people together through everyday events. If that is the case, do these same forces work through online dating? If Fortune's romantic hand guides potential partners through intuition, noticing, releasing blocks, and being in the right place at the right time, can a digital algorithm accomplish the same thing?

A telling statistic might answer this question. From 2013 to 2015, online dating tripled for 20-somethings and doubled among 55-64 year-olds. Yet, in the same Pew Research survey, among the 15 percent of Americans who used dating apps, only 5 percent met their significant other online.[6]

Five percent is not much magic. Perhaps online dating is governed by the mechanical world — the cause-and-effect world of Flatland which is ruled by the power of accident. Online daters hope that the two-dimensional world of the machine will open a third dimension of self awareness to their lives, and engage the fourth dimension by which Fortune flows.

6. http://www.pewresearch.org/fact-tank/2016/02/29/5-facts-about-online-dating/

I saw the two-dimensional machine in action through the following story: A friend knew a sad-sack guy whose wife dumped him. Feeling lonely, the guy managed to get a new girlfriend who, after four months, sacked him as well. This sent him deep into his doldrums, rarely leaving his apartment after work. One day, his office mates suggested Tinder, the dating app that drives 1.4 billion potential date swipes per day.

He filled out the form, uploaded his picture, and within a few hours, 60 female suitors flooded his inbox — some from out-of-state offering to get on the next plane. So, he went for it, sometimes three dates in a day, meeting at lunch, enjoying drinks after work, or diving into dinner and sex in the evening.

He went from emotional agoraphobic to swinger with a few swipes. He even jumped into bed with a tattooed tantra queen who took him to his kinky edge and beyond. You can imagine his excitement with his new-found digital magnetism. Was this real change or an illusion? I surmised that the excitement of Tinder's surging in-box distracted him from the subtle feelings of soul work.

In this way, my psychologist friend Miriam stresses that doors open by *noticing* — noticing opportunities that reveal themselves, often as thoughts and feelings that live just below the radar of awareness. For Karen, it's all about integration — the process of self-reflection, acceptance, and healing of the past. Integration allows one to live more in the present, more open to the mystery of romance.

Conversely, I have another close friend who *only* dates through online connections. "There's no difference," she argued. "It's just another way to bump into people. You still have to use intuition in your inbox."

For me, Fortune strikes a balance between pushing and patience. Patience means accepting life exactly as it. Pushing requires that we do the work of integration — facing our fears and healing the past.

My own "How I Met Your Mother" story was unremarkable, but also deliciously complex. I was in the middle of my Saturn Return soon after the Mevlevi Spring had collapsed. I loaded a rental truck and invited my girlfriend, Penny, to drive across the desert to greet Skylab in Los Angeles. I felt intoxicated with Penny at my side as I journeyed into adulthood.

Saturn returns at age 28-29 like a wind shift. In sailing, you must quickly respond to the shifting wind or the boat will stall. Wind and current work this way, but what about life?

I was always skeptical about astrology, so I asked my astrologer friend, Nicoli, whether Fortune unfolds according to the mechanical clockwork of the heavens or the deeper forces of destiny.

"Bruce, folks don't understand that astrology is actually part of our real world, of our solar system," Nicoli explained.

"The Octave is often called the Law of Seven and seven was an important number to the ancients who studied our solar system. Think of the seven days of the week. The days correspond to the seven planets of the ancient world: Sunday is the Sun's day, Monday is the Moon's day, Tuesday is Mars, Wednesday is Mercury, Thursday is Venus, Friday is Jupiter and the last one is Saturday — Saturn's day.

"Saturn is all about boundaries. Saturn is the end, the boundary, mortality itself. To the ancients, Saturn was the law of time, of incarnation: One is born, lives a life, and dies. It is a simple fact of nature. All that is born will die. Saturn was the Grim Reaper, Father Time, the ultimate restriction. Saturn was all about the awareness that time would eventually win out, and one would die."

I considered all the rockers who died at the approach of Saturn's Return: Jimi Hendrix, Jim Morrison, Janis Joplin, Kurt Cobain, Amy Winehouse, and countless others. Nicoli continued:

"This awareness of Saturn's boundary pushes one to do one's work in life — to master a craft, build a profession, discover your boundaries, and to get on with life. Saturn requires effort to get on with the task at hand."

As Nicoli described Saturn's boundaries, I remembered hitting age 28 and feeling the pressure of time — of reverse time. Life is like an enormous contra dance where you have the freedom to swing your partner and enjoy her eyes, but only within the chain of the dance, the command of the caller, and the time signature of the band. Nicoli continued.

"A Saturn cycle is approximately 29 years and dividing that into fourths, you get a wake-up call every seven years. These junctures are the conjunction, the square, and the opposition. It is all done with geometry in astrology. So one is born, and approximately seven years later there is the first Saturn square (90 degrees). Then at fourteen years there is a Saturn opposition (180 degrees), at twenty-one another (waning) square and at twenty-nine, Saturn returns (conjuncts) the same place it was when you were born (360 degrees).

"If one lives to be ninety, one experiences three Saturn returns. Our second Saturn return is at fifty-eight or fifty-nine years old. Saturn Returns bring a recurring lesson to be learned — the sign Saturn was in when you were born, the house it lives in your natal chart, and the aspects it makes to other planets. The lessons become more refined as we age and mature. Saturn's gift is manifestation and if we are willing, our life manifests in the present, and unfolds in time."

As Penny and I drove across the Utah desert during my Saturn's Return, all I knew about astrology was Reshad's exhortation that we don't need to be ruled by our chart, advice I ignored as I heeded Saturn's call to load up the van.

Penny and I rented an apartment together in Santa Monica. If online dating had been invented back then, my profile would have matched her in an instant (yeah, she shares a birthday with my mom). But, with Saturn in charge, our puppy love didn't stand a chance. After a few months, we went our separate ways.

My next two years fits into a short paragraph:

I spent my days building an audio-visual studio. At night, I would eat Chiles Rellenos alone in an empty Mexican joint, then get up in the next morning, fight the freeway and do it again. On weekends, I remodeled a bungalow I had bought.

Manifestation, manifestation, manifestation. Yeah, I was lonely and horny. But I couldn't see any reason to seek love at a cooking class. I knew my soul mate would be following a different star.

Around this time, a succession of young women — all students of Reshad — made it a point to visit me. I would take each one to an Italian joint run by a Colombian named Virgilio. We would order a garlic-laden, tomato-based aphrodisiac, split a bottle of Chianti, keep the empty bottle as a souvenir of our passionate dinner, drive back to the bungalow, and culminate the evening by not having sex.

Living in the fourth dimension messed up the sex part. I could see the entire plot (reverse time) in the blink of an eye: the passion, attraction, lust, and sex, followed by the misunderstanding, explaining, rationalizing, and finally the breaking of hearts. It sucks to have to share a Spoiler Alert with your date when you see how the story will end.

Around this time, a young nurse from Tennessee named Suzie had moved to the "Jungle," a ramshackle neighborhood of densely-built beach apartments in Playa Del Rey, just north of the LAX flight path. Considered to be the last stretch of beach Bohemia in Southern California, the Jungle was a big step up from the 38-foot sailboat Suzie had been sharing with her ne'er-do-well nurse boyfriend in the Marina. His unfortunate habit of sampling narcotics from the hospital where they worked brought that relationship to a quick end.

I bring this up because Suzie, the future Karen Miller, lived tantalizingly close to my lonely bachelor pad — about four miles as the crow flew. But Suzie had to complete her vision quest before our octaves would cross a few years later. I'll let Karen Sue pick up the story:

"Around my Saturn Return, I started to get more restless. I remember feeling the pressure to find my home, which was more than where I lived. I wanted to find my spiritual home. I was exploring spiritual paths, holistic health, Kundalini yoga, and alternative ideas.

"I convinced my roommate, Chris, to consider moving to Santa Cruz. So, we loaded her VW Squareback and headed to Santa Cruz. I sensed this feeling of excitement and possibility — as if a new door was opening.

"We had a good life in Santa Cruz. We cooked together and entertained. But soon, Chris got involved with a man and it was time for me to move out.

"I moved into a tiny guest house near the lighthouse where I lived alone. It was a lonely time in my life. I was constantly looking at other people and the things they had — particularly relationships. I was envious and jealous, and even resentful that I was not in a committed relationship. I wanted to be married.

"It was during this time that I stumbled upon a little pamphlet titled, 'Gratitude.'

"I had a wake-up call. I realized that I needed to change my attitude and focus on what I had instead of what I didn't have. I got into a place of trust, and everything shifted. I shifted into a different world.

"I had a vision of my future self, of the future coming in, and saw myself as an old woman. I saw myself with long white hair in a French twist looking pretty and lively. I saw my older self tell my younger self, 'Just hang in there. If you only knew what was coming.'

"I quit my job at the hospital and headed to Big Sur. I lived in my Ford Falcon for a few weeks. A friend showed me how to lower the seat, lay out a piece of plywood, and form a comfortable bed. I had a Coleman stove.

"I got to know some of the locals who showed me where the private beaches were. I also changed my official address so that I could go to Esalen after midnight and use the famous hot tubs. It was a magical atmosphere with natural hot springs feeding into candle-lit stone pools perched on the cliff. The moon illuminated the Pacific Ocean while giant waves crashed far below.

"During my time in Big Sur, I lived in a place of question: Where is my spiritual home? What do I need to be doing? Who is my teacher?

"I decided to perform a cleansing ritual to find my true voice. I didn't know what was going to happen; I was on a vision quest. I fasted several days and then drove to a secret beach that had a waterfall.

"I followed the steep, difficult trail to the beach, all the time opening myself to my question, going deeper and deeper: What is the next thing to do?

"I saw the waterfall and began to climb the slope. Once I started, it wasn't possible to go back. It was very steep and treacherous. I'm amazed I didn't fall. I climbed this rugged cliff full of rocks and debris, literally pulling myself up the hillside.

"As I climbed, I felt like I was a Native American on a vision quest. A vision quest is a sacred rite where you go into the wilderness seeking guidance and renewal, where you encounter your real self and let your old self die. I had been studying the Tarot archetypes for the Inner Guide, and I connected through those archetypes. It was very scary, but I just kept going.

"I sensed that there would be something beautiful at the top, but when I reached the top, there were lots of briars. It wasn't pretty at all.

"But now I needed to go down. I kept asking which is the way to go? I was in this place of total surrender, of asking where is my life calling me? At that moment, I found a way to surrender into the stream. I have been able to totally surrender a few times in my life, and it was quite profound. I was called to the stream, into the stream of life. But this was a real stream, and when I reclined to let go, the rushing water carried me over some rocks, and I got banged up, scraped, and scratched.

"I was pretty upset that I had gotten hurt, but I was also in a surrendered state. It was very similar to the place of trust I experienced with the brain tumor. On one level, I'm embarrassed that it happened, that I got hurt, but on another level, it took profound courage. That moment symbolized my seriousness toward the spiritual path.

"The sun was starting to go down, and I eventually reached the beach. I gathered my shoes and clothes and realized I had to get out of there, or I might die from hypothermia. Plus, I was hurt and banged up. I managed to hike out even though it had become completely dark.

"I got into my car, but wasn't quite sure what to do. I headed to Deetjen's Inn since there was nothing else for miles. As it turned out, Deetjen's was closed, so I walked around the back and went to the kitchen. I found some staff who wanted to take me to the hospital. I said, no, I don't need the hospital. I'm a nurse. Could you let me stay here? So they took me to a special room, Grandpa's Room, which was the original hand-built home of the Inn's founder, Grandpa Deetjen. It was beautiful. And in that room, I saw a sculpture of a nude woman leaning back in a state of total surrender. I saw myself in her.

"Throughout the night, people came and sat with me. They chanted at times and kept vigil. I felt held and loved and supported. And, I felt a confirmation. These people took me in, put me in Grandpa Deetjen's place of honor, watched after me, and took care of me.

"The next day, a friend from Santa Cruz picked me up and cared for me over the next two weeks. I realized that I couldn't reach my true spiritual station myself; I needed a teacher.

"At that time, rebirthing was the craze. I wanted to reconnect to my birth experience. During the session, there was a lot of breathing and guided imagery. When we completed, I mentioned how I had always enjoyed spinning 'round and 'round as a child. Out of the blue, the healer said, 'You need to meet Reshad Feild.'

"I kept Reshad's name in my thinking. I had this intuitive sense that Reshad would recognize me. Those were the words that came to me and I didn't really know what those words meant. On one level 'recognize me' doesn't make any sense. But those were the words — I needed to meet him and he would recognize me.

"I started my search to find Reshad at the Rajneesh Center. I asked, 'Do you know Reshad Feild and where he lives?' And they said, 'Oh yes, he lives right down the street.' I went there and met a woman working with roses. She invited me to come to a talk that very night.

"As it turned out, Reshad was ill and did not attend. Afterward, I mentioned that I was a nurse and if I could be of service, please call me.

"So, the next day, they called and invited me to lunch. They created this incredibly beautiful meal, maybe a dozen people around the table, and I was the guest of honor. I had never received this kind of attention.

"We finished the meal with Turkish coffee. Reshad instructed, 'Turn your cup over.' He gestured for my inverted cup, and I passed it to him. As he turned it around, observing the grounds, I got the sense he was reading me — not the grounds. He saw the shape of a crescent moon. 'You will travel very far in the work,' Reshad declared. I didn't know what to say, but I felt at home.

"I returned that evening. After Reshad's talk, again I became the center of attention. He took my hands and noticed 'how kind I was' by looking at my forearms. Soon I was in floods of tears. Someone took me upstairs and prepared a bath for me with fragrant lotions. When I came back downstairs, I felt completely recognized for the first time in my life.

"I immediately became part of the school. My job was to do the laundry. Once a week, I would also serve as Person of the Day — like a duty officer. My Ford Falcon had taken its last breath, so I would get up at 4:30 a.m. and bicycle thirteen miles in the dark from West Cliff to Aptos, fulfill my duty, then work the evening shift at the hospital.

"I have never shared my story about the waterfall before. I didn't think people would understand it, would grasp the mystery behind the events that change our lives. Going over the waterfall represented my willingness to sacrifice everything to live in the spiritual dimension of life. It led me to a school where people had dedicated their lives to living in this spiritual dimension, which is not the illusion, but the reality of life.

"I talked to Reshad about my serious desire for a partner. He directed me to his soon-to-be new wife. She told me how she fervently prayed for a spiritual partner and how she had made a list of the important qualities she was seeking. Shortly after that, she met Reshad.

"I didn't make a list, but I sought someone equally dedicated to the work, someone who lived to serve in a higher spiritual plane. I didn't need to verbalize these qualities, like wanting to have children, etc. I trusted in the intuitive nature of life itself — like me going to Deetjen's Inn and knowing that they would take care of me."

At this point, Karen's octave intersected with mine. While I was living alone, manifesting my Saturn Return, Reshad invited me to come to Santa Cruz to present a slide show on Geomancy, the sacred science of earth energies. I sent Reshad a letter to discuss preparations and in my flippant way, I added a postscript, something like: "While you're at it, why don't you set me up on a blind date."

Just so you know what's going on here, I'm interviewing Karen while we're laying in bed in the wee hours before dawn.

"That's your thing," Karen retorted. "You think you were so flippant. But, you weren't so flippant. You were serious too! But you won't admit it to yourself."

"What do you think I wrote?" I retorted, "'Dear Reshad, I'm lonely and horny and desperate. Please find me a wife!' Of course, I was flippant and ironic, and you're right, serious too."

"Reshad announced to the group that you had asked him to set you up on a blind date," Karen continued. "But he wasn't sure who to ask.

I didn't say anything, even though I secretly wanted him to choose me for the blind date — and he did. I was very shy, but it was not a casual thing. It was my first and only blind date, and he gave me permission to do whatever we wanted."

"What kind of permission?" I interjected. "Sounds *very* casual." Karen ignored me and continued:

"I remember being excited about it. Reshad played it up whenever we talked. The day came; someone picked you up at the airport and brought you to the house. You walked in the door, and Reshad made a big deal, like, 'This is Bruce and he is the one who started the Institute for Conscious Life.'"

I interjected, "What I remember was walking in the door and Reshad gesturing toward each woman in the room, saying, 'I was thinking about this one, and this one, and this one.' Then he pointed to you, announcing, 'But she is the one.' It seemed incredibly awkward."

"It was embarrassing," Karen remembered, "but I had come to expect that from him."

I interrupted again. "And after all the build-up, everyone in the house ended up going out on a group date. We saw the Incredible String Band guy followed by calamari at India Joze."

"But that wasn't how the evening ended," Karen reminded. "After everyone had gone to bed, we sat on the couch for a long time."

"How was that for you?" I asked.

"I told you that I was serious about being in a relationship," Karen remembered.

I interjected again. "What I remember was this whoosh of energy — and I'm supposed to be the cerebral guy. There was this whoosh of love energy. And I thought, 'Whoa! This is happening.' And by 'whoa,' I mean there was a sense of shock, like an octave shock."

"You found it shocking?" Karen probed.

"Not in that way," I explained. "But unlike the people who make their ideal partner lists — and I hate those lists — my list would have been all wrong. I would have ordered all the wrong things. You're so different from anyone I could have conceived."

"So, maybe you felt shocked, but…"

"There was this whoosh of energy," I continued. "You were completely present and connected in my being. And that was profound. At the same time, there was this shock, this holy-shit wake-up call. My preconceived notions of my partner were turned upside down."

"Yeah, but it worked out pretty good," Karen reminded.

"Yeah, but it's still a shock that it did," I countered.

Karen rolled over and snuggled closer.

"Now, no more talking. Give me my rubbies."

11

Alchemical Marriage

Creativity…is usually the clash of two value systems or traditions,
which, in collision, create a transcendent third thing.
David Brooks

"Stop the car; I need to pee," Reshad commanded. We were driving back from a talk somewhere in the middle of nowhere on a moonless New Mexico night. The driver pulled the car over, stopped the engine, and Reshad got out. We waited in silence under a blaze of stars.

Earlier that evening, I had asked Reshad whether the octave intervals, *Si-Do* and *Mi-Fa*, function in a descending octave the same way as they do in an ascending octave. I realized I had stepped into it when Reshad stopped putting on his coat, looked at me with regal bearing, and slowly replied, "I… am… the Octave."

Whoa.

Under the galaxy of New Mexico stars, I was still digesting this earlier statement when Reshad returned to the car. I tried to remain conscious of my breathing because that was what you were supposed to do when you were around Reshad. Reshad took a breath, then announced:

"Bruce, there is only one thing you need to know," he began.

The lengthy pregnant pause perked my ears. Then he dropped the Big One:

"The higher blends with the lower to create the middle."

And that was that, and we continued onward.

Reshad dropped little koans all the time — what he called "snippets." He even published two snippet books. I sensed this one was just for me. Reshad was a spiritual alchemist, and perhaps he was acknowledging that I'm one, too. That in the fraternal order of Men Who Pee Under the Stars, this was a transmission: "Get going, Bruce, do the inner work; you're an alchemist."

I spent months, maybe years trying to penetrate this little riddle. So creating the middle is the big idea? At the surface, it was something about the Holy Trinity, perhaps the relationship between spirit and matter, and certainly Gurdjieff's Law of Three.

Over time, I came to dislike the statement, but I wasn't certain why.

Eventually, I married an alchemist. Karen's alchemy is subtle and disarming. Her motto is not the Hermetic maxim of alchemy, "As above, so below." The maxim she lives by is: *"Things that don't go together, somehow go together."*

Karen did not get this out of a book or learn it in a lecture; it's one hundred percent who she is, a synthesis of contradictions fused in love. Like on our first date — after necking at the proverbial Pleasure Point, the cliff high above the Santa Cruz surf, and after the Jewish Chicago boy becomes smitten with her rolling tobacco and calling me "Darlin," I watched in awe as she casually crawled under her 1969 Ford Falcon. Karen whacked the gear linkage with a crowbar, put the tool back into its ready-when-needed spot, got back behind the wheel, and cranked the straight-six to life. I can't imagine a more seductive act to disarm my defenses. First date intimacy and girl-crawling-under-the car with a crowbar flowed seamlessly together.

Karen lives by an "all people are equal" ethos that ignores labels. In her eyes, the nurse's aide and the doctor are equal. She focuses on the person, not the race, religion or role. While this sounds moral and righteous, in practice, *things that don't go together, somehow go together* adds just enough creative tension to raise the vibratory rate. And since Karen's maxim holds the key to creative transformation — we should all take notice. It took me many years to drop the whole higher-lower thing.

Karen's maxim was on full display at her Presbyterian ordination a few years ago. She thought nothing of inviting Jews, Buddhists, Taoists, Hindus and Sufis to contribute to the ceremony. When the minister performing the actual rite finally got a turn, he masked his exasperation with a bit of dry humor:

"Thank you, everyone. And now it's time to focus on the religion that actually matters today…"

In Karen's view, *things that don't go together, somehow go together* is not a recipe for jamming contrary people and ideas together.

"I create space inside myself — a spaciousness — to hold the paradox," Karen explained. "The image of my arms open, ready to embrace comes to mind. I bring curiosity to the paradox and let the contradiction inform me. I also create space for the contrary elements to inform each other. Recently, I supervised an odd mix of students: Two mainstream Presbyterians, a gay man, two biblical literalists, and a transgendered male from Alabama. The challenge was to provide a holding environment where the students would feel safe. By creating space for their honest, authentic selves, the students were able to learn from each other without making assumptions or judging each other."

Karen's maxim also describes how creative people work together and how the reconciliation of opposites releases energy. Think Steve Jobs and Steve Wozniak, Siskel and Ebert, or my own right-wing/left-wing, control-freak/hippie-freak agency partnership.

When the clash of opposites works, the door to Fortune opens. Consider Bill Hewlett and David Packard of HP fame. They forged their relationship on a two-week camping trip. Like true gentlemen, they flipped a coin to determine whose name went first.[1]

The most celebrated alchemical marriage of all time was between

John Lennon and Paul McCartney. At their first meeting at a church hall performance of John's band, the Quarryman, the teenage John likely recognized that a creative relationship with Paul would be difficult:

> For Lennon it was a dilemma – should he admit a talented member who may pose a challenge to his own superiority within the group, or should he persist without McCartney, retaining his leadership yet likely consigning the group to failure?[2]

Joshua Wolf Shenk, in *The Power of Two*, describes how the two Beatles reflected the essence of creative tension and why things that don't go together, somehow go together:

> Paul and John seemed to be almost archetypal embodiments of order and disorder. The ancient Greeks gave form to these two sides of human nature in Apollo, who stood for the rational and the self-disciplined, and Dionysus, who represented the spontaneous and the emotional.[3]

Geoff Emerick, the engineer for many Beatles records, described how Lennon and McCartney worked together:

> Paul was meticulous and organized: he always carried a notebook around with him, in which he methodically wrote down lyrics and chord changes in his neat handwriting. In contrast, John seemed to live in chaos: he was constantly searching for scraps of paper that he'd hurriedly scribbled ideas on. Paul was a natural communicator; John couldn't articulate his ideas well. Paul was the diplomat; John was the agitator. Paul was soft-spoken and almost unfailingly polite; John could be a right loudmouth and quite rude. Paul was willing to put in long hours to get a part right; John was impatient, always ready to move on to the next thing.[4]

1. "William Hewlett & David Packard." 2015. Entrepreneur. Accessed October 24. http://www.entrepreneur.com/article/197644.
2. "6 July 1957: John Lennon Meets Paul McCartney | The Beatles Bible." 2015. Accessed October 24. http://www.beatlesbible.com/1957/07/06/john-lennon-meets-paul-mccartney/.
3. Shenk, Joshua Wolf. 2014. "The Power of Two." The Atlantic, August. http://www.theatlantic.com/magazine/archive/2014/07/the-power-of-two/372289/.

The collision of John and Paul made for great music. In fact, the Beatles' crowning achievement, the White Album was recorded in sessions described as "tense and unpleasant." This kind of alchemical fusion between spirit and earth, energy and matter, asshole and nice guy is the source of all creative power. At its ultimate expression, the sun itself is powered by nuclear fusion. Two nuclei collide at high speed, fusing to release the energy that powers the stars.

Reshad's *higher blends with the lower to create the middle* lacked the collision and conflict of high-energy fusion. He described an alchemical parfait — a creamy custard commingling with the berries below. "Blend" is the wrong word for talking about higher and lower. A Vitamix blends; alchemy transforms.

The two nuclei don't blend, they collide. And "middle?" That's not working, either. Middle means compromise, splitting the difference, hedging your bets. How about "create?" That almost works. Paraphrasing David Brooks, the clash of two value systems or traditions *collide*, but they don't create a *middle*; they create a transcendent third thing — something new, bigger, and original.

In writing this chapter, I discovered Reshad's source in Gurdjieff's opus, *Beelzebub's Tales*. In Gurdjieff's words: "The higher blends with the lower to *actualize* the middle." *Actualize* suggests that the third state is already here in latency, but just needs to be awakened from slumber.

And higher? Lower? You can describe spirit and matter as higher and lower, but if you do, the two will never fuse. Fusion occurs when vibration increases to the point that the two are *recognized* to be one and the same — Karen gets it right again.

I should add that higher-lower hierarchical thinking leads to all kinds of trouble in the world.

So in reality, alchemy is akin to nuclear fusion. The collision of contradictory points of view is resolved by letting go of judgment,

4. Shenk, Joshua Wolf. 2014. Powers of Two: Finding the Essence of Innovation in Creative Pairs. Houghton Mifflin Harcourt.

releasing expectations, and cultivating the common ground. Fusion raises the vibrational rate and releases creative energy.

The Beatles' masterpiece, "A Day In The Life," was created this way — a musical fusion of two songs. The piece begins with Lennon's surrealistic recounting of a newspaper story — the fatal car crash of a young London socialite. Halfway through the song, a rising glissando bridge explodes through the Mi-Fa interval and emerges as a different sounding song. In fact, it *is* a different song — a McCartney song. Remarkably, the 24-bar bridge section that connects the two songs was completely improvised by the orchestra. How often do you hear a full orchestra improvising? George Martin, the legendary Beatles producer, explained:

> What I did there was to write... the lowest possible note for each of the instruments in the orchestra. At the end of the twenty-four bars, I wrote the highest note. Then I put a squiggly line right through the twenty-four bars, with reference points to tell them roughly what note they should have reached during each bar... Of course, they all looked at me as though I were completely mad.[5]

At the end of John's song, a chaotic race of instruments swooshes upward until an alarm clock rings. Boom! Paul sings about waking up and falling out of bed. Interestingly, the alarm clock was a serendipitous mistake. The engineer counted out 23 bars and laid an alarm effect into the tape to indicate where the bridge should be inserted later. Because of the mix-down limitations of four-track recording, he couldn't remove the ringing effect.

The second song originated as a short piano piece written by McCartney about his morning commute as a young student. As Lennon described it, Paul "contributed this little lick floating around in his head that he couldn't use for anything."[6] That's an off-putting way to describe it, but When McCartney bursts in, the new song

5. Martin, George, and Jeremy Hornsby. 1994. All You Need Is Ears: The inside Personal Story of the Genius Who Created The Beatles. Reprint edition. New York: St. Martin's Griffin.
6. Sheff, David. 1981. "Playboy Interview with John Lennon and Yoko Ono." Playboy, January.

lifts the listener into *Fa*, the feeling of expansion — the expansion of the heart.

Emerick, the engineer, describes the scene when he played the rough mix for the first time:

> There was silence after we finished playing it back. It was like you were watching a black-and-white film, and suddenly there was color and Cinemascope. The feeling in that control room was just amazing. Nobody had ever heard anything like it in their lives.[7]

Why am I banging on about this song? "A Day In The Life" captures the essence of Fortune: Life unfolds like random newspaper events yielding the raw material for transformation. Two songs collide, like the primal forces of nature — attraction and repulsion, order and disorder — which release the creative energy needed for change.

Dramatic shifts in vibration signal the entrance of Fortune. What once was, is no longer. The death of the past, the birth of the present: this is the Octave — another word for the working of Fortune.

Listen to "A Day In The Life" at full volume. Let *Mi-Fa* bridge jolt your status quo. Sense the energy of the Octave as it carries you toward the explosive finality of the final *Do*.

The genius of The Beatles was the alchemical pairing of two opposites — John and Paul. Their magic also stemmed from their mastery of the bridge. In classic pop songwriting, the bridge is the contrasting middle section that breaks the sameness and lifts the listener. In this way, the bridge functions like the *Mi-Fa* interval. Listen to any of The Beatles songs, for example: "I'll be Back" at 1:03, "Things We Said Today" at 1:00," or "Something" at 1:15. Experience how the bridge shifts your emotional gears and quickens your heart. This is the sensation of moving through a *Mi-Fa* interval.

Lennon and McCartney are remembered for their music, but by the time they moved from Sgt. Pepper to the White Album, their engineer couldn't handle the creative tension:

7. "Geoff Emerick | The Beatles Bible." 2015. Accessed October 24. http://www.beatlesbible.com/people/geoff-emerick/.

I lost interest in the White Album because they were really arguing amongst themselves and swearing at each other. The expletives were really flying.[8]

Lennon brought Yoko Ono into the sessions, even bringing a bed into the studio to accommodate her needs. Paul couldn't stand having this new person intrude in their recording space. This "Yoko wedge" between John and Paul functioned like the control rods in a nuclear reactor — the creative reactor. Inserting the rods absorbs excess neutrons and prevents explosion, but also shuts down the generation of energy.

In Paul's words, Yoko Ono "attracted John… to another way of life." A short time later, Lennon and McCartney split.[9]

Alchemy doesn't produce a glue to hold relationships together. The alchemy is in the action. Alchemical relationships present wave after wave of difference to face and integrate. The challenge is to take two very different songs — two very different people — and combine them into living art.

The creative marriage is an alchemical marriage — one that is fueled by the Third Force, the love force, from its reactor. In the history of matrimony, the idea of love in marriage is a recent phenomenon. According to historian Stephanie Coontz, throughout history "love in marriage was seen as a bonus, not as a necessity." Historically, marriage had an economic basis, but as Coontz sees it, in the last two centuries, marriage has changed:

In this Western model, people expect marriage to satisfy more of their psychological and social needs than ever before. Marriage is supposed to be free of the coercion, violence, and gender inequalities that were tolerated in the past. Individuals want marriage to meet most of their needs for intimacy and affection and all their needs for sex.[10]

8. Lewisohn, Mark, and Paul McCartney. 2013. The Complete Beatles Recording Sessions: The Official Story of the Abbey Road Years 1962-1970. Reprint edition. Sterling.
9. "Paul McCartney: Yoko Ono Did Not Break up The Beatles - Telegraph." 2015. Accessed October 24. http://www.telegraph.co.uk/culture/music/the-beatles/9670368/Paul-McCartney-Yoko-Ono-did-not-break-up-The-Beatles.html.

According to Coontz, now that marriage is about love, marriage has become more fragile. In her telling, divorce is not a sign of moral failure, but the opposite. Today's fifty percent divorce rate suggests that more and more people are making the epochal effort to achieve the impossible, to find love through the reconciliation of opposites, and embrace the fragility of the alchemical marriage.

The goal of the medieval alchemist was to unlock the secrets of life to purify base metals into gold. Spiritual alchemy uses the processes of life to achieve a similar goal — purification of the soul. In this way, a conscious marriage offers direct access to the alchemical process.

The alchemical marriage brings two separate and discreet entities together to create an ephemeral substance. This third entity is what's known as the Philosopher's Stone — the legendary alchemical substance that is akin to the Holy Grail, the Elixir of Life, and Perfected Love. At its simplest, a man and a woman create a child, two musicians create a band, and two guys create a design agency. At a deeper level, alchemical marriage creates a new dimension akin to a universe being born.

Robert Bly describes this dimension as the "third body" that a man and woman build over the course of a marriage and share in common:

A man and a woman sit near each other, and they do not long
At this moment to be older, or younger, or born
In any other nation, or any other time, or any other place.
They are content to be where they are, talking or not talking
Their breaths together feed someone we do not know.
The Man sees the way his fingers move;
He sees her hands close around a book she hands to him.
They obey a third body that they share in common.
They have promised to love that body
Age may come, parting may come, death will come!
A man and a woman sit near each other;

10. Coontz, Stephanie. 2005. Marriage, a History: From Obedience to Intimacy, or How Love Conquered Marriage. New York: Viking Adult.

As they breathe they feed someone we do not know
Someone we know of, whom we have never seen.[11]
— Robert Bly

And with this picture in mind, Karen and I drove up the coast to Big Sur and Carmel. We had just started our project creating a third body. This was clear at our first date when I realized, "Whoa! This is happening," that "whoa" was the shock of encountering the third body, the love body.

We stopped at the Carmel Mission and headed to the courtyard, just by the fountain.

I hadn't practiced talking points or made much of a plan, so I opened my heart and delivered earnest proclamations of love.

Karen listened patiently until an awkward pause let her intervene:

"Are you going to ask the question?"

Startled by how bad this was going, I quickly changed course: "Will you marry me?"

"Yes, of course, I will."

Having taken our lovers leap, we continued up the coast to share the big news with Reshad — who in many ways, was still our third body.

---

11. Bly, Robert. 2000. Eating the Honey of Words: New and Selected Poems. New York: Harper Perennial.

12

Love is Reckless

Don't push the river; it flows by itself.
Barry Stevens

"Some gin and tonics for the ladies?"

Nick Saxton, our bad-boy friend, cracked the bedroom door wide enough to serve a trio of drinks to the bride, her mom, and her bridesmaid. It didn't matter that one of the ladies was pregnant and the other, her mother, was a teetotaler from Tennessee. In Nick's mind, the solution to any problem involved pot, sex, or alcohol.

The problem at hand was that we invited ninety-six people to our West LA bungalow to witness our five o'clock marriage in a postage-stamp backyard. I had planned to spend the day contemplating this passage toward family and responsibility. Instead, I frantically raced around town looking for plastic sheeting to cover the tables from a thunderous rain.

Weeks earlier, a friend had asked if we had a Plan B. I remember explaining, "Are you nuts? It has never rained in Los Angeles in August."

This was before the Internet. Now you can discover a weird historical anomaly for precipitation on August 18:[1]

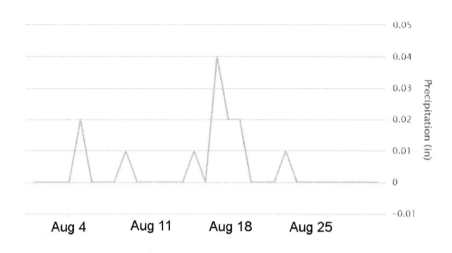

While the guests crowded inside to escape the rain, Nick continued to serve unauthorized gin and tonics to a growing group of men while Reshad regaled with his aristocratic swagger. I noticed the long-sober husband of my mom's best friend in this circle of sots and knew the wedding was out of my hands.

Lines were becoming drawn between two camps, Sufis and Jews, and each with their leader, Reshad versus my mom — and not the alchemical wedding we envisioned.

Karen and I saw ourselves as poster children for the alchemical marriage. Tall/Short, Northern/Southern, Jewish/Christian, Analytic/Empathetic. We used code language to describe our potency: White Meat/Dark Meat. We knew it wasn't going to be an easy marriage, but together, we made one whole bird.

Karen was warming me up to the Karen-axiom that *things that don't go together, somehow go together*. When I shared my concern

1. "Los Angeles, CA Climate in August." 2015. Accessed October 24. http://www.climatespy.com/climate/summary/united-states/california/los-angeles-intl/august.

about mixing energies at our wedding, Karen replied calmly, "Why wouldn't we invite everyone we feel close to?"

Traditional weddings acknowledge this axiom— the blending of camps. In Christian ceremonies, the bride's family sits on the left; the groom's on the right. In a Jewish ceremony, it's the opposite. Either way, the officiant opens his or her arms, invites the blending of two souls, ties the knot, and the couple kiss. The alchemical deed is done. The two camps become one family. Everyone drinks, dances, and is happy. Maybe it's a fantasy, but alchemical fusion is the goal.

Thirty years ago, if you weren't a church-goer, it wasn't easy to find a venue and officiant for a non-traditional wedding. As Fortune would have it, Reshad was hosting his two small children from England in California that August. He agreed to make a side trip to Los Angeles, children in tow, to marry us. It was not his custom to venture outside the bubble of his Sufi world, so we knew we were taking a risk by inviting him into my family scene. Reshad presented a list of demands and complaints, including "Five o'clock is the wrong time in the Octave to get married."

If there was any concern, it was Gerald and Helen — my closest family friends from Chicago. Fifteen years earlier, Gerald famously walked out on wife Helen in a classic sixties *Mad Men* move. Gerald packed his drum set, said, "Honey, it's been nice," and took off. As was the solution to every mid-life crisis back then, Gerald headed to California — but taking my mom's client, Betty, with him.

So, now Karen's axiom about everything "fitting together" would be acid-tested since Gerald and his new wife Betty insisted on coming to the wedding — as did ex-wife Helen and now-adult daughter Janie who would lay eyes on her dad for the first time since middle school at our wedding. Oy.

If I had a blind spot, it concerned the Sufis. I had known Reshad for ten years, and at each stop along his journey — England, Los Angeles, Boulder, Santa Cruz — Reshad would collect devoted followers, then piss off a growing portion of them. In making our invite list, we overlooked the fact that most of our dearest Sufi friends were in the pissed-off camp. Oy vey.

Somewhere during the planning, I wanted to honor my Jewish roots. So, I asked Nander, a Hungarian, vaudevillian, cantorial grandfather of one of my best friends, to lead a Jewish ceremony after dinner. It was meant to be a small thing, a side note, as a toast. Perhaps, I wanted to make my family feel comfortable. Maybe, I was trying to assuage my guilt for marrying outside the tradition. Or maybe invoking the God of the Torah in a second ceremony would add an extra layer of marital security. Truth is, we just wanted to stage a good show.

According to the plan, after the Sufi ceremony, everyone would be ushered to the street, tables of ten rolled out, and a sit-down catered dinner would be served from our phone-booth kitchen. For good measure, we squeezed a dance floor, band, and vocalist into the backyard. Richard, our architect friend, created scaled drawings to ensure that every person, table, and chair could squeeze in. Importantly, we visualized every step from greeting the guests to throwing the rice.

Visualization was an important practice in our school. Karen and I were both trained in J.G. Bennett's *Decision Exercise* which was taught as a sacred initiation and a way to contact one's essential self. The basis for the exercise came from Gurdjieff, who felt that people, in their normal reactive state, cannot "do" anything.

Bennett considered the Decision Exercise to be the most powerful method to awaken the inner ability to "do" — i.e. participating consciously in the manifestation of the creative world.

Mr. Bennett's exercise was deceptively simple: Before bedtime, you visualized a simple task. An example would be wiping off the top of the refrigerator. Breathing consciously, you visualized each step in your mind's eye: getting a paper towel, finding the spray cleaner, grabbing a step-stool, removing the debris, spraying, wiping, putting it all away, and most importantly, acknowledging completion. The key is to visualize *being in your body* — *feel* yourself climb the stool, *feel* your arm moving and wiping. You can even include your emotional state in the visualization. It might be a feeling of gratitude and ease.

So how does spritzing the fridge lead to enlightenment? In the Decision Exercise, the simpler the task, the more powerful it becomes. It is an exercise that builds a bridge between two worlds: between dream and materiality, between night thoughts and day thoughts, between the subtle world and the manifested world. By performing the exercise, what gets initiated in the subtle world as thought-form is consummated the next day as a completed physical action.

The Decision Exercise acknowledges that actions and events in the physical world — what we experience as Fortune — precipitate from an unseen, energetic blueprint. From these subtle visualizations, the physical act unfolds the next morning without effort — greasing the skids of creation. The goal is to live a creative life in a harmonious flow. The Decision Exercise serves as a warm-up drill to learn how to live consciously without struggle — a life in harmony with the formative world:

> Who says God has created this world? We have created it by our own imagination.[2]
> — Meher Baba

Our wedding was a highly-engineered event with lots of moving parts and conflicting camps in a too-tight space. So Karen and I quietly visualized each step of the ceremony and reception.

We must have visualized golden shafts of sunlight because at 5:00 p.m., the rain miraculously stopped, the ushers wiped the chairs, and the guests took their places.

As Karen walked down the aisle, I studied her grace-filled presence. "Who is this transcendent being?" I wondered. My wonderment shifted to a more pressing question. Can Reshad pull this off?

2. "Meher Baba." n.d. Wikiquotes. https://en.wikiquote.org/wiki/Meher_Baba.

Good news. Reshad delivered his opening remarks with the power and flourish of Peter O'Toole.

Bad news. Nothing coming out of his mouth made sense.

"I have had the privilege to be present at the marriage of many many people," Reshad began. "From halfway up Mont Blanc and all over the world. It is my privilege, the dignity that I have to have when I am there for a couple is TOTAL COMPLETE CONCENTRATION, that I am not there with my ME, if you follow what I am saying."

I considered turning around to see how my family was handling this, but I chose to stay the course. Just breathe.

"And I know all of you have come," Reshad continued. "Some of you people are Jewish, and some people are this and some Christians. Whatever."

There went half the audience.

"I have given a lot of radio shows recently. I said that I feel so strongly that this country, I feel so positive about. I'm not talking about politics. If only people will see and you will see how wonderful you are, and this beloved couple knows how wonderful they are."

I knew not to analyze Reshad's syntax, so, I surrendered to Karen's axiom, knowing that on some level, this all must go together.

"It is easier to bear the brunt of what is sometimes..." Reshad added a long theatrical pause, then thundered in his king's speech, "DIFFICULT. But we are one in Universal Love. All of us."

I peeked at Karen. She seemed untouched by the words — nor by anything in this world. Reshad continued.

"I am privileged to say that very few people that I have met who said 'I will' have not kept together..."

My inner cynic couldn't let this one slip. For reasons unknown, every marriage Reshad officiated had failed. So, I prayed... please God, let us be the exception.

Finally, it was Nick's turn. He was the poster child for reckless love, so we invited him to read from Rumi:

Love is reckless;

Reason seeks a profit...
Love gambles away every gift God bestows.
Without cause God gave us Being;
Without cause, give it back again.

If this was a reckless wedding, at least we had Rumi on our side. The rings came next, then Reshad sang to the heavens, beauty and grace flowed into our world, and we were married.

As was the custom in our school, Reshad led the Rose Ceremony. Karen and I exchanged a rose, then two, then three, all the way up to nine. With each exchange, I could feel an energetic substance grow between us. We were creating Bly's "third body" — the bigger "we" that would beget children and community, joy and suffering, and sickness and health.

"Give your wife nine roses, the number of perfected man and woman," Reshad instructed.

We placed the nine roses into a punch bowl of rose-scented water and sipped. The ushers served it communion-style to the guests.

As I Karen and I sipped the rose elixir, Fortune bestowed her bounty onto our marriage. For one fleeting moment, there were no financial calamities, no children with special needs, no marital dysfunctions, adopted strays, midlife crises — or even wedding crises. These could wait a few minutes.

Family and guests assembled in the front while the expert Sufi team turned the backyard from chapel to banquet hall. Five minutes behind schedule became ten, then fifteen. The corseted constraints of our brilliant program had begun to unravel. Thirty minutes is a long time for ninety people to mill about on the sidewalk, so Nick and Reshad retreated to the house to refortify with gin and tonics. Maybe, alchemical maxims have their limit — too many things that don't go together are too many things.

The food finally arrived as Karen and I made small talk from table to table. All this time, the Jewish ceremony loomed, but the time window was shrinking. What kind of cockamamie wedding has a second ceremony anyway? Like herding cats, a minyan pulled together, an impromptu chuppah raised, and Nander's resonant voice invoked the God of Abraham, Isaac, and Jacob. At the appropriate moment, Janna, our soul-singer friend sang "Sunrise Sunset."

Crush the glass. L'chaim!!

Janna and band segued into Ella Fitzgerald; Karen glided into my arms, and the universe overflowed into our hearts. As we danced, I heard strange rumblings from the sidelines. Nander wasn't happy about an African-American singing from *Fiddler on the Roof*. Reshad couldn't handle being upstaged, so he retreated inside, surrounded by devotees, further splitting the energy into two camps. The music picked up; my mom danced aggressively with Charles, an advertising guy who, true to the Mad Men ethos, was her growing love interest. My father, of course, was oblivious. Janie briefly and bravely danced with her deadbeat dad.

According to our visualization, the big send-off was slated for 9:30 p.m. — way too soon as the party had barely gotten started. A crowd followed us to the front, and in a blur, Karen and I shook off the rice, jumped into my Datsun, and left the unraveling scene behind. Glancing over my shoulder, the Hieronymus Bosch painting, *Ship of Fools* came to mind. Without a captain, the gathering seemed headed toward oblivion.

We drove to Santa Barbara where, given our exhaustion and Karen's nausea, our honeymoon night was more about realism than romance.

The next night we dined at San Ysidro Ranch, the setting for JFK and Jackie's honeymoon retreat. We couldn't afford to stay there — nor eat there — so we strategically split an entree and headed back to Los Angeles the next morning to entertain Karen's mom and little sister.

We pulled up to our house and walked inside. The trashed space had been transformed with flowers and stacked with gifts (good work, Sufis). Karen and I beamed with nuptial love as my mom shared the following words:

"I'm going to say this once, and then I promise never to mention it again."

I braced myself for the fact that my mom would mention it again and again.

"After you left, Reshad and his minions tried to throw me out of the house. I was sitting here at the dining table, talking to your cousins when all of a sudden they announced that the party was over; everyone had to go."

I was in no mood to spoil our happily-married streak — now two days old — so, following kid-protocol, I blocked it out. Blah-blah, mom-talking, blah-blah.

Flash forward exactly thirty years. For the last two months, I have struggled with this chapter. I've sent it to the discard pile several times and even consulted with Miriam, my oracle in such matters:

"No one wants to read about our stupid wedding," I complained to Miriam. "All weddings are the same. They expose the dysfunction at the heart of every family."

"You can't cut it out," Miriam cautioned. "It's the pivotal scene, the Oedipal split between you and your mother, and it sets up the inevitable confrontation between student and teacher — the 'atonement with the father' on the Hero's journey."

"Pivotal" seemed to overstate the case, so I skipped the chapter, wrote several chapters before and after, and still I drew a blank. Then it dawned on me: I HAVE NO IDEA WHAT HAPPENED AT MY OWN DAMN WEDDING!

So, I called my mom, age 91.

"Mom, do you remember our wedding?"

"I think so."

"Do you remember having a confrontation with Reshad?"

"I can't really remember. Is Reshad still alive?"

Like an amnesia victim trying to piece together the lost chapters of a misplaced life, my marriage story was officially missing. I couldn't leave it blank, so, I wrote to Kathleen, Karen's bridesmaid. She emailed in reply:

I would love to talk, I'm getting ready for an exhibition, so my brain cells are a little tapped out at the minute – ha ha! I'll have to dig back in the dusty old memories of that time. Of course, my most vivid memory is Richard taking chairs away from guests!

WTF! So, I contacted Janie, my childhood neighbor who danced with her deadbeat dad. She wrote back:

Just so you are aware, many years have passed, and my memory of your wedding is a bit blurry. I do, however, remember leaving with an orthopedic issue…"

Double oy! Karen and I argued and argued whether the chapter even belonged in the book.

"Just drop the whole thing," she advised. "What are you trying to accomplish?"

I called Hamid, my best man. He was pretty blunt:

"Mr. Miller, it comes down to this: Why did you have to have a second ceremony? When you are married, it is done. There is nothing more to add."

Okay, I'm Jewish. I screwed up. But I needed to know what happened.

I located Richard, our former housemate who served as stage manager for the event. We had not talked in twenty years. Richard had more to add, a lot more:

"So, Nick, Reshad, and the others were in the back bedroom, drinking pretty heavily," Richard recounted. "Reshad was mostly grousing about the second ceremony which didn't set well with him. 'There should only be one,' and 'I'm the only one.' That kind of thing.

"I was busy working. Kathleen, Daniel, and I served as the staff that night. We were just trying to keep everything flowing.

"After you and Karen left it started to get really difficult. Reshad started making a lot of demands and wanted the property cleared of all people. 'The party is over. Stop the party, stop the music, stop the dancing, it is done, everybody leave.'

"Being the chief of staff, Reshad summoned me to make it happen: 'Richard, I want this property cleared immediately. Make it done.' And I thought, 'Oh shit.'

"So, Daniel and I went out back, and this is the important part of the story because I did something I have had to look at. There was an older woman, and she moved to sit down — and I removed her chair."

As Richard painted this picture, I began to panic. An emotional truth postponed for 30 years was now tumbling into view. Richard continued:

"I said to this older woman, 'It's time to go.' And I started packing up chairs.

"Remember Chris from Boulder? " Richard continued. "He took one look at me and said, 'That is exactly the reason why I no longer have anything to do with Reshad and this school.'

"I looked at Chris, and at that moment I felt so upset that I had removed a chair from an old woman that I placed it back and immediately apologized to her. And I said, 'Chris, I understand; you're right.'

"So, I decided not to clear the property at that point. This decision did not go over well, and for the rest of the night, I was in the dog house.

"People were drinking. And at one point Janie and your brother were dancing, and she got thrown into the bushes and seriously sprained her ankle. And I thought, oh my God, now we have a sign that something is very wrong. Reshad was banging on, complaining 'It's wrong. Something is wrong.' Then, somebody passed out from dehydration and had to be whisked off.

"It got quite late and Reshad couldn't remember if he had eaten or not, because he never ate. And Nick reminded him that he had eaten fish and chips, which of course he hadn't.

"And then, your mother and Reshad got into it, really heavily. Reshad made a statement about you and him, and he being given the house, and that he was running the place. Your mother said, 'Sir, let's be perfectly clear. This is my house; I put the down payment down. And, you are a bad guest.'

"That went over really well. Your mother just took him out. One shot, one blow. Let him have it. She was like, 'I'm not going to put up with this shit. You're behaving badly. This is a wedding, and if you don't like it, why don't you leave?'

"So, that kind of stunned Reshad. And then your mom left.

"And you gotta be thankful to our Sufi group. They put a firewall around the situation. The Reshad scene inside the house was in flames; the backyard was having a wonderful party.

"So, I stayed outside for the rest of the night. Reshad was in a real state and was letting everyone have it.

"Finally, Reshad passed out and was whisked off to bed. Things pretty much died down at that point. But, it was not a bad night. It was an epic night. The Sufi school was on fire.

"We got up the next morning, and the place was trashed. Daniel had slept on the lawn. There was stuff in the bushes. It was a mess. So, we started to clean it up. Reshad got up and was a mess. He announced, 'That is the last wedding I will ever do. I refuse to perform one ever again.'

"And I think he knew that he wasn't flying with perfect colors that night. I think he knew it. He lost a lot of credibility. A lot of people were hurt that night. They were hit hard.

"While characterized obedience to the teacher is important, I had to make a choice between obedience — pulling chairs out from under old people — versus acting like a civil human being. I'm not blaming anyone for that. That is my interpretation. I thank Chris all the time when I bring this story up because he nailed it, really crisp, and really fast. 'That is not the school. That is not what it is about.' Bang, bang, bang. It was beautiful. That was a life moment for me. That was a pivot point for me and how I wanted to be going forward.

Still in shock, even faint, I sighed and said nothing. It was a lot to take in. Richard continued:

"So, what was the lesson?" Richard paused to reflect. "That it's not good to mix energies. You had your aspirations, Karen's aspirations, all these aspirations. And you crisscrossed them to create energy. As a friend, I hope to God that you stop doing that, but you're good at it. It's like lighting a powder keg. It works. You can kick some energy up.

"I talked to a doctor once who wanted to mix energies in her practice, different modalities, and now she may be up for malpractice because of it. If you mix energies, it can cause problems. You're orchestrating. You're being a wizard. You're affecting change."

Listening to Richard tell this story left me deeply unsettled. Our thirtieth wedding anniversary was coming up which demanded something special. I was looking forward to our annual dinner of Spanish-spiced lamb tenderloins with a glass of Zinfandel — but not this.

Richard's charge of wedding malpractice forced me to reexamine my alchemical precepts — the charge of willful wizardry, mixing of energies, lighting a powder keg, and practicing Karen's axiom without a license.

As Fortune would have it, Amy, another long lost friend, invited us to dinner while I was working on this chapter. She took us around her home, proudly pointing to the framed photos of her daughter Grace in her stunning wedding dress.

"Where's Dave?" I asked. Dave was Grace's dad and Amy's ex. "He's not in any of the wedding pictures. Didn't he give his daughter away?"

Amy looked at me like I was kidding.

"Grace considered inviting her dad for maybe a split second, but then opted not," Amy explained. "He would be way too unpredictable. Grace and her fiance wanted the wedding to be beautiful. Why risk it?"

Why risk it? WHY RISK IT? I considered Amy's pragmatism. Is love meant to be reckless or constrained? How much risk management is too much?

Consider the famous proverb, "Don't push the river; let it flow by itself." We are taught in life to push the river, make a splash, create a name for oneself. But pushing the river also comes with unintended consequences.

I asked Karen if we had pushed the river by mixing energies — "lighting a powder keg" trying to "kick up the energy."

"We knew Reshad was a loose cannon," Karen reminded me, "but it was inconceivable that we should be married by anyone else. So, we invited everyone important in our lives and whoever came, came."

It takes a bride and groom to have a marriage. But, there is also no marriage without witnesses. "Witnessing" provides the Third Force — the river of flowing energy that sanctifies and catalyzes the alchemical marriage.

Maybe over-engineering the guest list — the Witness list — is the true "pushing the river." Pushing neutralizes and sanitizes the Third Force energy. If there is a crime of wedding wizardry, it would be to exclude the loose cannons and not plunge into the river of life.

Finally, it dawned on me. We visualized each step of our perfect wedding right up to the moment of throwing rice. After that, Hieronymus Bosch was in charge.

If there is a postscript to this story, it also comes from my conversation with Richard, who shared:

"When it came time for us to get married, Kathleen and I essentially eloped. We hardly invited anyone. Do you know why? Because of your wedding."

I would add one more footnote: After thirty years — years that have been richly-lived and richly difficult — Karen and I are still married.

13

Giovanni's Gift

You have a right to experiment with your life.
You will make mistakes. And they are right too.
Anais Nin

"You mind if I smoke?"

Nick took a sip of our expensive single malt, lit up, and prepared to drop a pearl of wisdom:

"The thing about you girls is that you're afraid to look at the dirt in life. Like, somehow you're exempt."

Nick exhaled a small cloud while Karen instinctively held her breath. Karen was very pregnant, so she excused herself to our tiny kitchen. Kathleen, her bridesmaid, got up to join her.

Lori, Nick's girlfriend, gripped her empty glass.

"Come on, Nick," Lori complained.

Nick continued:

"If you're really honest with yourself, what you girls want is a fatter dick and a bigger wallet."

Having heard the line too many times, the girls grimaced. Nick continued on this tack, but now bellowing to the kitchen because Lori had lost interest.

"Heh, heh, come on, be honest," Nick blustered.

"Nicky, I'm getting tired," Lori whimpered.

"I'm just calling it how it is," Nick badgered. "Business, sex, religion, whatever — people size you up by what's in your wallet — and your pants."

Richard, Kathleen's boyfriend, made the strategic blunder of refilling Nick's glass.

"Thank you, Richard." Nick sipped and continued. "There was a time when I vowed never to shoot a commercial, and now I'm driving a fucking cab."

Nick sipped his Scotch and took a drag in succession.

"This town is about three things — money, sex... and money."

"That's two things," I piped in.

"Okay, money, money and fucking money — and it doesn't hurt to be Jewish. It's certainly not about art."

Nick bellowed over the kitchen noise.

"Do you realize that I worked with Antonioni on *Blow-Up?* And George Lucas — he wanted me. Michael Jackson, 'Boogie and the Beat.' Rick James, 'Super Freak,' and 'Give it to me Baby.' And the launch of MTV? Fucking Pat Benatar. Your good friend Nicky invented the music video genre."

Nick sensed that he had everyone's attention, so he queued up for the money shot:

"Benatar, 'You Better Run'... Rascals remake, what a bitch. She was angry and pissed, didn't want to be there and take direction like an actor, but I took her sassy little pouting cunt and turned it into something. You look at life; you see what nobody wants to look at — the dirt in life — and you discover art. That's what an artist does. But, you guys measure people with money."

"Nick, we love you just the way you are," Karen chimed in.

"Nicky, I want to go home right now." Lori pleaded.

"Lori, just breathe. Richard has poured another of his best Glenfiddich, so we mustn't waste. Isn't that what Reshad says, 'Wastage is the only sin.'"

"Glenlivet," Richard corrected.

"*My* best Glenlivet," I further corrected.

"Fiddich, Livet. Life is only real when you Livet." Nick laughed at his pun. "You got to live the moment and taxi driving seems to be my lot, fucked as that may be. But, Lori, why are you on my case? 'Cause I'm not meeting your high standards?"

"Nicky, I'm not on your case. I just want to see you do something with your life. All you ever do is complain. You're negative all the time."

Lori stood to leave the table.

"Then why don't you call a cab?" Nick snarled. "Oh, I am the cab."

And with that, Nick stubbed out his cigarette and started to stand. Karen returned from the kitchen.

"Nick, you *are* an artist," Karen offered.

She gave Nick a hug.

"Think of all the material you're getting," I added.

"Nobody wants to see the homeless rejects I pick up," Nick groused. "They want Robin fucking Williams pretending to be homeless. Let's go. And I'm sorry about all the smoke."

Lori collected Nick, installed him into her tiny Fiat, and waved goodbye. We returned to the kitchen to deal with the four-course aftermath.

I scrubbed burnt bits of steak au poivre and thought to myself, "Why am I attracted to these people — Reshad and Nick — with all their bluster?" If life is a game of collecting the right ingredients, what am I trying to bake? Knowledge? Fortune?

Years later, this question of collecting "ingredients" returned. I was directing a video for a company that laundered hospital linens. The private pilot who flew us from plant to plant was also the cameraman — a big stocky guy named Jack. The engine noise and bumpiness made it impossible to talk or read in the little Cessna, so I spent my flying hours studying Jack from the teeny back seat, trying to make sense of how he was put together. Jack was like an impenetrable mountain — all physical, Taurus-like, loud, and self-absorbed without the slightest drop of self-reflection. In my imagination, I would borrow small homeopathic doses of Jack — just enough to kick some ass if the need arose.

As I washed dishes, I wondered, "What ingredients am I seeking from Nick?"

Harville Hendrix, the famous marriage theorist, spoke of *maximizers* and *minimizers*.[1] Nick was a maximizer — he would explode his feelings defensively, act impulsively, and exaggerate his needs. He was a bit of a train wreck, but rubberneckers and news crews are drawn to the tremendous energy of train wrecks.

So, Nick became a source of "maximizing," who we kept around to spice up our young married lives.

Soon, we had a child, and our friendships gravitated toward couples with small babies and less and less of Nick and Lori. This explains why we failed to notice the day Nick disappeared. Poof, vanished, like gone. This was before email, social media, phone forwarding, or other digital fingerprints. Nick's disappearance was even more alarming because his girlfriend, Lori was pregnant.

When Lori asked Karen to be her suddenly-single-mom-needs-a-labor-coach, Karen knew this would be an awkward situation. We didn't know Lori; our guy was Nick. And worse, the elephant in the delivery room would not be there. So, when the long, lanky boy entered the world, everyone made a calculated effort not to state the obvious — Lori's baby looked exactly like Nick.

Lori was now a single, artsy, waitress mom with a newborn. Everyone helped out the best they could, but as a musician, Lori being a single mother in Los Angeles was unsustainable. Plus, we had our own challenges raising a high-energy toddler. Before long, Nick was pretty much forgotten.

§

Six months later, the phone rang. It was Nick.

"Hi... can't really talk." Nick rambled into my ear without any

1. Hendrix, Harville. 2001. Getting the Love You Want: A Guide for Couples. Reprint edition. New York: Holt Paperbacks.

back story. "I've been away; crazy stuff. Been to the moon and back. It will be a movie. This is very big, and I need to see you."

"Sure," I replied.

Cryptic phone calls never lead to good, and Nick babbling like an alien abductee should have been my signal to hang up, but the word "movie" was my sucker punch.

When soldiers come back from war, they are different. Nick was palpably different in that way. Without explanation, Nick came by the house to drop a screenplay in my lap.

"Read this," he said, "then we'll talk."

I picked up the script — *with two hands*. In the movie business, anything over 120 pages is suspect. If it's 160 pages, producers thumb to the end, see the page number and pass. After a certain weight, there's no thumbing; the script goes straight to the slush pile. I wasn't versed in these formulas, so I opened the thing, paged to the back, and noticed it was 250 pages. Nick had also cheated with the margin widths, another instant disqualification.

I considered the title, *The Fight for Love*. Clever with ironic possibility, but Nick didn't do irony. Too bad this will be on-the-nose — another disqualifier. I flipped it open and began to read.

I was mesmerized.

The story began at the time of Nick's disappearance. He was driving his cab around the Wilshire District when he got a radio call to pick-up a passenger at Antinori's, an Italian restaurant in Beverly Hills.

Nick pulled up as two guys stepped out of the restaurant speaking in Italian. They embraced, then one of them, Giovanni, entered the cab.

Nick described Giovanni as "built like a miniature sumo wrestler with impeccable manners, total confidence and an infectious sense of humor."

I devoured the screenplay as Nick punched the meter and pulled into traffic:

"So how's your day been?" Giovanni asks.

"I'm starting my day over," Nick scowls glancing in the rear view mirror. "How about you?"

"Every day is a happy day for me," Giovanni exclaims.

Nick isn't convinced. "For you, every day is happy, huh?"

Giovanni laughs. "For years it's been like this."

Nick checks out Giovanni in the mirror and replies, "Well, my days are wonderful and terrible. Sometimes, all in the same day! So, tell me how you do it."

"This is possible because I don't care about a fucking thing," Giovanni boasts.

Nick turns around to look Giovanni in the eye. "And this is what makes your days happy?"

"Yes. This is the secret to a happy life."

I was troubled and intrigued by Giovanni's don't-care-about-a-fucking-thing formula for happiness. Giovanni was either a realized being or a sociopath.

Nick smoothly changes lanes.

"And what kinds of experience led you to this exalted state of detachment?" Nick asks.

Giovanni smiles.

"Six divorces, seven children, and I produce over thirty movies."

"Oh, yeah? Anything I might have seen?"

"Foreign films, mostly."

Nick is skeptical.

"Name one."

"*La Strada.*"

"*La Strada?* That's one of the greatest movies ever made!" Nick exclaims. "You worked with Fellini?"

"No!" Giovanni thunders. "Fellini, he worka for me!"

"Any others?"

"*La Dolce Vita, Divorce Italian Style...*"

"Tell me more!"

Giovanni laughs. "If I tell you more, you gonna be masturbating for three days."

"Hey," Nick pipes in. "I worked on some low-budget movies myself, but they were awful."

Giovanni goes to the heart of the matter: "It doesn't matter what you do; it only matters that you do it."

The ride was over, and Giovanni hands Nick a twenty.

I put down the script. *"It doesn't matter what you do; it only matters that you do it."* This odd aphorism ricocheted in my brain. Being good, breathing consciously, serving the guest, helping humanity, transforming energy, raising vibration, saving the world — all this *doing good* had been my mantra and now this crazy koan pulled the rug right out. *"It doesn't matter what the fuck you do…"*

Nick continued to grouse about his sorry life in the cab until, a week later, another a radio dispatch crackled into his life:

"677… Pick-up at Orlando Orsini's."

Nick grabs the mike, "Yeah, yeah… I'm on it."

Nick performs a lazy U-turn, oblivious to oncoming traffic. He is clearly upset. Earlier that day, the alarming pink from Lori's home pregnancy test had put him into a state of shock.

Nick pulls up to the restaurant. The door opens.

"Take me to the Westwood Marquis,"

Nick glances up with a double-take. "Aren't you the maestro de cinema I picked up at Antinori's."

"Yes. That's me."

It's Giovanni.

"I remember your voice," Nick offers.

"Hey, I'm going back to do movies, kid. I need the money. Four days after I see you, I lose forty million dollars in the oil business."

"Wow."

"This time, I gotta make it all happen with the mirrors. If they catch you broke in the movie business, they gonna eat you alive. I gotta make two movies next year. We going to shoot the first one in Arizona this June, then we going to Paris."

And with that, Giovanni — the ultimate vector of Third Force shock — collided into Nick's irascible world.

Fortune double-dips into our world to make sure we're paying attention. The actress Rosie O'Donnell tells a great double-dip story.[2] She was on a flight, sitting in coach, just after starting out as a newbie on VH1. She sat next to a bitchy woman who complained bitterly to the flight attendant that she didn't get the salad she ordered. To calm her down, Rosie made a game of offering her salad in exchange for the woman's dessert. Soon, the woman lightened up and shared that she was a new agent at William Morris.

Six months later, Fortune double-dipped. Rosie was on another flight, and the same woman was sitting next to her.

"What are you doing?" the woman asked.

"I got offered *Win, Lose or Draw for Kids* on Disney," Rosie replied. "They're gonna pay me $50,000 a year, five-year contract to host the show."

Her seatmate said, "No, you're not. And I'm now your agent, and we're too close to God for me not to intervene… and it's too weird to sit next to you twice!"

In that same too-weird-to-be-true way, Fortune double-dipped for Nick:

> Close up on the answering machine. Lori and Nick listen to the message.
> "I knew he'd call!"
> "You meet with him tomorrow?" Lori asked.
> Nick smiles. "I'm coming out of the cab on this one, babe. I can feel it."

The next day, Giovanni visits Nick and Lori at their apartment. Giovanni needs help finding angel investment to start a production company. Nick calls a few friends but fails to score. As the scene begins, Giovanni paces back and forth facing Nick and Lori on the couch.

2. Rosie O'Donnell. 2015. Accessed October 24. http://www.wnyc.org/story/299360-rosie-odonnell/?utm_source=sharedUrl&utm_medium=metatag&utm_campaign=sharedUrl.

"I'm angry tonight kid. Very angry," Giovanni growls.

"Relax. Have some wine," Nick offers helpfully.

Giovanni clenches his fist, throws some imaginary punches, then turns to face Nick.

"I don't want to relax. I don't want any wine. I'm angry, Nick. I'm angry with you!"

"With me? Why?" Nick is confused. "Because my friend wouldn't give me the money?"

"Nooo. It's because you no positive. You're very negative. Look at your life. What happened, Nick? You say you work with the biggest superstars, and now you drive a taxi. It's because you give up. You choose to throw away your life. You choose to be negative. You do!"

Nick rubs his face and laughs nervously.

"Shit, man," Nick complains. "Everyone in the business lies to me. Fuck."

"It's no joke. I'm very serious," Giovanni warns. "If you no willing to look at the dark in your life, how you going to wake up? You a masochist is what it is. You no willing to go through the pain, but it's worse where you are! If you no change your attitude, you gonna die!

Nick glares at Giovanni. "Get outta my house!"

Giovanni gently changes gears. "Believe me, Nick. I no say these things to hurt you. I like you."

The following day, Nick and Giovanni meet at Paddington's Tea Room in Beverly Hills. Giovanni offers to help Nick.

Giovanni bores in with penetrating clarity. "Either you live, or you die. You do, or you don't."

Giovanni takes a bite of kiwi pie, letting a big glob of whipped cream plop on his shirt. He casually wipes and continues.

"This is your last chance, and you're not going to get another one. I hope you see this. Personally, I don't think you got the guts to do this. But I tell you one thing. If you do, you got a friend over here. I'll answer your questions and give you help if you want it."

"Okay…" Nick is uncertain. "So what do I do now?"

"This afternoon. Go to a church. Any church. It doesn't matter. Go and sit for a couple of hours. And you don't have to pray, 'Oh, please

God…'" Giovanni puts his hands together in mock piety. "No, talk to Him with FORCE!!"

Nick runs up the steps of several churches and pulls at the doors. Being Los Angeles, they are all locked. Finally, Nick finds a small chapel. He sits amid the empty pews. Tears run freely.

"Help me, Jesus. Forgive me," Nick sobs wiping his face with his sleeve. "Fuck. I'm tired of living a lie. I wanna be free. I don't wanna die. I wanna live."

I was spellbound. Was this our insufferable Nick? Was this real change? Was he surrendering the mass of garbage that stood in the way of his life?

Two days later, Nick called me again. He asked if I would like to meet Giovanni. Holy shit, what was I supposed to say?

I drove to the Hollywood apartment where Nick was staying. I was startled by the new Nick. The post-Giovanni Nick was much slimmer, better dressed, and more focused. Nick noticed my surprise as he stepped into my car.

"Yeah, this is my fighting weight," he laughed patting his gut. "This is what you get after living on coffee, cigarettes, and apples for six months — and occasionally sex."

"So tell me about this Giovanni guy," I asked, pulling into traffic. "Is he your guru or something?"

"I have no idea who he is. I always wondered if a man of knowledge, a guru, a teacher, a realized being, could exist without any kind of label. A man of power, but also completely hidden. Maybe, Giovanni's my answer."

"So, Giovanni is a man of knowledge?" I asked.

"All I know is that he popped into my cab — twice — and the next thing, I'm in a kind of school without any name, without any tradition — just me pushed to my limits… way beyond my limits."

"But he's a film producer, right?" I pressed.

"Uh huh. Remember the campaign to save the Hollywood Sign?"

"Yeah," I said. "Late seventies. Hugh Hefner was behind it."

"Giovanni showed me this little plaque of the Hollywood Sign. He carries it everywhere."

"Like a calling card?" I asked.

"Exactly. So, I called the Hollywood Chamber. They told me that Giovanni Mazza, Italian film producer, gave $27,777 to restore the first O. Alice Cooper donated the last O. He is who he says he is."

"Really? So, what's the plan? Is he producing your script?"

Nick smirked in an off-putting mystical manner.

"You mind if I smoke?"

As Nick lit up, I continued driving toward Beverly Hills fighting the surreal pull of it all.

Nick exhaled out the window. "If there's a plan, I will be the last to find out."

"But, you've been with him for a year."

"And I know less and less each day," Nick smirked again. "Pull over here."

We parked on a Beverly Hills side street. Nick got out and walked toward a rooming house. I waited, unsure what to do about the expanding rabbit hole under my feet.

A short time later, Nick and Giovanni returned. According to the script, Nick "walked like a pimp" and Giovanni "carried himself like a king." Seeing the pimp and the king together, I flashed on the great buddy films — Abbott and Costello, Joe Buck and Ratso Rizzo, Butch Cassidy and Sundance, the Odd Couple...

"Hey, give me a cigarette, kid." Giovanni elbowed Nick playfully. "You're not holding out on me, are you?"

They both laughed. Nick pulled out a Dunhill like a gentleman.

"So, this is your good friend, Bruce?" Giovanni asked.

Giovanni was immediately disarming. Picture Danny Devito with ten times the gravitas or Donald Trump the size of a cannon ball with an Italian accent.

"I hear you want to be in the movie business," Giovanni poked with the force of a charm bomb.

"Yeah, it's true," I replied.

Giovanni's mojo quickly extinguished my skepticism. In fact, Giovanni focused his heat-seeking charisma at anyone in sight, including an unsuspecting passerby carrying a pizza box.

"Pizza, pizza," Giovanni seduced with basso bluster. "Give me a piece of pizza."

The shocked passer-by opened his pizza box to oblige. Sensing Fortune's open door, Giovanni grabbed two slices.

I watched in fascination as Giovanni leaned against a parked car, folded the slices, and devoured them with pleasure. He caught my gaze.

"What? What are you looking at?" Giovanni scolded. "It's no criminal to be hungry, and my good friend here is very generous. Thank you. *Grazie!*"

The pizza guy smiled woozily and hoofed it out of the scene.

"Before we talk about movie production," Giovanni deftly interjected, "I have a little business to attend to. I need $240 to settle up where I am staying. I'm waiting on a check from Milan."

I looked to Nick. He was supposed to be my guidepost toward reality in this situation, but I was not clear whose team he was on.

Okay, stop the story. The astute reader is probably thinking "con man," get out of there, this is the oldest ruse since Popeye and Blimpie. But, Nick was not a con man. He was my friend and Reshad's friend and Nick read "Love is Reckless" at my wedding and Nick wrote this *heavy* script and seemed transformed and I wanted to be in the movies, and the price of admission was a hamburger today for a major motion picture on Tuesday. So, I wrote a check for $240.

You may feel morally superior and convinced that you would have behaved differently, but Giovanni was not a *normal* person in any sense of the word. Think Alice in Wonderland. The rules of gravity did not apply.

Let me digress on an axiom of Fortune: *The doors of Fortune open through another human being.* I will take it even further. The door of Fortune *is* another human being. That's right — octaves intersecting with octaves.

Consider the cheesy business people who go to networking events, all swapping their business cards; they understand this "door of Fortune" business, but on a very superficial level.

J.G. Bennett once explained that success is the *measure of opportunities* in one's life. So, maintaining a thick Rolodex of connections, having a close network of friends, knowing an inside guy in the movie business — these are all measures of opportunity. Taking it up several levels, raising one's vibrational rate also increases opportunities — exponentially — because you are living closer to the source of creation.

And so, I had Nick. He was my doorway, a shaky door at best, but my friendship with Nick opened a door of possibility called the film business. Giovanni must have picked up on this when he suggested we name our production company Friendship Productions. And just like that, I was a movie producer, and we were producing Nick's script

When Karen met Giovanni, she assumed he was fully vetted — trusting me, and I, in turn, trusted Nick. The fact that Giovanni was a film producer *and* a con man was immaterial. What I was seeking was access to my personal power. The Giovanni school was a school for power — self-actualized power. It's all laid out in Nick's screenplay:

It's late at night at the Moustache Cafe in Westwood. Giovanni takes a bite of chocolate souffle. Some of it falls on his shirt, and he looks puzzled.

"You know what you see in me, Nick?" Giovanni takes another bite of dessert.

"I'm not sure." Nick replies.

"I got power. Real power."

Nick is uncertain, but Giovanni goes for the kill.

"There's no many men like me on this earth."

"How many?"

"No many… People in Hollywood, they see me coming, and they go, 'Ohh shit.'"

"Why's that?"

"Nobody can bullshit Giovanni. I always know when somebody lie.

Some people in this world are very different, kid. I'm one. If you break the trust with me, it's finished."

And with that, Nick hit up everyone he knew to borrow money to finance Giovanni's venture.

While the tut-tutters will find this deplorable, in the Giovanni school it's about "clarifying your mind," and more specifically by liberating yourself from the psychic bondage around money. How? By throwing yourself into terrible financial jeopardy.

So, when Giovanni asked if I could raise $30,000 in forty-eight hours to launch a film production company, there were two possible answers. The first was: "No, I'm a small-time guy with small-time friends, so this is impossible, and by the way, you're a con man, so again, the answer is no."

The second was, "I'm at a crossroads in my life, and this is an opportunity to summon unexplored personal power and break through the mental and emotional limitations that stand in the way of Fortune, so I'm game. Let's make a motion picture."

And just like that, I chose the latter — the key word being "power."

Let's diverge to talk about power. In chapter two, when I squatted eye-to-eye with Philip Shepherd and let it rip, breaching my cathartic edges, I was tapping into power. Power is a tricky business. As Lord John Acton famously stated in 1887, "Power tends to corrupt, and absolute power corrupts absolutely."

Everyone knows this famous aphorism. They're not aware of the second part which is always omitted: "Power tends to corrupt, and absolute power corrupts absolutely. *Great men are almost always bad men.*" Boom![3]

So, according to Lord Acton, if you want to learn about power, you must sit at the feet of a "bad man." In my experience, politicians, CEOs, CMOs, ayatollahs, movie stars, and spiritual teachers confirm Lord Acton's truth about bad-ass power.

3. "Acton-Creighton Correspondence - Online Library of Liberty." 2015. Accessed October 24. http://oll.libertyfund.org/titles/acton-acton-creighton-correspondence#lf1524_label_010.

In the Sufi tradition, there is a power called *himma*, or spiritual will. In the words of Ibn 'Arabi, the 12th century Sufi mystic, *"Himma has the power to create real, actual outcomes that are not associated with illusory projections of the psyche."*[4] In other words, *himma* is not some abstract idea; it's the power that the biggest baddies embody to make things happen.

To understand *himma*, you have to move beyond concepts of good and bad. It is a force. Consider when Donald Trump ejected Jorge Ramos — the Walter Cronkite of the Hispanic world — from Trump's press conference on live television. As Ramos asked an uncomfortable question, Trump turned his head toward his security goon, gave him the eye, and poof, Univision's celebrated news anchor was taken away. And then, two minutes later, in an act of calculation and *himma*, Trump brought Ramos back.

In 2002, when the Bush Administration was plotting behind the scenes to invade Iraq, the Bush people blew off fact-based journalists, contemptuously calling news people "the reality-based community." It was a particularly cocky act of *himma:*

"We're an empire now, and when we act, we create our own reality," a Bush senior adviser told the Pulitzer Prize-winning journalist Ron Suskind. "And while you're studying that reality — judiciously, as you will — we'll act again, creating other new realities, which you can study too, and that's how things will sort out. We're history's actors... and you [journalists], all of you, will be left to just study what we do."[5]

Henry Corbin, the famous Ibn Arabi scholar, describes this vital force:

This power of the heart is what is especially designated by the word *himma*, a word whose content is perhaps best suggested by the Greek

4. Moss, Robert. 2010. The Secret History of Dreaming. New World Library (discussion of Corbin, Creative Imagination in the Sufism of Ibn Arabi)

5. Suskind, Ron. 2004. "Faith, Certainty and the Presidency of George W. Bush." The New York Times, October 17. http://www.nytimes.com/2004/10/17/magazine/faith-certainty-and-the-presidency-of-george-w-bush.html.

word *enthymesis*, which signifies the act of meditating, conceiving, imagining, projecting, ardently desiring — in other words, of having (something) present in the thymus, which is vital force, soul, heart, intention, thought, desire... The force of an intention so powerful as to project and realize (*essentiate*) a being external to the being who conceives the intention.[6]

If *himma* is the power, exercised through will, to make things happen, my core question remained: *"Does Fortune result from 1) Destiny, 2) Chance, or 3) Will?"*

With all the ingredients for the perfect Fortune experiment, Giovanni let me test option three. For the next forty-eight hours, I became Bruce the Himma Machine. Exercising my thymus (which according to the ancient Greeks is the seat of courage), I worked my contacts from end to end. The $30,000 pitch went something like this:

"Hey Judy, this is Bruce. How are you? I have something important to share with you. An opportunity to bring something significant into the world has come into our lives. Our friend, Nick Saxton has written a screenplay about the Work, about real transformation, all based on a remarkable journey that he took. We are working with a producer, and we are asking our friends to help move the project forward. We are seeking small investments that would be repaid with interest in six months. Would you be able to help?"

Perhaps I was stretching the truth — the screenplay wasn't really about the spiritual work, there wasn't real transformation in Nick's story — he hadn't even figured out a plausible ending — but, I had stumbled into Giovanni's school where the ends justify the means. What's more, Giovanni would have never offered to repay, let alone with interest, but my *himma* was not up to that task. At best, I wanted to tap into my seat of power and fulfill my motion picture destiny.

So, back to Lord Acton, was I now a "bad man?"

6. Corbin, Henry. 2014. Creative Imagination in the Sufism of Ibn Arabi. Translated by Ralph Manheim. Princeton, N.J.: Princeton University Press.

Today, with a few clicks, you can anonymously request thirty grand with a Kickstarter campaign and not have to face your friends or tap into your thymus gland. Just click, submit, then go out to dinner.

But this was my Luke Skywalker moment, to bring in $30,000 in forty-eight hours — about $60,000 in today's money. Just reaching someone on a landline phone required good Fortune.

Karen, Nick, Kathleen, and Richard gathered around as I cranked up the calls, a hundred here, five hundred there, maybe a thousand. All the while, an untapped power was being born.

As Corbin explains, the working of *himma* creates "a being external to the being who conceives the intention." In other words, exercising this power creates a "being" or "world" of its own.

Friendship Productions was that being. The plan was for Giovanni to go to New York, stay at the Essex House, act like a "player," drink expensive cognac at the bar, and seek investors for the film. There were two little problems with this plan:

First, I didn't realize it at the time, but Giovanni, with his insatiable gluttony, was the spot-on reincarnation of Jabba the Hutt. I didn't realize that such a person could exist — someone who lived simply to consume. If Giovanni was a man of power, he exercised it in the same way that a black hole engulfs a universe.

I first glimpsed "Giovanni as Jabba" when we went to the bank for cash. I was awestruck watching his stubby fingers handle the money in a lustful, sensual, almost orgasmic fashion.

The second problem was more serious. According to Ibn Arabi, "you will not attach your *himma*, the power of the heart's intention, to anything other than [God]."[7]

Whoops.

We launched Giovanni on his mission to New York with high hopes and expectations. But over time, the back and forth communications began to wane. Our lofty hopes began their queasy

7. Journey to the Lord of Power. 2015. Accessed October 25. http://books.simonandschuster.com/Journey-to-the-Lord-of-Power/Ibn-Arabi/9780892810185.

descent when it became apparent that he was using the money to launch his daughter's fashion line.

Karen and I, sickened to our stomachs, whiplashed between hope and fear, fear and hope. As Rumi explains:

"Show me a fear without hope, or a hope without fear. The two are inseparable."

Like two wings, hope and fear allow the human soul to fly. Yet, Rumi flips your thinking about which is which:

Know that the station of fear is the one in which you are safe. Know that the station of security is the one in which you tremble.

Then Rumi goes all in:

The seaman is always on the planks of fear and hope — when the plank and the man get annihilated, there is nothing but immersion.[8]

Before long, Karen and I were immersed in the wrenching feeling that we had done something dirty and disgraceful. Making matters worse, we had borrowed the money from our Sufi friends.

We traveled to Santa Cruz to visit Reshad and were greeted like spiritual lepers. Reshad advised us never to mention Giovanni's name lest the negative energy infected the Work.

Thirty grand poorer, but now owners of an un-producible screenplay, Nick and I teamed up to turn our lemons into a viable script. I sat at the keyboard while Nick paced with his umpteenth cigarette. We worked hours, days, and weeks on the thing. There was one glaring problem. While *The Fight for Love* was a memoir about personal transformation with a con man as the spiritual teacher — a fabulous ironic premise with box office potential — Nick had not embraced the Mephistophelean fact he had given his soul to a con artist.

8. Schimmel, Annemarie. 1993. The Triumphal Sun (Persian Studies Series): A Study of the Works of Jalaloddin Rumi. Albany, NY: State University of New York Press.

He should have known because Act III laid it out:

EXTERIOR — OAKLAND BAY BRIDGE — DAY

A silver Rolls-Royce commands the roadway high above San Francisco Bay. Nick is driving Giovanni to the Lake Tahoe Caesar's Palace. Shadows from the bridge flicker over the shiny Rolls. Giovanni is in the front passenger seat scratching an endless roll of lottery tickets.

"If you gonna win big, you gotta have the courage to lose big," Giovanni declares. "People are afraid to do this. They don't understand the power of money."

"Which is?" Nick asks.

"To be able to do what you want and get other people to do what you want."

Giovanni continues to scratch tickets and adds, "But not to be an asshole. You manipulate the people with the bullshit. You're a classic asshole. Understand?"

"Hey," Nick complains, "take it easy. This is graduation day, remember?"

"Graduation day" refers to earlier in the day when Giovanni and Marcello, the Rolls Royce's owner, consoled Nick at a North Beach Italian restaurant. In this earlier scene, Nick bawls freely, letting the snot and tears drip to his sleeve.

"I just feel that the baby is here, man," Nick sobs. "It's time,""I can feel it."

"You wanta go back to Lori? Giovanni challenges. "She's waiting for you right now. It's your decision, kid. I'll give you the money to go back to Lori now, if that's what you want."

"Fuck," Nick exclaims wiping his sleeve onto his pants. "I can't go back to her. I have to let it go. It's over."

"Congratulations. You justa finish Giovanni's school."

"What?" Nick is shocked.

"The old Nick is dead," Giovanni proclaims. "Now it's time to build the new one."

"God..." Nick is overwhelmed.

"You feel it?" Giovanni asks.

"I do...I don't feel attached to my past at all. It's weird."

"It is what it is to be born again," Giovanni laughs. "Not like a Christian. Before, you always trying to take a bag full of shit with you."

Nick starts to cry again. This time out of gratitude. Marcello touches him on the shoulder.

"Sometime the storm comes to clear the air," Marcello consoles. "It's all right for a man to cry. It's like tears from the fog. After it clears, you can see again."

Inside the Rolls Royce, we see Giovanni scratch off another dud ticket:

"Just because school is over," Giovanni cautions, "doesn't mean you don't have lots of work to do."

"Are you going to be busting my balls for the rest of eternity?" Nick complains.

"I'm gonna bust your balls until you are right."

They continue to drive until they reach the eerie landscape of Mono Lake. Nick and Giovanni get out of the Rolls to stretch their legs. Giovanni speaks with force.

"You can bullshit the whole world as long as you're truthful and you don't hurt nobody. Life is a con job, kid. And everyone is a con man."

Nick, feeling troubled, refutes back, "I don't know if that's exactly true."

"Can you show me somebody who never tell a lie?" Giovanni counters.

"Well, no."

"You never did?"

"No, I did," Nick confesses.

"It's like Jesus say, 'Let him without sin throw the first stone...'"

"Okay."

Giovanni looks Nick in the eye. "So you either a con man who tries to build something good or you trying to destroy. You understand?"

"Uh-huh." Nick struggles with the principle, then asks, "How did you learn this? Or were you born with it?"

"No," Giovanni replies, "I pay very dearly."

"By knowing yourself?" Nick asks.

"Uh-huh. It's what I try to do for you from the very beginning. Get you to know yourself and be a leader again."

"Oh…" Nick is quiet.

Giovanni breaks the silence. "I hate con men. They hurt people."

For a moment, they watch the shadows fall across Mono Lake. A full moon rises in the Eastern sky.

Nick and Giovanni pull up to Caesar's Palace. It's late. With grand gestures, crisply-dressed doormen open the doors. Startled by the attention, Nick hops out and follows Giovanni to the casino floor.

"How about giving me a hundred so I can play a few games myself?" Nick suggests.

"No way," Giovanni replies. "I need your energy with me. As long as you breathing and stay positive, we gonna win."

By the end of the evening, Giovanni has a huge pile of hundred dollar chips stacked in front of him. He pushes ten five-hundred dollar chips over to tip Vivian, the red-headed dealer.

"Thank you, sweetheart. You've been very good to me tonight. I'm sorry I make you suffer."

"See you tomorrow, Giovanni," Vivian seduces.

Giovanni stuffs his pockets full of chips and retreats to the bar.

He and Nick toast their success with a bottle of the most expensive cognac. Giovanni puts his cognac down and turns toward Nick.

"Nick, tell me," Giovanni asks. "What do you think is my real talent in life?"

"Well, you're a genius with people," Nick replies. "And, you're a good gambler."

Giovanni smiles. "What else?"

"You're great at getting rid of the garbage."

"And?"

"It has something to do with money," Nick adds. "You're very good at getting people to give you their money."

Giovanni sips his cognac, looks straight at Nick and slowly proclaims:

"I am the greatest con man on earth."

The pit boss comes over to the bar.

"Excuse me, sir. Your suite is ready."

Nick and Giovanni head to the elevator. It's very late. Nick presses the button and collects his thoughts.

"I was thinking maybe God is the greatest con man on earth," Nick suggests.

Giovanni smiles cryptically and replies.

"He is. *Forgive me, God.* He makes the people believe on Him."

At this point in my life, I wasn't ready to accept *"Con Man"* as a Name of God. And Nick was in too deep to see Giovanni as a con artist, especially after stiffing every friend for money.

Nick's stormy seas played out like stages of grief, evidenced by the ever-changing titles to his screenplay. When Nick realized the desperate mess he was in, *The Fight for Love* became *Terrible Trouble*. When he reached the pleading with God stage, he re-titled it to *"YYYY."* My choice, laden with layers of meaning, was *Confidence Man*. Nick, of course, rejected it.

In the end, Nick's spiritual transformation turned out to be an illusion, not because the lessons weren't real, but because Nick was unable to integrate them into his life. There aren't real teachings and unreal teachings. All experiences offer alchemical fuel — if you use them.

We printed and registered the script and proudly sent the first copy to Mort. Mort was a true mensch who knew the film business. We had high hopes a week later when the phone rang:

"Well," Mort began, speaking in his characteristic upbeat manner, "I found it a bit like Frankenstein."

"Like the horror movie?" I asked dumbfounded.

"No, no, no," Mort replied with a hearty laugh. "Like with Frankenstein, all the bolts holding the character together are exposed. The same with your Nick character — there's nothing likable, nuanced, or sympathetic about him."

Oh my, God. We created a Frankenstein.

According to the Octave, our third year of marriage was supposed to invite an outside shock, but Karen and I weren't expecting to birth a Frankenstein.

The real estate market was sky high, so we sold our tiny Los Angeles bungalow, made an obscene profit, and paid off the $30,000 and the interest. Nick was not so lucky. He became deeply mired in a dark psychic swamp.

Flirting with destiny, Karen and I weighed Seattle versus Atlanta and chose the latter to restart our lives. I cut the Oedipal business ties with my mother, bought her aging Cadillac, and prepared for a midnight dash across the Mojave desert. With hugs and tears, the entire neighborhood gathered on a hot summer night to see us off.

Lolo, our dearest neighbor, embraced me with a Brazilian hug:

"I'm gonna miss you guys. I see doors opening for you, big things, so much good Fortune ahead."

"Lolo, I feel good about it too," I replied. "Love you."

And with that, Karen and I tucked our toddler into the back seat and headed East in search of Fortune.

14

Hazard

If man sees hazard as a misfortune
rather than an opportunity,
he will seek to close the door to freedom
rather than keep it open.
J.G. Bennett

"Bruce, something's gurgling in the bathroom!"

We had been living in our restoration project for a week — a house that had once been slated for demolition to make room for rapid transit. Given its turn-of-the-century pedigree, Karen's urgent cries no longer alarmed me.

I headed downstairs, paint brush in hand, to discover brown muck oozing toward our stack of precious belongings.

"Karen, quick. Help me move these boxes!"

Beyond the immediate crisis, my parents were flying in that evening to celebrate our purchase.

I flipped open the phone book and thirty minutes later, a ReddiRooter guy and his ReddiRooter son pulled up in their truck.

"Don't you worry 'bout a thing," the elder Rooter assured me. "You probably got yourself a bunch of roots from that water oak and some clay tile pipe. We're going to dig you a little pit to catch all that sewage so you can have you a party with no worries."

I pictured my mom pulling up to our new home, marveling at the neoclassical columns, the grand porch, the graceful water oak — and the open cesspool.

"How much is this going to cost me?"

Mr. Rooter scratched some numbers on a scrap of paper.

"Get you back into shape for twenty-two hundred bucks."

Since this is a book about Fortune, this is a good place to recount how Karen and I left Los Angeles to buy a ticket to *The Money Pit*.

After much considering, we chose Atlanta to build our married lives. It was preferable to our rainy runner-up, Seattle. Our destination shifted to Atlanta when, on a Friday afternoon, we got a call from Julie, a friend in Atlanta.

"I drove by this old two-story house and immediately thought of you," Julie said. "It could use a bit of work, but it's a unique historic home."

The words "immediately thought of you" put my synchronicity sensor on high alert.

"Listen," Julie continued. "There was something about a developer. You need to call the owner, like now."

"Now" is another ear-perker that signals the hand of Fortune, so I called.

Tim, the owner, explained the situation. He was leaving the architecture profession to try his hand at law school and needed money. The buyer, a Snidely Whiplash character, owned a contiguous piece of property and made a low-ball offer for Tim's property so that Snidely could slice off the back yard for office condos. The neighbors were furious that Tim agreed to sell to Mr. Whiplash in the middle of a fight to save the historic neighborhood.

"This developer just made us an offer," Tim explained. "But, he wanted it notarized and the notary's closed until Monday. Can you come now?"

I turned to Karen.

"The owner wants to know if we can come now."

"Fly across the country to check out a house?" Karen asked with a double take.

"I could go," I offered.

"No, we all have to go together."

And with that, we headed to LAX, purchased three tickets for the red-eye to Atlanta, and boldly stepped through this door of opportunity before it slammed shut Monday morning.

If you haven't figured it out by now, I'm an opportunist. I sense opportunity and go with it. I sensed an opportunity with Nick's screenplay and took the plunge. Purchasing three walk-up fares to look at a house was a similar roll of the dice. A realist would have backed away, knowing from experience that the chances were slim that we would pull up and meet our dream house.

J.G. Bennett describes this level of risk as "Hazard" — the combination of *uncertainty* with *significance*.[1]

Uncertainty surrounds us — mostly unnoticed. Will my email get hacked? Credit card compromised? Lose my keys? Will this funny zit become cancer? Even in the most mundane affairs, a level of uncertainty exists. If you head to a Mexican joint for steak fajitas, the chance exists they will be out of steak. But there is no significance to this risk because you can order chicken fajitas instead. So, this kind of uncertainty is not Hazard.

If I plunk down $3500 to look at a house in Atlanta, I have exposed myself to Hazard. Three walk-up airfares represented most of my monthly income.

While Hazard seems obvious, it can be hard to wrap your head around the fact that outcomes can go either way. Our mind is wired around *expectation* — that we *will* fall in love, that our bets *will* pay off, that we *will* achieve our goals, that our children *will* do well, and so on. In the long run, our affairs usually work out, *but not as expected*.

According to the Octave, there is never a straight line from A to B.

1. Bennett, J.G. 1991. Hazard: The Risk of Realization. Revised edition. Santa Fe, N.M: Bennett Books.

Hazard injects risk into every significant enterprise — and usually at Octave intervals.

Bennett uses the ancient game of backgammon to explain the workings of Hazard, a game that leverages chance with skill. The word *hazard* derives from Arabic, *azzar* the die. In backgammon, Hazard enters the play through the roll of the dice. The board consists of two rows of triangular points, or openings, where the player's checkers can land. With each roll of the dice, the player takes action, moves his checkers, the landscape changes, opportunities quickly close and new opportunities emerge. It is a fast and fluid game of uncertainty and decision.

In life, we see the board but deny the working of the dice. We are oblivious to the fact that deep within us, our cells are dividing, 10,000 trillion times in a lifetime. A known, predictable world might offer more comfort than living at the edge of uncertainty, but nature's throw of the dice creates the mutations and genetic diversity that drive life's complexity, beauty, and fresh expression.

To achieve a perfect score of 10, an Olympic diver must push an envelope of ever-increasing risk. The potter must risk the collapse of clay to create a graceful vase. To experience love, one must open oneself to rejection and failure. In the movies, Hazard is the vivifying force that pulls us into the drama. In the words of the Russian filmmaker Victor Kossakovsky, "Doubts are crucial for making art."[2]

How one deals with uncertainty is the most-telling feature of a human being, whether they shrink with fear or bluster with cocksure certitude.

Insurance companies make it their business to leverage uncertainty. They purport to tame Hazard through actuarial science. They know that 9600 people in my age bracket will die in Georgia this year, and they will price my policy based on this level of risk. Whether or not "I

2. "Documentary Director Viktor Kossakovsky's 10 Rules of Filmmaking." 2015. Desktop-Documentaries.com. Accessed October 25. http://www.desktop-documentaries.com/Documentary-Director-Viktor-Kossakovskys-10-Rules-of-Filmmaking.html.

die" is not *significant* to them — although it is tremendously important to me.

Hazard is not random chance or statistics. It is a dynamic, enlivening force that enters into events of significance. According to Bennett, "As long as there are risks to be taken, dangers to overcome, there is life." Conversely, the ultimate, predictable stasis is death. In death, the checkers no longer seek out openings.

My son, Nathaniel, travels the world every summer without a companion, itinerary, or much money. A few years ago, he used a Birthright ticket to fly free to Israel, then got off the tour bus and ventured across the Sinai to Cairo. For his parents, he subjected himself to an unacceptable level of Hazard. But for him, it became an unplanned adventure to set foot in Tahrir Square immediately after the Egyptian Revolution.

As an opportunist, I borrowed $30,000 to invest in Nick's screenplay and lost it all. Was this an acceptable level of risk? Looking back, it was nuts. But as a long-long term investment, my eternal optimism still feels the final results aren't in. Not every return measures in money.

In this way, Giovanni's dictum, "*It doesn't matter what you do, only that you do it*," makes hazardous sense. We could have just as easily chosen Seattle and had a different life. Karen could have decided against going over the waterfall and not met me. Had the asteroid not hit planet earth, dinosaurs would be roaming down Sycamore Street instead of three jet-lagged Angelenos pulling up to a love-starved historic house. But we plunked down our airfare, flew across the continent, and opened ourselves to Hazard.

We pulled up to the house straight from the airport with the first light of dawn. There was a deja vu sense to the mission, having traveled from L.A. to Santa Cruz four years earlier to meet my blind date. Like a mail order bride, our blind-date house was showing her age. The cracked columns, peeling paint, and sketchy roof teased me in a beguiling way, "Hey big boy, want to have an adventure?"

It was too much to absorb and too early, so we left and returned later. After breakfast, we toured the house. The high ceilings, double doors, and spacious rooms seduced our feelings of grandeur. We excused ourselves and retreated quietly to the overgrown carport.

"What do you think?" I asked. "It's a lot to take on."

"It feels like fate," Karen observed.

"Well, I'm game," I ventured.

"So am I," Karen concurred.

And that was that. We were all in.

There was one little problem with this roll of the dice: I didn't have a job.

At this point in my life, I had confused opportunity with Hazard. Hazard is a force, not a magic carpet for wishful thinkers or passive participants in the game of life. With Hazard, you must summon your *cajones* to surf against the full hydraulic force of Mother Nature.

On the backgammon board, doors of opportunity open and shut all the time. There's a subtle distinction between the player who steps through a door with conviction, *leveraging* the opportunity and the player who expects Fortune to work things out as imagined. More often than not, the happy-go-lucky opportunist becomes a victim of circumstance. Bennett speaks to this distinction:

> To learn how to live in a world of hazard is not merely to *have* possibilities; it is rather to *create* possibilities. Hope does not consist in the realization of potential, but in the augmentation of potential. This is objective hope. Gambler's hope [is] expecting the law of hazard to do for you what is not its function at all, that is, to give you something for nothing. One of the great misinterpretations is to see the law of hazard like this. We are very prone to it. We go in for this sort of hope on a very large scale, of expecting unearned profit from the law of hazard. This is not how the world is actually put together.[3]

Hazard does not violate the laws of nature. It is a method of mining the energy that accrues from risk. Objective hope acknowledges this force — this augmentation of potential.

---

3. (Bennett 1991)

If a hurricane makes landfall, the $100 an hour guy who responds with a chainsaw has augmented potential to his favor — assuming he had the foresight to stock up on gas and oil before the storm. Or as Wavy Gravy announced at Woodstock, "There's always a little bit of heaven in a disaster area."

When Julia ditched her boyfriend, she opened herself to Hazard. As the events worked out, she bumped into her friend's sister on a random street in Boston, was invited to a party, met her fiance, and got married. Rather than bemoaning her fate, she augmented the rawness of her new situation, stayed in the crux of uncertainty, and stepped into a new opening on the board. But not every lonely heart bumps into Prince Charming. As Julia explained:

> "Why do you make a choice? It's because of the state you are in and how open you are to a scenario. And then there are all the coincidences that lead to these choices. It's strange, and it's unexplainable."

My friend Miriam recounted how, years ago, "the state you're in" shifted her Fortune in backgammon while competing with co-workers during their overnight hospital shifts.

"There was something about backgammon that was like life," Miriam told me over tea. "You're throwing the dice, making a move, back and forth between chance and decision. If you roll doubles, you get to play the numbers twice. I was playing this guy and kept getting doubles. Inexplicably, I hit doubles fourteen times in a row. I would apologize, roll again, then slaughter him."

Julia and Miriam seemed to have added something to the mix — *the state you're in*. In this way, they augmented the opening created by Hazard. This something is intentionality — not intention to snag a husband or beat the opponent; the play could go either way. Intention is a constant, an energy outside of time. Intention channels the energy of Self.

Last night, while talking about this chapter, Miriam shared another experience:

"I was walking between author events at the Decatur Book Festival feeling very alive when I noticed a Lottery sign above a convenience store. I don't play the Lottery, ever, but I stayed with the feeling, stayed with the impulse. Next thing, I'm in the store. I had a split-second sensation that said *blue,* but I ended up buying a green ticket. I scratched it off and won twenty dollars. That was fun, and that was that. I was about to leave when I remembered my original impulse. So, I returned, bought the blue ticket, and won $250."

"You had this urge and stayed with it?" I asked.

"Yes," Miriam replied. "And then it happened again tonight. I stopped to buy a newspaper at the Chevron station, bought a two-dollar ticket, and won $15."

"So, when does this flip?" I asked. "When do you become convinced of your gambling powers and lose everything?"

"There's the *self* that lives here," Miriam explained placing her palm against her face. "That *self* wants to win, will get hooked on the Lottery, and will likely lose. And then there's the *self* that lives about ten feet behind your head. It's not invested in winning. It simply witnesses. If you can stay with that one — that's where Fortune unfolds."

I began to wonder if by purchasing our stately home we had bought the winning ticket or the losing ticket. A wiser person might have taken the proceeds from our Los Angeles sale, bought four cracker-box bungalows, rented them out, and enjoyed thirty years of passive income. Our fling with Hazard tested our resolve, yet, our home has also served as the spiritual hub for grand affairs, programs, and community events. We have been able to augment our home's potential, but in the process, we've had to lash ourselves to the rudder and ride out the storms.

Back to the story. We had placed all our chips on the *Money Pit* and rolled the dice. Soon, our brief winning streak began to sink with the sewage.

For the next six months, Karen and I worked tirelessly to whip our muck-mansion into shape. It should have been a bonding experience, but the strain of living in a construction zone also carried a toll.

Of greater concern, I had used this all-consuming project to avoid facing the fact that I didn't have a job. My wishful thinking — the opportunist — assumed that everything would work out.

It's not that I didn't have a plan. Even as a small child, I have always been entrepreneurial. My plan was to re-start my Los Angeles audio-visual business in the back of our renovated house. Somehow, I missed the important fact that the corporate AV world was shifting from slides to video. Naively, I thought I could transplant my previous life.

More importantly, I ignored the fact that my mom had provided my funnel of clients. With my Oedipal split from my mom, I no longer had any business connections. A realist would have spotted this fact. But maybe a realist would not have taken the leap at all. As it painfully worked out, Karen had to go back to her nursing career while I became the frustrated house husband with a full-time, full-energy preschooler.

I paint this young-married picture, not because our problems were unique, but to explore why we failed to roll doubles or get the blue lottery ticket. Did I miss subtle promptings that said *blue,* or was this my karmic fate?

I used to feel snarky about people and their problems — that it's all in your mind. If you just trust the river's flow and follow Deepak's and Oprah's "energy of attraction," life will provide. I took my bias from Li'l Abner's Joe Btfsplk character — the guy with the permanent rain cloud over his head. When I was younger, Joe gave me one of life's great stoner insights — that we create our own dark clouds and call it reality. The lie, of course, being that Deepak and Oprah don't have dark clouds.

Now that I'm older, I can share my elder perspective that there is never a time in life when we eliminate problems. There is always a problem *du jour* consuming one's attention until a new problem takes its place.

We give our problems labels: financial, marital, health, or existential. We might even see the psychological roots of a problem.

But to go deeper, all problems reflect discomfort with *uncertainty*. Will he love me or leave me? Will I get the promotion or lose my job? Will my cancer come back? Can I rebound from this setback? How can I recover from this debt load? Will I ever be happy again?

Uncertainty exists within the framework of time, the expectations of the mind, and the inability to trust. Unlike Miriam, there's no way I could follow an alien impulse to buy a Lottery ticket. I'm wired to think the Lottery is for losers. Irrespective of the odds or ethics of Lotto, it's one's constrictive resistance — our wiring rather than the circumstances — that creates the experience of problems.

As I write this, after ten chapters of backstory, I still have a big-time problem. I still don't have a stable source of income after the collapse of my business. The money left over to pay the monthly mortgage on our still-unsold office building officially ran out yesterday, so now I'm burning through savings. All of this gnaws at my edges and keeps me churning: Is there a stone unturned? Am I complacent? Do I need to get a job-job instead of writing this book? Where is my Blue Ticket!

But, if all problems stem from uncertainty, why not follow the "21-Day Abundance Meditation," find my Buddha nature, embrace the present moment, follow the flow, and trust? Or, is it trickier than that? If we follow the inner quest, do we risk new problems, and expose ourselves to bigger, more existential crises?

Reshad used to say, "There's no such thing as a problem, only unattended situations." When he said this, I didn't quite know what to do with it. I would either feel deficient because I still had problems, or superior because I was privy to the secret knowledge that problems don't exist. More likely, I felt deficient and superior simultaneously, which sums up the New Age.

But back to the story. After our triumphant move, we now had three problems: 1) Money Pit house, 2) no source of income, and 4) wife forced back to work. I should also add: 5) my midlife crisis was looming on the horizon. If Saturn's Return arrives at our fourth Octave (7×4 = 28 years), the midlife crisis hits at the sixth Octave (7×6

= 42 years). My forty-two-year midlife crisis was approaching, but unlike the movies, I wasn't forewarned by an ominous soundtrack.

Feeling desperate, I bargained, "Hey, God. I'm a good provider. I'm clever, and since there are discernible facts to this problem, I should be able to figure this out." And, the bigger trap: "God, must certainly be on my side, because I've been good."

You never know how your midlife crisis will hit. Everyone else can see it coming a mile away: "Poor schmuck, he's got it coming." But us schmucks are always oblivious.

It was the seventh year of our marriage (Si-Do) and three years into the *Money Pit* (Mi-Fa), and forty-two years into my life (the note Sol) when all of these octaves and intervals lined up, and my midlife crisis hit. Karen sent Nathaniel off to another room, closed the door, and signaled that weird low pressure that precedes a storm. Without a southwest corner for escape, my emotional body felt exposed.

"I want a separation," Karen calmly said.

"Shit…" A chasm opened in my stomach. "What? What! What are you talking about? Where is this coming from?"

"It's just not working for me, Bruce. You're not there for me. You seem… oblivious."

"What?," I protested in a stunned ramble, "I'm under pressure working morning, noon and night to make this thing work. Why are you doing this? We're together; I love you; I've always loved you. Why drop this insane bomb now?" I took a breath. "What about our son?"

"He will be fine. The last thing he needs is to grow up in a house where his parents aren't emotionally connected."

"Wha, wha when are you planning to do this?"

"Steve Brown offered his rental house. I'll be moving in a few days."

For the amateur psychologists scoring this at home, let's put a few markers on the game board:

• Bruce: Cerebral guy, narcissistic mom, parents not emotionally connected, not fully engaged with his sexual/emotional sources of power.

- Karen: Feeling gal, hypercritical mom, abusive father, abused as a child.

Might as well throw the elephant in the room onto the board:

- Reshad: Surrogate father figure, multiple divorces, encourages students to transcend psycho/emotional issues to achieve a spiritual state.

Your board may look different, but equally unsustainable without a crisis to get the markers moving.

With Karen's announcement, I sunk into an emotional vortex that forced my heart's brittle casing to crack. As Robert Bly wisely explains, the naive, passive man must travel the road of ashes, descent, and grief:

> The naive man will lose what is most precious to him because of a lack of boundaries. This is particularly true of the New Age man, or the man seeking "higher consciousness." Thieves walk in and out of his house, carrying large bags, and he doesn't seem to notice them.[4]

A few days later, Karen sent over a couple of goons with a truck to move furniture out of our house. ["They were not goons!" Karen interjects while reading the draft.] I felt paralyzed watching the citadel of our marriage crumble. My options seemed limited to just one: to experience the pain crushing my heart.

Like a condemned man, I dragged myself to the back of the now empty house where I had built my unused audio-visual studio — part of my unsuccessful business plan. I shut the door, curled to the floor, and let Bonnie Raitt's *I Can't Make You Love Me* play over and over. This may sound saccharine, but grief is palpable. I let the sobbing

---

4. Bly, Robert. 2004. Iron John: A Book About Men. Reprint edition. Cambridge, MA: Da Capo Press.

course through my body and surrendered to an emotional whirlpool that had no bottom, knew no end.

Bly continues:

> The mark of Descent, whether undertaken consciously or unconsciously, is a newly arrived-at lowness, associated with water and soul... The lowness happens particularly to men who are initially high, lucky elevated. ...what is proper next for the man is the whirlpool, the sinking through the floor, the Drop, what the ancient Greeks called *katabasis.*

As I sunk into my grief, I reasoned, why stop? Why not go all the way? I let the whirlpool of *katabasis* take me deeper and deeper to the depth of my core brokenness — a fetal-like descent to a place that was strangely similar to my opening atop Reyes Peak. Yes, the infinite runs in both directions. Bly explains that:

> ...the man can use the divorce — like any other serious collapse — as an invitation to go through the door, accept *katabasis*, immerse oneself in the wound, and exit from his old life through it... One has the sense that some power in the psyche arranges a severe *katabasis* if the man does not know enough to go down on his own... In depression, we refuse to go down, and so a hand comes up and pulls [us] down. In grief, we choose to go down on our own.

The Biblical Job faced *katabasis*, and brought forth the theological question: "Why do the righteous suffer?"

Like Job, the English poet and artist, William Blake, was impoverished and unrecognized in his life. Blake's plight explains his fascination with Job's misfortune. In one of Blake's twenty-two engravings of Job, the Biblical figure reaches the nadir of despair, encased in suffering, yet surrounded by stars singing for joy. The stars seem pretty happy about what Job was going through. They get it.

When I was a film student, I sensed that great art drew from these private depths, so I dropped my screenwriting class to avoid these dark and inaccessible realms. Later, when Mory challenged,

"Why do you want to be an artist? You just end up in the cuckoo house," he might have been protecting me from this torment. He understood *katabasis*.

But, here I was in *katabasis* anyway. Alchemy describes this stage as Nigredo, the "putrefaction" where matter decomposes to its primal state. The old form dies. The suffering grips the soul like the squeezing of a sponge so that it can absorb clean, clear water.

Job is traditionally interpreted as a story of good deeds and bad, retribution and restoration, and Satan and God. Through the lens of *katabasis*, the story shifts to one about alchemy, transformation, and wisdom. That God alone knows the meaning of the world, of death, and resurrection.

After the hurricane hits, the task at hand is to bring out the chainsaws and rebuild. If you live through enough storms, wisdom accrues. You understand the cycles of life, that storms continue through good years and bad, and through ups and downs. But, you no longer live in hope or fear. You know how to ride out the storm.

Judgment is born of a life lived, of *katabasis,* of looking Hazard in the eye as both friend and foe. Yeah, I played a hand and lost. But Hazard also reshuffles the deck, providing ever more potential to leverage. To play the game means participating with Hazard, not feeling separate from it, not hoping that a benevolent God will hand you winning cards, but working with the ace you've got. That one ace is your gift, your grace, your lucky streak. Play it.

It could have been five minutes or five years, but I pulled myself up from the floor and straggled outside. My friend, Susan knew to appear at the front porch at that moment.

"Susan, I need to go for a ride."

"What's going on? Are you okay? " Susan asked.

"Karen left."

"Where do you want to go?"

"I don't know."

We drove and drove and drove. Like newborn skin, my rawness needed to re-acclimate to the world.

"Stop. Let's go there."

I motioned to a nightclub. It was three in the afternoon.

We went inside. A bartender was prepping the bar. He nodded welcome without words. I heard a mournful saxophone coming from upstairs. I pointed toward the stairs. He nodded again.

Susan and I went up the stairs to a darkened room full of empty cocktail tables. A shaft of daylight cut through the emptiness hitting a sax player playing alone on stage. I watched him explore his inner Coltrane without audience or appreciation.

My *katabasis* needed some Coltrane. John Coltrane's music could be raw, soulful, spiritual, or conflicted. This guy's sax growled and sang to me that way, taking me on a journey from *katabasis* to Being. In Coltrane's words:

> Some people say [my] "music sounds angry," or "tortured," or "spiritual," or "overpowering" All a musician can do is to get closer to the sources of nature and so feel that he is in communion with the natural laws.[5]

And now, I knew this story. Natural laws brought me to this club. Natural laws also brought me into the club of men who get closer to the sources of nature by knowing their brokenness.

5. Wilmer, Valerie. 1962. "Conversation with Coltrane." Jazz Journal, January.

15

How I Met Your Mother - Part II

The doors to the world of the wild Self are few but precious.
If you have a deep scar, that is a door,
if you have an old, old story, that is a door.
...If you yearn for a deeper life, a full life, a sane life,
that is a door.
Clarissa Pinkola Estés

In the movie *Water for Elephants,* Jacob, a college veterinary student learns during his final exam, that his parents were killed in a car crash, that his father left huge debts, and that the bank had foreclosed on the family home his father mortgaged to pay for college. Given the sudden collapse of his world and with nowhere to go, Jacob hops a passing train in the night.

Jacob awakes to discover that the train belongs to the Benzini Brothers Most Spectacular Show on Earth. He befriends a kindly drunk named Camel who takes the young Jake under his wing and gets him a job with the traveling circus.

Living alone, I grieved the sudden collapse of my world. Like Jacob, I wanted to hop a train and reboot my life. I wanted to jump an inner train that would carry me across my emotional abyss.

As a literary device, trains propel passengers through the Octave, across time and through dimension, oblivious to speeding steel on steel. Trains plunge into tunnels where unseen forces transform young lovers. Circus trains bring all the archetypes together — strongmen, gypsies, roustabouts, wild animals, musicians, freaks, and ingenues — all with the purpose of transporting audiences into the illusion and then back into the real world.

My opportunity to hop a train arrived in the form of an invitation. Reshad had left the United States in search of more fertile ground. He found his opening with the Swiss. Unlike American students who questioned authority and had no money, the Swiss eagerly followed Reshad's direction and had the money to stage a triumphant spectacle, a spiritual circus called Johanneshof.

Johanneshof was set up as an international school where people from different countries could work in a cross-grained cultural setting, and where transformation could take place. There would be lectures, meditations, breathing exercises, Whirling Dervish training, cleaning and cooking, plus all the struggles of multiple languages. More importantly, Reshad's invitation was the train to carry me across my personal abyss.

In our Sufi school, we called this attitude "living in the question" — a way to remain open to the octave coming in. You can jump onto this train at any moment by acknowledging that the future is unknown. My efforts to make my life work had backfired, and now I felt trumped by the universe. In times of crisis, we try to fix our problems by drawing from experience, but it usually doesn't work. You can't shift into second without a stint between gears.

Reshad held a grand vision for an international spiritual school for all the years I had known him. Twenty years earlier, Reshad huddled over a map with dowsing rods to find the exact location for his big center. Armed with the map, a friend and I drove to the ordained spot 25 miles east of Los Angeles. We pulled up to a barren field; a stray dog tried to get into our car, and that was that.

Over the next twenty years, Reshad developed a substantial body of work, but nothing like a real school. All of this would find its culmination at Johanneshof.

As I entered the magnificent villa, Stefan, Reshad's new right-hand man, greeted me. It was odd to see a Swiss guy performing my role and even odder to see the full glory of Reshad's aristocratic British vision in Swiss drag. Person of the Day, washing walls with rose water, using a burning pan to clear thought-form, visualizations, the Octave, movements — Reshad's entire bag of esoteric tricks had transplanted to Swiss soil without losing anything in translation.

The Swiss hit all the high marks with great earnestness, including impeccable manners, consciously-prepared food, and precise scheduling. I had seen this show before (albeit on a smaller stage), so I could see beyond the practiced perfection. I knew that the real teaching would emerge later when the train fell off the tracks. It wouldn't be long before Reshad's fatal flaw — his drinking — would throw a few spanners into the works.

It was taboo to mention the flaw or point out the obvious. But, I knew that no path has it together. The best you can hope for is "half together." In every enterprise, there is always the *hidden half* — the buried, sublimated side that must not be spoken of. The dark side of the moon provides the real juice of a school. The job of the student (and they don't tell you this) is to wrap your head around the light *and* the shadow; it's a package deal. The excruciating contradiction between shit and Shinola *is* the teaching. This is the Law of Three — Affirming Force and Denying Force. The Great Work is to reconcile these two in your being.

So, it came as no surprise that on Day One of this glorious enterprise, within the magnificent historic villa of Johanneshof, nestled in a formal rose garden overlooking the Lake of Lucerne, and ringed by majestic snow-capped Alpine peaks, that Reshad's faithful and beloved wife (wife number three) abandoned the scene — and him as well.

And now, on with the show.

Reshad made it clear over the years that a teacher or healer must never engage in the work of transformation without the grounding of a partner. I didn't have one either at this point, so I couldn't judge. As you might imagine, I was interested to see how this episode of *The Bachelor* would play out.

Fortunately, I had come for the opening act, before the Octave would take its natural course over Johaneshof's two-and-a-half years and deviate — as per the natural tendency of vibrations — into a mirror-like impostor of the original intention. This was before Reshad would briefly fall for a young dancer named Renata, before his spurned secretary would be placed on life support on Maui, before he would replace his American wife with a Swiss one, and before his Swiss students would realize that they had given their life savings for the slim chance to pass through the eye of the needle.

If this sounds sour, it shouldn't. There are no straight lines in life and my path also brought me to this glorious experiment. As Reshad spoke, I looked out toward Lake Lucerne and the Alps beyond to reconnect with the sense of purpose that had guided my life. Reshad challenged us to make contact with our original, instinctual essence:

"The baby instinctively knows when it is hungry and where the food is coming from," Reshad explained. "There is a total dependence on the parents, and that alone is a subtle form of communication."

"Later, as we get older, this instinctive gift can easily be covered up and forgotten, and so we cease to realize that we owe our total dependence to God, who is the All-Provider.

"When this is forgotten, that form of communication is also forgotten. In the understanding of our total dependence on God, what we need can be communicated to us from the higher worlds, but we have to be empty of the impediments deep in our subconscious.

"There is also communication between the different worlds within us... They long to tell us things, simple things sometimes, but necessary things. We may have lost the art of communicating with them... We may have lost what I call our primal innocence."[1]

1. Feild, Reshad. 2011. The Inner Work. Books on Demand.

I had come to Johanneshof for a psyche rewiring. I wanted to erase the old circuitry deep in my subconscious and find my primal innocence — the loving openness that implicitly trusts in the beneficence of life.

Maybe, I was in my primal innocence when I noticed a quiet woman working alone in the garden. A Cinderella of sorts, I don't think anyone noticed her. I watched as she tended to the plantings without stirring a molecule of atmosphere. I was struck by the fact that she worked barefoot — marvelously muddy feet. You never see the Swiss without their Bally's or their hiking boots. Her bare feet said, "Hey, I'm connected to my primal innocence. Come, let's play in the mud." So, I approached her.

"Hello," I said.

"Hi," she replied shyly, but with smiling eyes.

There wasn't anything more to say after that, because a different form of communicating took over.

"Hi," I stumbled again.

"Hi," she replied in her best German-English.

The conversation didn't go much further because — poof — I stumbled into my primal innocence.

At this point, you should ask, "Poof? What are you talking about?"

I'm not entirely certain. Maybe, souls really do have mates. We're so busy bumbling through life and putting out fires, we fail to notice. But then, every few lifetimes, our soul might bump into its mate for a quick, "Hey, how's this human thing working out for you?"

As it turned out, Irmgard was Austrian, not Swiss. I don't think the Swiss knew what to do with her, she being so shy and sensitive, so she was given to tending the garden. Professionally, Irmgard worked with small children using music therapy to help them access their preverbal period. So, here I was, accessing my eternal, preverbal state.

Stumbling into transcendent love with your barefoot soul mate in the middle of a seminar, a few days before heading back to the States, made for an interesting dilemma. There aren't any dating books for this type of situation.

Mercifully, Peter and Anne Cunz, who were Reshad's principal sponsors in Switzerland, invited Irmgard and me to visit their village. And just like that, Irmgard and I were whisked from Reshad's high-pressure drama to parts unknown.

After an hour of driving, Peter asked if we would like to go up a funicular railway. "Sure," I replied. Maybe, this was my chance to hop my train across the abyss.

Mount Neisen stood alone among the Bernese Alps with its angular features. For this reason, it's called the Pyramid of Switzerland. We parked, Peter bought tickets, and we climbed aboard.

With barely a lurch, the funicular started to climb the 68 percent grade alongside the longest stairway in the world — all 11,674 steps. Irmgard and I held hands through tunnels and watched the tree line pass below until we reached the rocky, barren summit.

The funicular lifted us high above the treeline to the top of the world. The train stopped, Irmgard snuck under a barrier, and I followed. Balancing from rock to rock, we danced with the gods. The crystalline air blended with our shared dimension of Self.

Soon it was time and the cables and pulleys gently brought our tram back to earth. We continued driving to Kirchdorf where Peter's wife, Anne, greeted us with three Swiss kisses. She wanted to know everything about our fledgling relationship, but didn't understand that our "thing" was only three days old. Anne served us rosti, the traditional dish of her canton and soon it was time for bed. She cautioned us not to stay up late; there was a big parade in the village in the morning. Irmgard and I ignored her advice and stayed up to co-mingle in the fragile atmosphere of self-subsisting love.

The next morning we learned it wasn't just any old parade, but a once-each-decade festival that brought the entire canton together to celebrate traditional culture. "Quick," Anne announced, "There is still time!"

Anne supplied us with bicycles, pointed us in the general direction, and soon we found ourselves cycling the parade route —

inadvertently as the grand finale. Little girls with flowers and hundreds of village folk in traditional garb lined the road cheering us on. We passed cows blanketed with flowers and wagon cornucopias stacked with perfect produce. Men in costume blew 12-foot alphorns while choruses yodeled and sang in every direction like a Tolkien dream. The message seemed to be, yes, you live in a loving universe — but you gotta get your timing right, and we did.

We cycled back to Peter and Anne's with the realization that all things that go up the mountain must come down. Anne drove us toward my parting point, the Zurich airport. Much of the ride was in silence knowing that the forces that brought us together were now taking us apart. I gathered my bags at the curb, held Irmgard's hands, and looked into her eyes.

"Irmgard, I don't know what to say…" I felt stumbly and bumbly but plowed on. "A doorway opened for us. What does it mean beyond that?" I looked more deeply, beyond her eyes. I could feel the fairy tale losing altitude, but plodded on. "I've always been afraid of this kind of love because I was afraid of breaking hearts. I don't want that."

Irmgard nodded.

"I have to go home and see what's there, see where this path takes me… takes us. That doesn't diminish the love I feel for you."

"I understand, completely," Irmgard said. "You have a wife and a child."

I turned toward Passport Kontrol feeling confused, joyous, and shitty all at the same time.

I let myself stay in the not-knowing during the long flight home. The Swiss flight attendant asked if I wanted my water "with or without *gassata*," I chose with. I sipped the little bubbles marveling at transformation — that water could so effortlessly transform from solid to liquid to gas.

When I arrived home, the house was just as empty and cavernous as it was before — maybe more so, but little bubbles of consciousness seemed to have carbonated my being. Something had shifted.

Irmgard and I continued to exchange letters and photos, but we avoided mentioning our relationship. In one letter Irmgard shared, "Reshad is now very gentle and kind when he talks to me. That amazes me because he is not so gentle with everybody."

Immediately after returning, I led a seminar in Santa Fe — anything to get out of the house. More importantly, my voice and authority began to emerge. I decided to avoid parroting the official Reshad teaching and let the students claim their experience as unique, empowering, and important. This was a radical notion.

At about this time, Dr. Bhagwan Awatramani, a former medical doctor from India was visiting Switzerland. I tell his story because it illustrates how, in the spirit of Fortune, teachers and their teachings cross-pollinate. It also speaks to the Buddhist proverb, "When the student is ready, the teacher appears."

Bhagwan's story begins in 1947 with the partition of India. Fourteen million refugees were forced to flee from the newly formed states of Pakistan and India in the throes of genocidal violence. Half a million people died. As Bhagwan tells the story:

> We lived in what's now Pakistan, so we had to seek refuge in India. After fleeing, we became a joined family with my grandfather, his three sons, and their families living together. There must have been ten or fifteen of us. Adding to the stress of being uprooted, I was sent to boarding school at age five.
>
> There was tremendous pressure at boarding school to do well. Since I couldn't get affection from my family, I sought affection from my teachers. And they would only give it if you did well. This intense pressure to achieve continued. By the time I was ten, I was getting peptic ulcers — something normally suffered by worried businessmen. And because of that, I knew I wanted to be a doctor. I wanted to understand this pain.
>
> After school, I went to college in Bombay — an enormous, chaotic city of ten million back then, thirty million today. In this chaotic situation, I couldn't adapt; it was too much.
>
> So, I sought help from a psychiatrist to help me with my

confusion and stress, and to help me adapt to the new situation. He introduced me to the Indian spiritual teachings. Normally, a psychiatrist wouldn't do that. He sent me to a spiritual teacher in Bombay.

I attended this teacher's lectures for a year, but he focused on the Bhagavad Gita and the Upanishads. His teaching was theoretical, but it was nice to know that there was a path to follow. My teacher explained that there was no hope that you could overcome your state. Only once in a hundred years does someone get enlightened.

After a year of this, a new teacher appeared in Bombay. This teacher wasn't theoretical; his teaching went straight to meditation. And, I was just blown by that, so I followed him to the letter, to every word he said.

My teacher estimated was that you could get a glimpse of enlightenment in nine years if you were reasonably regular. If you were very regular, maybe six years. And, if you were extremely interested, maybe in three years.

I was full of hope, so I followed him to his ashram in South India, which was quite a journey — two nights by train. I stayed there for six weeks and did a lot of meditation.

This second teacher was teaching Ramana Maharshi's teachings. This was unusual because no one did meditation in those days, not even in India. In the medical college, I was probably the only one doing it. It must have been strange for them that I was doing such things. But this particular approach of Ramana Maharshi was also rare. Ramana was not well known, not even in India.

Ramana's approach is called self-inquiry. It tells you to inquire within to discover who you are. Am I the body or do I experience a body? Are you your thoughts, feelings, memories, pain and your struggles? Is that who you are? You inquire, and you come to the realization that no, I am not my thoughts. I am the thinker of my thoughts. I am not my body and mind; I am the *experiencer* of the body-mind.

And when you do this, the mind starts getting quiet because you're not fueling the mind. You're not giving attention to the mind, so the mind subsides. And that's the process of meditation.

I started this form of meditation before starting medical practice. You couldn't earn a living teaching meditation; that was unheard of. In India, meditation was free. So, I had to practice medicine, and of course, I was obliged because I had a medical education.

I practiced in a poor area of Bombay, a slum area, where anyone could just walk in without appointments. They were lined up like in a refugee camp. I charged one rupee per person, approximately two cents in today's value, or about 25 cents back then. So, I had to see a large number of people, on average over one hundred patients per day. The maximum was 160 patients in one day. So you could hardly spend two minutes per person.

In those two minutes I would ask the person's name, what they were suffering from, examine the person, diagnose the person, give an injection, and give instructions of follow up, and ask the person to leave — all in two minutes.

To be able to do that, patient after patient, takes tremendous focus. If I was in a state of meditation, I could easily grasp what the patient was experiencing, what he was suffering from, and what was the appropriate treatment. This way, I could use meditation to diagnose and treat a large number of people. Meditation gave me the compassion and focus to deal with the stress without any loss of energy. Of course, at the end of the day I was exhausted, but that was likely midnight.

After twenty-five years of practicing medicine, I felt that was enough. Giving medication to tranquilize people, what's the point? When the real thing is meditation, what's the point in distributing tranquilizers and pain killers? I put another doctor in my place who gradually took over my practice.

During this time, I met some Swiss travelers who had come to India for past-life reincarnation therapy. I explained to them that it was a lot of rubbish. They had come to my village at Matheran and then some neighbors sent them to our little resort. They were doing meditation amongst themselves and learned that I knew something about meditation. They invited me to join them. And when I joined them for meditation, they experienced a different quality of meditation.

They invited me to their home in Basel, Switzerland where they had organized a gathering of forty people. I was pleased about this as we gathered in the garden to meditate. I told them that we would meditate for an hour, which is too much for beginners. And so I sat there with my eyes closed in front of forty people. An hour later, I opened my eyes, and they were all gone — all except two Germans.

I asked the two Germans, "Why did you not leave?" And they said, "We were so embarrassed. You came all the way from India and everyone has left so we couldn't leave."

They took me to Germany to meet their teacher who had a large following. She spotted me immediately. She was a doctor who was dying from cancer. I went to visit her in the hospital. From her hospital bed, she phoned six or seven centers in Germany, asking them to organize seminars for me. It was as if it was made to happen.

The next year she died, and suddenly, everything collapsed.

It's a longer story, but the person I was staying with in Switzerland invited me to a birthday party. I didn't know the person, but the party was for one of Reshad's organizers. And then this friend of Reshad invited me to stay at his house. At that time, I was willing to stay at anyone's house because I had no accommodations, no money, no nothing.

One Thursday evening, my host invited me to accompany him to Johanneshof. There were around eighty people in the meeting room. I sat in the back, almost hiding, just to watch what was going on. And then Reshad announced, "Has anyone come here for the first time? Please raise your hand."

I did not raise my hand because I was hiding. Reshad asked again, actually three times. And the third time, he was emphatic: "Please raise your hand."

Reshad noticed me and commanded, "Come here." He introduced me to everyone and invited me to give a little talk.

I mentioned to Reshad that I was flying to the States the next day. He said, "You must go to Atlanta and meet my friend Bruce."

And here, our octaves intersected. One afternoon, after Irmgard and while I was wallowing in my bachelorhood, the phone rang. It was Reshad:

"Bruce, listen to the sound of my voice," Reshad declared.

"Oh God…" I grimaced, sensing the set-up for an outside shock.

"I have fixed it for you."

I mused at the oddity of Reshad's statement. "Fixed?" When Reshad explained that he was sending an Indian guru to my doorstep, my inner complainer griped, "Guru fixing not wanted at this time, thank you very much."

The challenge was that in our Sufi school, receiving the guest was paramount. It's called a*dab*, or respectful courtesy and manners. We made a big practice of greeting guests with flowers at the airport, putting flowers in their room, and serving a cup of tea. We also washed the walls with rosewater, prepared fancy meals — it got crazy. The point was to not "presume" the guest. The traveler represented the Third Force, a vector of opportunity that could open your small world into a larger world. Conversely, the traveler, having left his normal world behind, had the opportunity to be received in love — and by this know he or she is loved. *To know you're loved* was the overriding theme of Reshad's school.

When I pictured myself hanging out with Bhagwan in my bachelor pad, I realized the whole *adab* thing would fall flat. So, I called Karen.

"Karen, I need your help."

"What is it?" She asked.

"Reshad is sending an Indian guru our way."

Whether it was *adab* or ulterior motives, Karen jumped right on it.

"Okay," she said, "Let's talk about menu, flowers, rosewater…"

I'm a little fuzzy about what happened next. So, I asked Karen to refresh my memory. This conversation takes place in bed:

"Karen, remember when I asked you to help me host Bhagwan?"

"Why are you asking me this? It's like four in the morning."

"I know. That's when I think about these things."

"Okay, but this will cost you," Karen yawned. "I remember being part of those conversations about Bhagwan coming. I think we were spending time together, but living separately."

"We were co-parenting. That was it," I reminded.

"It was more than that. You asked me to come back to help you."

"Yes, but during Bhagwan's visit, we were still living apart," I insisted.

"I had that apartment down the street," Karen reminded, "but I'm pretty sure I moved back in with you. In fact, I know I did because, during the time of his visit, Bhagwan and I went to a lot of movies. Afterward, I would talk to him about our relationship. I don't think you shared what you were going through, but Bhagwan and I talked a lot."

"You and Bhagwan talked about you and me?"

"Absolutely," Karen recalled. "And he would talk about the whole idea of the Lover and the Beloved and the difference between having a lover and marriage. That marriage was about having children and having a stable life. He explained that there is an ever-changing balance between lover and beloved."

"A changing balance?"

"Yes. In some relationships, you're the lover and in other relationships, you're the beloved. And, I think in our relationship, in some ways, you have been more the lover, and I have been the beloved."

"Really…"

"It wasn't like you weren't my beloved," Karen reassured. "But in the sum balance of a relationship, in loving relationships, it's often one way or the other. Not that one is more important than the other; it's just the nature of relationships."

"I remember peeking out the window when you returned from the movies," I reminded, "and seeing the two of you talking in the car."

"We saw a lot of movies, including *Forrest Gump,* which was about being in the right place at the right time — just like your book. In the movie, Forrest fell in love with his childhood friend. He adored her, but she would never open herself to his love because he was mentally challenged. Eventually, through trials and tribulations, she opened to his love, but maybe too late. They got married right before she died, presumably of AIDS. But they were very very happy."

"Was the tide turning for your feelings toward me when you were with Bhagwan?" I probed.

"I think the tide was turning before Bhagwan. At the time, I wanted to reconcile, and just talking to him, the tide turned, something turned."

"You felt something shift in you?"

"It wasn't just in me," Karen explained. "It was a door opening. It was the whole Fortune thing. The door had been closing. You were pursuing this relationship with Irmgard, and I was going to do my single thing, but it seemed that there were greater forces at work. Somehow Bhagwan came at that exact time."

"But, that's all circumstantial. What were you feeling?"

"It wasn't so circumstantial."

"But that was the context."

"I was definitely feeling, before Bhagwan came, that I wanted to get back together. And you did not want to get back together so much. That's what I remember. And something happened in talking to Bhagwan."

"And it wasn't just because of Irmgard."

"No, Irmgard played a role too." Karen explained. "She played a role. Sometimes, something is needed to wake us up. Irmgard was a wakeup call for me. She played a role."

I was still curious how the ship turned around, so I asked Karen again.

"You two would be at the movies and then it would be time to talk. Were you reaching out to Bhagwan to help sort this out?"

"Bhagwan offered a helpful frame of reference — about the nature of relationships. He also has very Eastern ideas from having an arranged marriage. But, he also had this real appreciation for the solidity and importance of marriage. He became my ally in helping to turn the ship."

"Do you remember me being resistant to this?"

"I think you were understandably resistant."

"But you were coming on to me with your sweet eyes."

"Yeah, I was. But it was all genuine. I think Bhagwan became the Third Force. At that point, a third force was needed to shift things."

"And do you remember me being invited to go upstairs to have a session with him?

"Yeah, I remember that," Karen replied. She started to drift back into dreamland. "Is that enough?"

"I think so," I replied.

"Good. We did it. We did it," Karen yawned. "And now that calls for rubbies." And with that, she turned over, wanting to be caressed.

With Karen's recollections, my memory rekindled. I remember seeing her in a deep place. I just watched, expecting to be served with some kind of "summons."

The day came during their *Forrest Gump* phase when Bhagwan asked if I would like to sit with him. I dreaded the thought of it, but since Karen sternly vibed a "better-get-with-the-program" look, I had no choice.

I trudged up the stairs to an empty room where Bhagwan sat in a folding chair. Yes, the empty bedroom that had been cleaned out by Karen's mover-goons two years earlier.

"So, tell me about this woman, Irmgard," Bhagwan asked.

I told him the whole story with just enough synchronicity to support my case: In short, since Irmgard entered the story like a divine intervention, why step back into a dark and painful marriage?

Bhagwan was understanding, but did not seem moved.

I pleaded my case: "Bhagwan, if there is only One Love, there cannot be two. You can't have all sorts of doors opening everywhere. I feel guided."

Bhagwan paused to absorb my question, then replied:

"This business with one love can be confusing. Yes, there is only One Love, One Beloved, but that love can take many appearances. There is the love you have with a child, or with your parents, or with a guru. And so it is with marriage."

I could follow his argument, but it wasn't winning me over.

Bhagwan continued. "I remember being a young man. And my family made this big event for me to meet my future wife. With food and family, my future bride waited for me to join the festivity. And I was telling them, why do I need to do this event? If this is my destiny, I will have to love her anyway, love her completely. So, just let me be and meditate."

Bhagwan laughed heartily. I didn't get the analogy. Maybe it was the whole arranged-marriage thing. I remembered my arranged date in Santa Cruz years earlier. Maybe he had a point.

"Let me explain how there can be two and still be One," Bhagwan continued. "Do you know the story of Radha and Rukmini?"

I stared blankly.

"There were these two women in Krishna's life," Bhagwan explained. "With Radha, it was a transcendent love, *mahabhava*, the quintessence of love. It was not a worldly love. It was beyond the ego. Radha and Krishna are simultaneously one and different."

He continued. "Rukmini"s love is called *kanta-bhava*, the love of wife. This love is bounded by our duties in the world to bring forth children and have a home. With Radha, in your lifetime, you may never even meet this soul. It's enough to know that this kind of love exists. With Rukmini, this is who you are in this world; you are bound in this love."

I think I heard the word, "bound" and not much else. I was still married, so I was bound. Being bound either feels good or it doesn't. At that moment, something let go. It wasn't where I wanted to go, but I accepted being bound.

Jews bind their arms. Chinese women bind their feet. Babies like to be swaddled. Yoga is about being "yoked." Even the expression "tying the knot" comes from a Celtic tradition of binding the bride and groom's hands during the wedding ceremony. In a way, I was relieved that I didn't have to choose between the two. I was bound, and accepted that I didn't have to make a decision.

I wrote to Irmgard, offering a detailed chronicle of how I ended with Rukmini rather than Radha. I don't know if the analogy worked for her either. Even though our relationship lasted just a few days, it had a timeless quality, so I'm sure she was hurt.

Bhagwan became a source of spiritual work for Karen and me and a disruptive force in my relationship with Reshad. Where Reshad was a showman, Bhagwan was hidden. "Pay no attention to the guru," Bhagwan seemed to say. "Turn your attention completely toward your experience of self." This was radical and refreshing.

My pivot toward Bhagwan forced me to reconcile the paradoxes between East and West. One day, Bhagwan approached me looking perplexed: "What is this thing about the Octave?"

I did my best to explain how in Reshad's school, we viewed transformation as a quickening of energies that follow natural harmonics. When Bhagwan gaped at me with a puzzled look, I realized that in his world, there was nothing to transform. Life is All One, Right Now. In my world, life offered different lenses to view the unfolding drama — and the Octave was one of them.

Needless to say, the Octave was performing its magic. Immediately after Bhagwan's vist, Karen moved back in and we relaxed into the soul place that holds marriages together. She even went to Johanneshof a couple times. As she recollected:

"The interesting thing was the second time I went to Johanneshof, you and I had reconciled. Irmgard was there and seemed heartbroken. It was not so great for her to see me.

"I sought advice from people for how to handle her. And, I wrote her a letter while I was there. I don't think we ever talked about it, but she wrote me back and said that she so appreciated me writing. Something opened because I did that. I was very intentional about reaching out to her because I didn't want my happiness to be the source of someone else's distress."

When Karen returned from Johanneshof, I got on the phone to invite our friend Susan to join us for a celebration dinner.

"Susan, can you bring a bottle of wine, maybe a loaf of bread?" I turned to Karen. "I'm on the phone with Susan. Anything else?"

Karen called out from the kitchen. "Ask Susan to pick up a pregnancy test kit."

"Karen wants you to pick up... A WHAT?"

Susan heard this and shrieked. She had followed our two-year separation and had chalked us up for divorce.

We didn't wait until morning. The tell-tale pink strip appeared before dinner like a burst of Fortune — an eleven year hiatus, and now, boom, a second child, and a true second marriage, but to the same person.

Karen gave birth in May, culminating nine months of new-found love and extraordinary Fortune. She continued to work as a nurse in her labor and delivery unit right up to the last week. Then Fortune's other shoe dropped. Until then, Karen generated the only stable paycheck in the family. So when she announced, "I plan to stay home with this one," I knew I was heading toward trouble.

I went into overdrive to ramp up my work as a freelance corporate scriptwriter. But, with Atlanta's Centennial Olympics seven weeks away, my plan was precarious. Over 197 countries, 10,000 athletes and two million visitors were headed to a city of 400,000 people, putting every project in the city on hold for three months. People fled and businesses shuttered. I now had plenty of time to tend to Karen and baby; the bigger problem was living on zero income.

By the third month, we were getting notices about utilities, the mortgage, credit cards — the usual suspects. I couldn't fathom how I got into this predicament a second time. I wanted to be a loving, protective father and spouse — not a deadbeat dad. If only I knew where to push, what clever idea to launch, maybe cold calling, direct mailing, or just pleading with God.

When the foreclosure notice arrived, I crumpled into a chair. "I can't keep doing this," I muttered. A Reshad tape was playing in the house and I heard these words:

"Expectation blocks the world of possibility."

Whoa… Expectation blocks the world of possibility? I repeated the phrase over and over in my head. So, what is this expectation — expecting a pony for Christmas? Or something more insidious? Rumi says that there is no death worse than expectation. But still, I couldn't wrap my head around it.

I contemplated the words: "Expectation, expectation. How does expectation block possibility?"

I began to see expectation as energetic, a mental knot that squeezes the free flow of life. Here I was, living in that flow, but not trusting it. Every ounce of worry was a testament to my distrust. But, it was trickier than that. I couldn't be so naive to think I could sit back like Bennett's happy-go-lucky guy and "expect" unearned profit from the Law of Hazard. As Bennett explained, "This is not how the world is actually put together."

Like a trapped rat, all my exit strategies seemed blocked. Should I push the river? Outwit the river? Augment the river? I couldn't just trust the river. That would be too irresponsible. Our house could be gone tomorrow.

For Sufi's, one of the names of God is Al Samad, the Satisfier of All Needs:

"He is the One God: God the Eternal, the Uncaused Cause of All That

Exists. He begets not, and neither is He begotten, and there is nothing that could be compared with Him."

Al Samad exists beyond the scope of causal thinking, but I wasn't ready to give up mental management. Experiencing life as a self-sufficient flow from an Uncaused Cause could only take me to a scary place. My heart got heavier and heavier. In a panic, I got on my knees. There was no way out. Tears began to flow. I can't let go; can I let go? All other strategies had failed, so, I simply let go. If the universe has its own fucking agenda, why not let it run the show.

There seems to be a pattern here. Like Mercury retrograde, I keep coming back to the same conundrum. Every time I let go, it's not enough. I'm asked to surrender again and again.

The next day, the ringing phone jolted me out of my funk.

"Hello?"

"Is this Bruce Miller?" the voice asked.

"Yes, it is."

"You may not remember me. My name is Patty Andonian. We worked briefly together on a job for IBM a couple of years ago. I have a friend, Bob, who is looking for writers and I gave him your name. Please give him a call at this number. That's all I know, but nice talking to you, Bruce."

"Nice talking to you, Patty."

Who is Patty Andonian? Beats me, but I called Bob anyway.

"Hello, my name is Bruce Miller. I was given your number."

"Can you come right now?" Bob asked.

"Can you tell me what this job is?"

"Do you know anything about banking technology?" Bob asked.

"Not a thing."

"It doesn't matter. I'll meet you when you get here."

I drove thirty minutes to the new headquarters for CheckFree Corporation. CheckFree had bought out an Atlanta software company and was moving in. I scanned the sea of empty cubicles and bumped into Bob Oliver, the freelance writer I had talked to on the phone.

"Here," he said. "This is a list of products that need sales sheets. It's a big push. About a page and a half each would be good."

Bob didn't know a thing about banking technology either. He filled his pages with flowery copy.

I sought out a tech guy who knew something about the product. He explained that CheckFree's products used the ACH to transmit money. I asked a few questions and was apparently good to go.

I chose a random empty desk, plopped down, fired up Word, and started to write. Two years later, I was still at the same desk, working forty hours at my freelance rate, and making more money than my boss. The brass would regularly plead with me to become salaried, but at that point, I was the only one in the company who understood every product. So, I shrugged, "Anything wrong?" and kept plugging away.

Our boss, the Vice President of Marketing, would often give us half-baked assignments at five p.m. with five p.m. deadlines. I think he was trying to pad his portfolio using hacked advertising ideas — ads he traced from magazines.

Being creative guys, we didn't do that. I would huddle with Mathew, a young designer in his twenties. Together we would announce, "Time for a design coup!" We made a habit of ignoring our boss's stolen ideas. We were emboldened, so much so, we got our boss fired and won the Max Award for the best marketing campaign of the year.

Triumphant, we brought the beautiful Chihuly glass trophy back from the award ceremony to sit in the CEO's office. Two days later, the entire marketing department was invited to meet with the new VP of Marketing. "We are in the process of transition," the VP explained. And, with that, the entire department was fired; they had chosen an outside agency to replace us.

Yes, it was a dark day. But, one of the themes of this book is to tap the energy of adversity, augment opportunity, and make some lemonade.

Mathew and I invested 250 bucks each, set up shop in my unused

AV studio, and started Design Coup. It took a year for CheckFree's new agency to fully take over. We enjoyed a full year of high-ticket work as CheckFree's agency of record during the transition. Do I hear Fortune?

It was a remarkable run that produced a vacation house, stock investments, and flush times — until the day, fifteen years later at the bank, that I drove a stake through Design Coup's failing heart, and then raced to the hospital with Karen on New Year's Eve.

16

Karen 2.0

"God created beings not to act in a morality play
but to experience what is unfathomable, to elicit what can become,
to descend into the darkness of creation and reveal it to him."
Richard Grossinger

"Okay, Annie, before I go down for surgery, you have to promise that you will get yourself some support hose," Karen said firmly.

"Oh, I promise, Miss Miller," Annie replied. As a $9 per hour nursing assistant, Annie was not used to being on the receiving end of so much attention.

I marveled at how Karen chatted up the steady stream of hospital staff. Personally, I would have been more concerned about having part of my brain removed, but my beloved seemed to have entered into a new realm, what we affectionately called "Karen 2.0."

Transformation is a noble aim, but I question whether people actually jettison much baggage on their life journey. Karen seemed the exception. By any measurement, Karen seemed palpably transformed, empowered, forthright, perhaps even blunt.

"Annie, you need to get prescription compression stockings. Get a doctor to write a script."

"Oh yes, I will. My legs do hurt," Annie replied.

"Okay, then let's go. I'm ready," Karen announced to the assembled.

And with that, the two orderlies began to wheel Karen down to surgery.

After four days of hospital love fest, the main event was about to begin. I headed down to pre-op to catch the next show. If this sounds glib, I'm trying to paint a picture of Karen's 2.0 attitude — particularly in the face of brain surgery. As Karen recollects:

"I don't remember being that scared. I was in a pretty surrendered place. I knew that I needed to have surgery to save my life. And, I liked my doctor. I was a concerned that he had just driven back from Florida and would be tired because my surgery was in the early evening.

"It was scary to have brain surgery, but it was also necessary. I didn't know what might happen; it was just the journey I was on. I was just going with it. I was completely going with it.

"It was like being on the whitewater rapids in the boat. I knew that if I became all emotional and upset about it, that could turn the boat over and cause a lot more problems. So, I chose to be surrendered and relaxed, particularly with the anesthesia, because I knew that by being relaxed, it would all go better."

When I arrived at pre-op, Norma, an older nurse, was twisting and pulling at Karen's wedding ring. It occurred to me that even during our painful separation, our rings never came off.

"It hasn't come off in nearly thirty years," Karen warned.

Karen didn't miss an opportunity to be 2.0.

"So, Norma, how long have you been married?" Karen continued.

"Thirty-five years," Norma answered, still tugging.

"You need a second honeymoon."

"Yeah, I do work too hard."

Norma produced some cream and the ring finally let go.

"Wow," Karen exclaimed.

Jennifer, the charge nurse, wheeled up her touchscreen.

"I need you to sign several places for consent," Jennifer explained.

I marveled that there's even an app to click for partial brain removal.

"Do you have babies?" Karen asked.

"I do," Jennifer replied.

"Enjoy every moment of affection," Karen insisted. "They get big on you fast."

Jennifer smiled.

I held Karen's hand, a superfluous gesture given the river of energy coursing through my being.

"Karen, this is a crazy moment to share this, but whoa… I feel so in love."

Karen smiled.

"Isn't it funny," she confided, "I feel myself entering a space I long dreamed of. When I was young, I imagined what it would be like to surrender into love without any shame — a kind of freedom to be myself without inhibition or fear."

I felt the irony that such tenderness would emerge with Karen wired to the gills. And then, the moment was gone.

"Hi, I'm Doctor Solomon. I will be your anesthesiologist, today."

"Where are you from?" Karen asked.

"New York," Dr. Solomon replied. His brash Brooklynese cut through our tender moment like a brisket cleaver.

"I once had a Jewish boyfriend in New York," Karen shared coyly. "I like Jewish guys."

"Mazel Tov!" Dr. Solomon badda-boomed. "Ours will be a match made in heaven. And these are my two assistants, Dave and Joey."

"Hi, guys," Karen smiled.

Dave and Joey unplugged the tubes and cables and started to wheel Karen away.

"Wait," I called out. "One more goodbye." I held Karen's hands and whispered, "I won't miss a breath. I will hold you and be with you. We won't be apart for a second."

"I love you, Honey."

And with that, Dave and Joey wheeled Karen away. All three continued to kibbitz.

"I've never had anesthesia before," Karen warned.

"It's just like tequila," Joey explained. "But stronger."

I went to the lobby to wait out the hours — day four of pure adrenaline, not much food, and little sleep. When I'm frazzled, I'm better off writing, so I started to type:

> I am sitting in the waiting area with my friends. Our day has been blessed with many visitors. Karen's niece and her partner drove down from Knoxville, a chaplain friend sang for Karen, and Cindi, our unexpected angel who works with neurological patients at Shepherd, offered a daunting picture of the recuperative path ahead.

We also received calls from old friends. It was so helpful to know that Karen was being remembered in places like India, England, Switzerland, Canada and beyond.

I emailed Bhagwan even though he was off the grid in the mountains of India. To my surprise, Bhagwan pecked back using his low-tech phone:

> Dear Bruce,
> Unexpected News.
> I will keep. Her in my thoughts.
> Tell her all will be OK
> Love and best wishes
> Bhagwan

I savored every syllable from Bhagwan, especially, "All will be OK."

After a long three hours, Dr. Chandler joined us in the lobby. When you think "brain surgeon," any of the Star Trek characters might fill the role: Patrick Stewart, William Shatner, or Leonard Nimoy. But Dr. Chandler was closer to Bill Murray — a loose, easy-going guy who wore sneakers as he opened brains. I was encouraged to learn that Dr. Chandler had assembled a neuro dream team that attracted patients from all over the country. Maybe, our soul was watching over us on this one after all.

Dr. Chandler took me aside and casually delivered the news. It could have been a sports update.

"Yeah, Karen is awake and fine, moving and talking. I was able to remove the entire tumor, clean lines, looks good. We'll get the full report on Tuesday."

I waited another hour, then ventured toward the recovery room — a vast space with only one patient. I made my way to the far corner and stepped through the curtain. Karen looked like a train wreck.

"Hi, it's me," I ventured.

Karen's deep grumble emerged from the other world.

"Hi, Honey," she groaned in her best Hanibal Lecter. "This is some weird ass shit. I don't want to get used to surgery. That's all I got."

Karen slipped back to the netherworld, but the staff seemed ecstatic with her progress.

Feeling pummeled and drained from too much adrenaline, I headed home to collapse into my first real bed in days.

The shower and sheets were fantastic, but Karen's side of the bed spoke to a canyon of emptiness.

The next morning, I visited Karen again. She was queasy and groggy, but chatting up nurses the best she could. She kept asking for her nerdy Jewish anesthesiologist, Dr. Solomon. Karen has a thing for skinny Jewish men.

A nurse asked if we remembered a particular doctor's name.

"Don't look at me," Karen growled with what was now a Bette Davis voice. "That's the good thing about having a brain tumor; you don't have to remember those things."

Given her progress, the doctor gave Karen a free pass back to her regular room, bypassing the ICU a second time. Karen settled into bed and drifted asleep.

I called my friend Daniel and gave him the report: "Karen's doing great. I'm the one in trouble. I was freaking all night. I don't see a way through this."

The Bette Davis voice awoke from the netherworld: "The mind is a perfect doubt machine."

"Shit," I mumbled. "It's Karen 2.0."

Karen pulled herself up. Her words did not come easily, but she had something important to share.

"I had an amazing night last night," she muttered with a subterranean growl. "When I woke up in the recovery room, I felt like I was in a chapel, a white room at the top of a building. There was a peaked ceiling filled with light. I was in this in-between place. I felt the support of these beings, this support from the other world. They have been with me the whole time I've been here. I was desperately trying to wake up in my body. But I couldn't wake up, and I couldn't quite move my body. I don't even know if words were coming out when I was talking."

As Karen described her experience, the room felt strangely translucent. She continued.

"These two African-American nurses were with me all night. I would call to them, and they gathered around me to pray. I asked them to sing, 'Come on in the room; Jesus is my doctor.' They knew it, and we sang.

"Then I asked if they knew, 'I Give Myself Away.' They also knew it, and they sang it to me. It was a holy experience that I had come through from the other side. When I finally woke up, the two nurses prayed with me and gave me their blessing. It was so important. I felt connected to the meaning of my life."

Dr. Chandler came into the room, checked out Karen's cognitive and physical abilities. All was well. Karen had some visual impairment on her right side.

"She won't be driving for a long while, maybe never," Dr. Chandler said.

Partial vision loss seemed a small price for a complete Karen upgrade. It was also fascinating to watch Karen 2.0 in action. Even though a layer of heavy meds tempered her personality, Karen's playful feistiness emerged with new vigor. Everyone who entered the room — doctor, RN, transport or trash man — got the 2.0 treatment. You couldn't simply do your job. First, you had to reveal where you were from, favorite recreation, books, and marital status. Then you had to go directly to the soul place with Karen.

"I want you to meet Brian," Karen announced as Brian wheeled her back into the room after an MRI.

Brian was tickled but unsettled by the attention. He turned to leave, but Karen interjected.

"Brian, I hope you find a nice wife…" Brian looked stunned, so Karen deftly added, "OR A HUSBAND!"

Karen's 2.0 manner forced me to consider the function of illness.

Years earlier, in the months before the 9-11 attacks, Nick, our pirate screenwriter, was diagnosed with terminal lung cancer. We invited Nick to live with us during the remaining weeks of his life. Our impulse was compassionate, but maybe we were victims of Nick's final con. Either way, we didn't want Nick to die alone, and we expected our generous gesture to be met with a dying man's open-hearted gratitude. Ha!

Nick passed his dying days by becoming increasingly mean, ugly, seductive, demeaning, and demanding. For years he had practiced the high art of freeloading. Somehow, the uninsured Nick kept the game going by convincing Emory University Hospital to provide him with leading-edge lung cancer therapy and a private room — gratis! The doctors performed an experimental photodynamic bronchoscopy procedure, but unfortunately, during the procedure, Nick famously and secretly dropped acid. This little stunt earned him a trip to the ICU and pissed everyone off royally — especially the anesthesiologist who was required to account for every particle of substance in Nick's bloodstream.

Nick's bad-boy-in-hospice caper forced me to turn the mirror around, not focusing on the patient, but on the karmic function of illness. When I did this, a different picture emerged. I saw how Nick's cancer squeezed his being like a wringer squeezing a lifetime of residue from his emotional body.

The Sufi term for the wringing process is *fana*, which means annihilation of the illusion, of the temporal self. *Fana's* complement is *baqa*, the permanent, the real, and the eternal subsistence in God. The ego is hard-wired to avoid *fana* at all costs. As *fana* squeezes, *baqa* expands. Wring and release, little by little the karmic corset loosens its hold — ideally over a lifetime and not all at once at the end.

The pendulum of *fana* and *baqa* swings back and forth, creating the push-pull path of transformation described by the Law of Three and the Octave. I wondered if Nick tried to hasten the process by taking LSD during anesthesia. But the big lie that fuels addictions, distractions, and indulgences of all kinds is that we can bypass the implicit suffering of *fana* and *baqa*.

The night before Karen was discharged (yes, forty-eight hours after brain surgery) our friends gathered in her room for a "Sushi Love Fest." While we dived into little boxes of sashimi, Karen held center stage with her loopy, lovey 2.0-ness. I marveled at the striking difference between Nick and Karen's cancer journeys. Both had lung cancer, both were in their second Saturn Return, and both were on the Sufi path.

The experience of the Tibetan Buddhist teacher, Sogyal Rinpoche, is instructive here. As a child, Sogyal witnessed the death of two monks. The first monk endured intense pain and suffering which the young Sogyal recognized to be part of the natural process of purification. The second monk died seamlessly, which Sogyal felt demonstrated spiritual mastery — the result of a lifetime of inner work.[1]

Adversity is a great purifier and Karen displayed a remarkable equanimity. As I mixed soy sauce into my wasabi, Annie returned to administer a blood test. I watched Karen gently scold Annie about compression stockings. Karen asked her if she knew the song, "I Give Myself Away."

"I do. I sing it in our church choir," Annie replied.

1. Rinpoche, Sogyal. 2012. The Tibetan Book of Living and Dying. Edited by Patrick Gaffney and Andrew Harvey. San Francisco, Calif.: HarperSanFrancisco.

"Please sing it," Karen asked.

The room hushed as Annie sang:

I give myself away
I give myself away
So You can use me…
Here I am
Here I stand
Lord, my life is in your hands
Lord, I'm longing to see
Your desires revealed in me [2]

As Annie obliterated my "perfect doubt machine," tears flowed freely. And yes, there are quiet, solid, reliable people with spiritual knowledge, but they don't become spiritual teachers — they become nurse's aides.

The next day, it was time to leave. I was surprised how easy it was to break out of the Big House. We didn't have to pass the rumored test by the physical therapist, nor was there a visit from the business office presenting a six-figure bill. We just called the nurse, "We want out." The nurse removed Karen's last links to the beeping machines, and we split.

As I pulled out of the hospital garage, I couldn't suppress my urge to text and drive: "We out!"

Immediately the texts started beeping back like a news ticker:

"Yay!!!"
"Yay for Karen coming home."
"Woohoo!
"What a miracle!"

I called home to warn the boys, "Hide the dishes!"

I drove up the lawn to the door and supported Karen's measured steps. I lit a fire while Karen snuggled into the couch. Being in

2. McDowell, William. "I Give Myself Away." Lyrics. Delivery Room Publishing, 2008.

the hospital sucks, yet returning home was no picnic. The most immediate challenge was dealing with the meds. In the hospital, drugs magically appear at appointed times. You give your birth date; they scan your wrist and bzzit; it's all documented and tracked.

At home, the meds play out like a brain teaser: one every 4 hours, one tablet twice daily, one upon waking, one before retiring, two with symptoms and on and on.

Basic tasks immediately became a challenge. With no bed tray, I took a leaf out of the dining table and cantilevered it across an arm chair. Next, the bath. We put a folding chair in the shower — the first real shower in nearly a week. The crazy part was that Karen would make simple requests that cascaded like Lucy and Ethel in the chocolate factory.

Eventually, we got into bed. The OT and the PT were wrong — Karen made it up the stairs. As we snuggled together, I remembered the canyon of emptiness days earlier. "Wow, Karen is still in this world." But, I didn't have the energy to savor the sweetness. We were out.

The next morning, I made little notes whenever Karen shared her wisdom. I titled the page, "Thus Spake Karenthustra." Here are a few snippets from Karen 2.0:

"This morning I was just being aware of how I was pushing. Pushing to get better, pushing to do more. It's connected to anxiety. I'm just sort of over it."

"I am looking at the whole idea of pushing and learning not to push. It is a very subtle, energetic thing. I am learning that not settling into myself and just keeping busy are connected to shame."

"It feels more real to discover how deeply relaxed I can be. Not feeling I have to strive for something outside of myself. My job is to respond, not to push. There is plenty of movement and energy in being in yourself without having to have an idea about what needs to happen. It is much more alive to inquire into the nature of things. It's about the dance of life."

"One of the things that has been so pleasurable for me is holding peoples' hands. Love itself is so deep and nurturing; you can only experience it. You can't put words to it."

"It's like the thing that happened with me and all those nurses. These were the people coming into my room. So, that's where the love could happen — right there in my room."

"Some days you are glowing, and some days you are just living."

The next day, we officially entered the World of Cancer, a $200 billion theme park ride that is seductive in its sense of certainty, maddening in its lack of curiosity, and driven by obscene amounts of money.

The cancer industry's clinical approach at every level can be summed up in three words: "Kill the bugger."

You can imagine our discomfort when our radiation oncologist took us through an illustrated tour of Karen's illness. He clicked through multilayered PET scans, CAT scans, and MRIs that pictured the tumors like alien invaders.

The challenge was what to do with this information. If healing is ultimately a mysterious, yet natural process, the clinical detail seemed counter-productive. Karen's challenge was to take ownership of her healing journey without becoming a passive passenger on the cancer industry roller coaster.

Susan Sontag famously wrote *Illness as Metaphor*, on how the classic diseases (tuberculosis, AIDS, cancer) carry a sense of societal shame — that having a disease reflects a character flaw.[3] Before meeting Karen 2.0, I would subtly scrutinize cancer patients for their tell-tale flaw — is it diet, a psychological obsession, an emotional predisposition? Living now in the World of Cancer, I could see how my mindset wasn't all that different from Jerry Falwell blaming 9/11 on homosexuality.

All diseases are social diseases. The Arctic Inuits famously have fifty words to describe snow, yet we don't question the implication of having 13,000 words to describe illness, which now, according

3. Sontag, Susan. 1978. Illness as metaphor. New York: Farrar, Straus and Giroux.

to the ICD10 has exploded five-fold, using 68,000 codes to describe disease.

Naming bestows substance, and the word *cancer* carries a stigma that is cultural, psychological, and energetic. The word infects its victim like the disease itself — maybe worse. The challenge is not to succumb to the sinking weight of the C-word, a scarlet letter that hijacks thinking and sinks one's feelings with corrosive fear, shame, and despair.

Karen and I chose not to absorb the sinking weight of the C-word. Unfortunately, a well-meaning deluge of advice, books, and consolation flooded the emotional bilge on our leaky boat.

Three days after brain surgery, our friend Daniel drove us home from the first of countless doctor visits. Despite traffic jams, accidents, and exhaustion, Karen managed to remain upbeat.

"I just enjoy being together," Karen beamed as the traffic ground to a halt.

"We shouldn't have left the freeway for the side streets," I complained, but Karen wouldn't have it.

"I enjoy seeing these neighborhoods where Daniel used to drive his cab."

At that moment, Karen's disposition parted the scarlet sea. A magic word appeared that would guide us through the grueling journey ahead. And the word was *buoyancy* — the upward force exerted by a fluid that opposes the weight of an immersed object. When they said Jesus walked on water, maybe it was mistranslated Aramaic for *buoyancy*.

So Karen and I learned to walk on water.

Cancer is chaos. It reflects the chaotification of the world — within and without. We absorb chaos in many forms throughout our lives — mental, emotional, physical, and environmental. Even the simple act of watching television injects static into our brainwaves. Modern living generates energetic cancer whether it manifests physically or not. The first step in healing is *recognition* — so a cancer diagnosis is a healing event. No more presuming or pretending. It's time to start clarifying and redeeming the energy of cancer.

Looking at it another way, one part of us is living, the other dying. The C-word focuses on the part that is dying. In buoyancy, we align with the part that is laughing and loving, knowing and growing. Buoyancy is the affirmation of life.

The cancer doctors determined that Karen had "High-Performance Status" (i.e. buoyancy) on the Karnofsky scale, so they chose to aim their biggest guns (maximum chemo and radiation) and go for a "cure." My hope was that the cure wouldn't kill her first.

I sent out a message asking everyone to shift their thinking away from words of concern and consolation and encourage our buoyancy. The word *encourage* has "heart" (coeur) at its root. I wrote to our friends:

"Continue your love and support to keep our spirits and energy buoyant. See Karen walking on water, loving up the medical people, healing and being healed on her journey — and mine."

Karen said it better: "I am not into people worrying about my diagnosis. That is blah blah blah. I am on a healing journey."

If you've been around cancer, you know the drill — daily radiation, all-day chemo, debilitating nausea, a basket of pills, a collection of hats, and a comb full of hair. Karen was determined to begin her dream job, so it took a village of volunteers to shuttle her to and from work and to her multiple daily appointments.

Friends came every evening to give Reiki, polarity therapy, green smoothies, clay baths, sound therapies, and caster oil packs to counter the effects of the medical regimen. Karen also walked two miles per day with an "I will survive" attitude that pooped me out.

This same attitude propelled her to her annual spiritual retreat in Estes Park, Colorado. This last bit of 2.0-ism (from the girl not into pushing) pushed her doctors to adjust her absolutely-non-negotiable radiation schedule. Somehow, she managed the 9,000 feet altitude with a radiated lung.

Karen recounts the challenges of the trip:

"I got to the Denver Airport, and I couldn't figure out how to make the ticket kiosk work. Until that moment, I failed to realize that chemo and radiation fog your brain. So, I went outside to the curbside check-in. When I approached the agent, he noticed I was struggling to breathe, and he ran to get a wheelchair. I cried and cried all the way to the gate by the stress of it all."

Karen was a fighter. If she was going to battle cancer, she would fight it expertly. Her radiation oncologist suggested a plant-based diet and ka-wumph, the next day we were baking paleo muffins. A friend suggested a rare bentonite clay and ka-sploosh, Karen soaked her feet in a bucket of very expensive muddy water night after night.

Because Karen continued to work, she had to receive treatments while teaching her students. Five months into this, I felt exhausted, but Karen maintained an unwavering focus. Karen 2.0 was a life reboot — remaking herself while enduring a brutal regimen and without discernible evidence that any of it was working.

After five grueling months, Karen felt triumphant. Everyone marveled at how well she was doing, how she continued to teach and function while being given killer doses of "everything they got."

As we headed to the oncologist, I praised her spirit and strength. We entered Dr. Tien's examining room and waited to find out who won: Karen or the C-word. Ha Tien is the sweetest, most caring oncologist you could hope for, but her face foreshadowed the news.

"The tumor that was here is completely gone," she explained pointing at the scan. "And the second one, it has shrunk significantly. Almost completely gone. But right here, there is some new activity. This is what I'm concerned about."

I reached for Karen's hand and held it tight. This benign-sounding diagnosis — "new activity" —hit like an asteroid. Our sacred buoyancy was shattered, devastated, destroyed. The biggest guns had failed.

"I'm so sorry," Dr. Tien said, giving Karen a tearful hug.

17

Breadcrumbs

"You must lose in order to win.
You have lost something to gain everything.
Meher Baba

Karen and I were heartbroken. We had hoped to step off the World of Cancer's body-battering roller coaster, but instead, we bought another ticket. The PET-scan-sugar-excited something could be cancer; could be inflammation. It's not like a conventional boo-boo where it hurts; it scabs, and you watch it get better.

No, this problem only existed as a story. Someone unnamed saw something, or the blob of something, on a monster gamma-ray machine while the insurance company continued to bill us tens of thousands because they couldn't determine in-network from out-of-network, and unlike everything else in our lives, this something robbed us from any sense of charting our destiny, because we were caught in the grip of the medical-industrial complex.

Fortunately, we learned that a leading-edge, genetically-targeted drug was available for Karen's mutation (why didn't they give it in the first place?), but unfortunately, the drug can cause nasty side effects, and a one month supply cost the equivalent of what I paid for my first three automobiles combined. This was not too much to pay if the something turned out to actually be something, but we couldn't know without performing a biopsy — a biopsy that the doctor strongly advised against.

Sorry for the rant, but my sense of powerlessness in the medical house of mirrors was pissing me off.

We started getting calls from CVS Specialty Pharmacy asking us to make arrangements for the super drug — thirty little pills cost $7,500. Karen didn't want to take it, but hey, OPM (other people's money), so we agreed to take delivery — just in case. After several calls back and forth, CVS put the super drug on super-duper-expedited status. Fortune must have intervened because the drug never arrived.

I tried to find some comfort hanging in the Unknown — the attitude Reshad called "living in the question." Not-knowing is not easy; it threatens your sense of identity. But if you can settle into a state of trust and allow the bread crumbs to take you where they lead, real change is possible. Today was Day One for letting the bread crumbs direct our healing journey — aka The World of Alternative Medicine.

I was heartened that the very next day after Dr. Tien's heartbreaking news, Fortune was sending us to the beach, to the Meher Center. Julie, our beloved friend, nurse practitioner, and alternative healing savant had invited us to the beach — 500 acres of beach-front wilderness snuggled between the towering condos of Myrtle Beach and North Myrtle Beach, SC. Julie was a "Baba lover," the affectionate designation for people who follow the Indian saint, Meher Baba. She had a premonition that Karen would benefit from Meher Baba and had reserved two cabins at the Meher Center a month earlier. Julie's partner Hugh had been on a cancer journey for several years, and as a result, Julie and Hugh were familiar with the furthest fringes of alternative healing.

The tranquil Meher Center seemed out-of-place with thousands of Harleys roaring through Myrtle Beach Bike Week. We spotted the hidden drive off the tourist trap highway, and immediately the scene shifted from *Mad Max* to *Blue Lagoon*. At the gatehouse, two attentive Baba lovers presented an odd list of dos and don'ts (Ouija boards, tarot cards, and the I-Ching were strictly prohibited). Free from divination, we drove through a primeval forest of cypress, palmetto palms, and hanging moss to our cabin. Deer pranced across the drive while alligators slithered into the ponds. Baba-lovers lovingly raked footpaths throughout the property. Not a speck of asphalt anywhere.

A little background: In the 1950s, Meher Baba visited this unspoiled expanse of property. It had been given by one of his followers as a gift to future generations. I didn't know much about Meher Baba apart from the fact that Pete Townsend of the Who wore a Baba lapel pin at Woodstock.[1] I also knew that Baba was a renunciant who communicated using an alphabet board and hand gestures. Baba is considered an "avatar" by his followers which puts him in the same league as Jesus. As such, Baba lovers attributed a host of miracles to him.

In one account of Meher Baba's death in 1969, it was reported that his body did not show signs of decomposing. After a week, and with a doctor's blessing, they entombed him anyway. An American who was there described the screening of a film that was shot at the entombment:

> About halfway through the film the photographer is right on the edge shooting a closeup of Baba with a normal lens, and Baba opens His eyes. His eyes flash here and there like in the other films of Him. He has a soft smile and looks delighted with how things are going. Then for four or five seconds He looks right at the camera with a direct smile, then continues looking up and around. Then His eyes stop moving, and He closes them with a satisfied look. Then He goes back to the death-mask look we are familiar with. There are a couple of cries from the rear [of the audience]. Jal [Baba's brother] is sitting to my left, and he leans forward to twist around and check me out, how am I taking this? He shrugs and smiles as if to say, "That's the sort of thing my brother does."[2]

---

1. Townsend can be seen displaying Meher Baba on the lapel of his jumpsuit on the cover photo of his first solo LP, *Who Came First.*

Meher Baba visited the Myrtle Beach property three times in the 1950s. Today, every element from those visits is lovingly preserved. For Baba lovers, visiting the property is like making the Hajj or praying at the Wailing Wall.

According to Baba's directive, the purpose of the Myrtle Beach property was to be for "rest, meditation, and the renewal of the spiritual life." No seminars, practices, yoga, healing, nothing. Just sink into Baba's vibe.

Early each morning, Karen and I headed to the beach, watching alligators slide into the lake while a cacophony of birds filled our senses. When we reached the dunes, *kawhoosh*, the sun would pierce its fiery glow above the roaring surf. For the most part, we hung around for seven days letting it all sink in — something I hadn't done since hanging with hippies at Big Sur forty years earlier.

The 1950s brick bungalow where Meher Baba lived during his brief stays forms the focal point of the property. At scheduled times, the bungalow shrine was opened to the faithful like a Shroud of Turin.

I watched devotees enter Baba's bedroom, fall to their knees, lay their hands on his bed, and release their burdens — often in floods of tears. My burdens didn't release — no different from my non-experience in 1973 when Swami Muktananda bopped my head with a peacock feather while those around me swooned from Swami-induced kundalini.

I approached Baba's bed with quiet respect and breathed. All of a sudden, unexpected kundalini seemed to tingle in my thigh.

"What the *f*?" Realizing it was my phone, I gathered my shoes, left the shrine, and liberated the vibrating intruder from my jeans pocket.

"Hello?"

"Hi, Bruce. This is Leila."

---

2. Beckett, Barry. 2015. "Was He Still Alive?" *Avatar Meher Baba Manifesting*. Accessed October 25. http://www.meherbabamanifesting.com/did-he-speak/was-he-still-alive/.

Leila was a friend from my Reshad days. I was delighted to hear her voice but wasn't happy with her timing. Leila sounded shaky.

"What's up?" I asked, now feeling a bit pissed.

"I'm in the hospital.

"Oh, no. Are you okay?

"I don't know. I was leading a kundalini yoga class. It was at the end where you do *mula bandha.* You pull in your perineum and sexual organs to send kundalini energy up the spine. I closed my eyes and all of a sudden I was just blown open; there was no shore to hold on to, and I just blacked out. I can't remember anything, how I got to the hospital, what's going on. I need your prayers."

"Okay…"

I found a bench in Baba's garden and did my best to let Baba's healing energy connect to Leila and her crisis. Later I learned that the medical staff, needing a code, decided that Leila suffered from Transient Global Amnesia. Checking the 68,000 non-Inuit names for medical misfortune, I learned:

ICD-10-CM G45.4 — A sudden, temporary episode of memory loss. Your recall of recent events simply vanishes, so you can't remember where you are or how you got there. Episodes are usually short-lived, and afterward, your memory is fine. Events that may trigger transient global amnesia include acute emotional distress and sexual intercourse.

I would add Kundalini yoga to the ICD-10 list of triggers, but that's how it is at Baba Beach. Random events fuse with your thoughts, feelings, and sense of time into an inseparable buoyant glow.

Two days later, the Meher Center opened Baba's house again. Karen announced that she wanted to release her burdens to Baba. Giving her space, I chose not to go.

"I love you," I whispered with a kiss.

And with that, Karen and Julie took off on their little pilgrimage. Karen recounts her experience:

"I was surprised that Baba's house was so ordinary — just simple brick with basic decor. I would have expected something fancier. The artifacts were a bit strange. They even had a pillow where he laid his head after his car accident.

"When I entered his bedroom, I felt tension building inside of me… from the scary new thing the doctors found in my lung and from working so hard with all the treatments. I felt a deeply loving energy, and also this sense of devotion — not to Baba, but to life and the Divine Principle. It was beautiful, and it drew me to let go."

When Karen returned from Baba's bungalow, she appeared unsettled.

"I couldn't do it in front of all of those people," Karen confessed.

"Couldn't do what?" I asked.

"Let it all go."

And with that, Karen started to cry inconsolably — a cathartic release that was both startling and seamless with the surroundings. I'll let her continue the story:

"When I returned to our cabin, the anxiety from the cancer journey had been building up. I had put myself through so much following all the treatments, and then I just started to cry. The immensity of my pain and suffering had reached a breaking point. I had worked so hard, all those months, and now it seemed for naught.

"At that moment, in our cabin kitchen, I felt held, that I could let go. I remember the quiet of the forest while we walked the sandy trails. I felt connected to the earth without any complexity. Now I know why Baba asked that the property should be undisturbed, undeveloped, and uncomplicated. The land didn't demand anything from me. I didn't need to maintain any layers between me and the earth.

"I asked to go to Julie's cabin, and when we arrived, she put her arm around me, sweetly saying, 'Just go with it. Let it come.' And so I did.

"I was sobbing with tears, yet it seemed so completely normal. This was the norm around Baba. I just let myself cry until it was all cried out. I would cry, then pause, then another wave of grief would rise — the grief of the diagnosis, but also the grief of a lifetime."

With Karen in floods of tears, I had no choice but to go with the flow, too. The forest received both of our tears without judgment. In Baba-land, the turtles and deer and alligators seem to be used to this sort of thing. Even the deer don't scamper when you come up close. With all the gray-haired hippies around, I dubbed the place Bambi for Boomers.

Two weeks later we were in Dr. Dunbar's office (the brain doctor). Given the lung report, we were anxious to receive the next official results — an MRI to the brain. If there was a lurker in Karen's lung, what could be hiding in Karen's occipital lobe?

Nikki, the office assistant, took Karen's vitals. Then, nurse Kia entered the exam room and started typing data into the system. After a minute, Karen 2.0 blurted out:

"Can we just get right to it? I am incredibly anxious about my results."

Kia looked up surprised.

"Didn't anyone tell you, everything is great," Kia reported. "In fact, we have never seen such a significant filling in of the void left by the tumor."

"Stop." Karen took a breath. "Let me sit for a minute and take that in."

Karen took a long inhale and out. Our eyes connected and with a wink, we vibed each other, "Like holy shit, what a concept, *good news!*"

If cancer was akin to obstetrical labor, this was the point of "transition" — where our journey shifted. In our case, from mainstream to alternative medicine.

To launch our alternative journey, Julie told us to watch a seven-part Webcast called "The Truth about Cancer."

That night, Karen and I snuggled in front of the TV with growing anticipation. The Webcast centered on cancer patients who had taken personal control of their healing journeys through nutrition, energy work, and natural therapies. According to the program, chemo, surgery, and radiation focus on killing the tumor (and often the patient) — and not on healing. With the right nutrition and support, our bodies heal themselves.

We watched with rapt conviction, letting our mainstream medical blinders fall away. The host told the story of Dr. Kelley, a small town Texas dentist who cured his own incurable stage-four, pancreatic cancer in the 1960s. Kelley had the curiosity of a medical researcher, but not the degree. He was convinced that there must be a metabolic or immuno basis to the disease. He experimented with enzymes and saw significant results. Soon, he treated all sorts of people with success.

Who was this Dr. Kelley? While watching the program, I clicked Wikipedia (boldface added by me):

> William Donald Kelley, DDS, MS (November 1, 1925 – January 30, 2005) was an orthodontist who developed the Kelley cancer therapy, an **ineffective** alternative cancer treatment based on the **unsubstantiated** belief that "wrong foods [cause] malignancy to grow, while proper foods [allow] natural body defenses to work."
>
> Kelley received no training in oncology; according to Quackwatch his ideas are "largely **speculative** and **invalid**." Not only is his therapy **ineffective**, but people with cancer who take it **die more quickly** and have a **worse quality of life** than those having standard treatment, and can suffer serious or **fatal side-effects**.[3]

Groovy. Two conflicting streams of information, one on the TV and one in my hand, had now formed a cognitive car wreck in the middle of my brain.

And who is Quackwatch? Another quick search. Apparently, Quackwatch is just one guy who doesn't hold a current medical license, operates out of his basement, makes a living testifying in lawsuits against natural therapies, but is cited as a reputable evidence by the American Cancer Society.[4]

Whoa… With $800 million in annual revenue, the ACS can't find a better debunker — at least one with a medical license?

Karen and I next watched the next story, about a young medical

---

3. "William Donald Kelley." 2015. Wikipedia, the Free Encyclopedia. https://en.wikipedia.org/w/index.php?title=William_Donald_Kelley&oldid=660296107.

4. "Quackwatch." 2016. Wikipedia, the Free Encyclopedia. https://en.wikipedia.org/wiki/Quackwatch .

resident named Dr. Gonzalez. Gonzalez had graduated from Cornell to take a position at the famed Memorial Sloan-Kettering Cancer Center in New York City. Gonzalez worked previously as a journalist, so he asked his superior if he could conduct an investigative report about Dr. Kelley, the goal being to uncover the quackery of Dr. Kelley from a medical-scientific point of view.

Dr. Gonzalez flew down to Grapevine, Texas under the auspices of Sloan Kettering to get the skinny on Dr. Kelley. Kelley was happy to give Gonzalez access to his records. Gonzalez became so intrigued by what he learned, that when he flew back to Sloan Kettering with his report, he delivered the *wrong* conclusion. In a moment of conscience, Dr. Gonzalez abandoned his medical position and returned to Texas to study full-time with Dr. Kelley. Out of this experience, Dr. Gonzalez developed the Gonzalez protocol.

Again, I turned to Wikipedia adding my boldface:

> Nicholas James Gonzalez, M.D., is a New York-based physician known for developing the Gonzalez regimen (or Gonzalez protocol), an **ineffective** cancer treatment. Gonzalez's treatments are based on the belief that pancreatic enzymes are the body's main defense against cancer and can be used as a cancer treatment. His methods have been **rejected** by the medical community, and he has been characterized as a **quack** and **fraud** by other doctors and health fraud watchdog groups. In 1994 Gonzalez was **reprimanded** and placed on two years' probation by the New York state medical board for "**departing from accepted practice**."[5]

Wow. Facing loss of license and lawsuits, Gonzalez was forced to submit to psychological testing and undergo retraining to realign his ideas with conventional medicine. Welcome to the Gulag.

Okay, let me see if I get this right. In 1964, Kelley had stage four pancreatic cancer, 18 months to live, and a one percent five-year survival rate. He died 45 years later at age 79. For this, he was vilified?

---

5. "Nicholas Gonzalez (physician)." 2015. Wikipedia, the Free Encyclopedia. https://en.wikipedia.org/w/index.php?title=Nicholas_Gonzalez_(physician)&oldid=684903885.

Dr. Kelley famously treated the actor Steve McQueen. According to Gonzalez, Steve McQueen "had failed radiation, failed immunotherapy. He had been misdiagnosed for a year. The reason he ended up with Stage 4 mesothelioma was because he was misdiagnosed by his fancy conventional doctors in Southern California."

Against the advice of Dr. Kelley, McQueen chose to have his tumor removed and died soon after.[6]

When the Steve McQueen story hit the tabloids, the medical authorities denounced Dr. Kelley and took away his license. He also lost his house and medical records to a mysterious fire. They even threw Kelley in jail.[7]

A local district court affirmed by the United States Supreme Court, made it illegal for Kelley to distribute his self-published booklet, "One Answer To Cancer" because of the "grave, immediate threat of irreparable harm and a clear and present danger of physical or mental injury or harm to the members of the general public." According to Gonzalez, Dr. Kelley is the only scientist in U.S. history forbidden by court decree from publishing.[8] First Amendment anyone?

You can imagine my cognitive whiplash as I seesawed between the "Truth About Cancer" and the truth-y Wiki critiques. With our mental compass spinning, Karen and I vowed to follow the breadcrumbs anyway. The next afternoon the crumbs took an interesting turn.

We were sitting on the dock of our cabin, still disoriented, when Karen announced she wanted a mentor — someone to guide her alternative healing journey. We have many holistic friends and practitioners in our life, but Karen wanted to expand her resources. She called a prominent natural health store and left a message:

6. Mercola, Dr. 2015. "A Special Interview with Dr. Nicholas Gonzalez." Accessed October 25. http://cafemlm.com/wp-content/2011/10/InterviewGonzalezOnSteveJobs.pdf.

7. Fassa, P. (2010, October 15). The Dentist Who Cured Cancer. Retrieved October 02, 2016, from http://www.naturalnews.com/030050_dentist_cancer.html

8. Barrett, Dr. Stephen. 2015. "Injunction against F William Donald Kelley, D.D.S. Upheld." Casewatch. Accessed October 25, 2015. http://www.casewatch.org/board/dent/kelley/appeal1.shtml.

"Beep… Hello, my name is Karen Miller. I have metastatic lung cancer. I would like to reach Jane. Since Jane is in contact with a daily flow of customers, I thought she might know who was achieving good results and the healing modalities they used."

Two hours later, Jane called, but she first wanted to probe our "eccentric factor," or how health crazy we could get. Karen told Jane that our kids used to see the local naturopath, Dr. Berryhill, who was famously investigated by the State of Georgia for prescribing *belladonna,* a benign homeopathic remedy with a lethal label. Berryhill also famously gave our small child a replica AK-47 for Halloween. Jane seemed impressed, so we must have passed the crazy test.

"I'm going to give you a contact, Bob Gelder (not his real name)," Jane said. "I'm forewarning you; Bob is rather direct. *Fearsome* is the better word."

We drove an hour east to Nowhere County Georgia and tried to locate Bob's off-the-grid house with Google Maps. The street number didn't exist, so I gave him a call.

"Turn around, go about half a mile," a gruff voice commanded. "I'll be there to open the gate."

I spotted Bob by the gate of his small horse farm. He invited us inside and dispensed with the small talk. Pressing us like a Force 5 whirlwind, Bob explained that he almost died as a young man from multiple chemical sensitivity, which set him on a 40-year healing journey. At the time, he had young children and could not opt to become disabled. From this, Bob became a naturopath.

"Yes, I studied with some of the best," Bob proudly proclaimed, "including (insert drum roll), Dr. William Donald Kelley."

Karen and I rolled our eyes with the same breadcrumb thought: Two days after watching the suspect program, we were now sitting with the protégé of the infamous Dr. Kelley.

We spent the next five hours in a converted bedroom, filled floor-to-ceiling with remedies, as Force 5 Bob pressed my fragile wife:

"Got a gas stove?"

"Yeah…"

"It's gone."

"Do you dye your hair?"

"When I had hair."

"That's over."

"Cosmetics?"

"Uh huh."

"Not anymore."

"Shower filter?"

"Uh, no."

"Chlorine will kill you. How about fruit? Do you eat fruit?"

"I love fruit."

"Say goodbye to fruit."

"My God," I thought. "We're going to die from fruit?"

"Ever have a coffee enema?"

"No."

"You will now. I've taken one every day for 25 years, sometimes twice in one day."

Bob hooked Karen up to the Quantum Xeroid Consciousness Interface (QXCI) – a blinking box that stood between a tired old laptop and a tangle of electrodes connected to Karen's head and limbs. The machine was developed by a former NASA guy and identified genius, Bill Nelson, who worked on the navigational system for Apollo. Nelson had a son with autism, possibly the result of his wife taking Zofran during pregnancy. Nelson threw himself at the autism problem with the zeal of a scientist. His inquiry led to an exploration of the body's subtle energy systems.

From Bill Nelson's bio:

In developing his system, Bill Nelson has integrated the sciences of mathematics, quantum physics, electronics, naturopathy, homeopathy, chiropractic, energetic medicine and computer programming... The QXCI gathers bio-energetic data from the body via fifty-five channels simultaneously. The information is prioritized to help the natural health practitioner zero-in on the body's current specific needs. The program offers information specific to subtle energies, emotional and mental stresses, nutritional needs, food sensitivities, digestive and cleansing needs, etc. In the hands of a trained health practitioner, the imbalances in the subtle energy field are tracked to determine the most probable sources of ill health. In addition, the QXCI has the capability to apply approximately 50 different corrective energies to help the body establish energetic balance for health and well-being.[9]

For the next several hours, Bob drilled Karen without letting up.

"I'm as extreme as they come," Bob declared with a perverse pride. "Haven't touched a carrot in thirty years. See that pool out there? Never been in it. Do you have a pool or a hot tub?"

"Our friend has one in the mountains that we…"

"Do you want chemicals in your God-given body?"

Bob dabbled in conspiracies, politics, and garden-variety paranoia. In his defense, Bob had a genuine desire to see Karen get well. He was also blown away by Karen's fortitude. From 10 a.m. to 3:00 p.m., Bob never took a break.

Interestingly, the QXCI found all sorts of things that corroborated its accuracy, including a blood sugar spike, presumably from the fruit smoothie we made earlier with our new Vitamix. The QXCI also found environmental toxins, fungus, and other nasty critters. To our surprise, there was one thing the QXCI did not find. Insert drum roll: CANCER.

"I've tested you from one side to the other. Every form of cancer comes up negative."

Hmmmmmmm!?!!

We were starving at this point, so there was no time to ponder the disconnect between Bob's blinking box and Dr. Tien's Positron Emission Tomography. I paid Bob with a wad of twenties because, as he explained, "What I do is highly illegal in the state of Georgia."

With two big bags of remedies, we loaded the car and drove home watching the fast-food chains fly by. Starving from the ordeal, I longed for an ammonia burger, salmonella sandwich, or antibiotic

9. "Dr. Bill Nelson." 2015. The Quantum Centre. Accessed October 25. http://www.quantumcentre.com/footer-pages.php?page_id=37.

chicken finger — anything, even a verboten raw carrot (71 glycemic-index).

Later, we shared our adventure with Miriam. She was horrified at the idea of coffee enemas ("you're stimulating a poison response from your liver,") but Karen was undeterred. Proponents claim that coffee enemas cleanse the liver and gallbladder and purge the body of bile, waste, and accumulated toxins. I won't go into the details, but Karen became quickly adept with the flushing paraphernalia.

With the liver flush complete, the next step in Bob's protocol was a colonic. Julie suggested a visit to the legendary Horace, aka the Colonic King of South Carolina. I'll let Karen and Julie tell their story:

Karen: Julie, you suggested we visit Horace, and I thought, "If I'm going to have a colonic, why not go with the best, even if it's off the beaten path."

Julie: Exactly. Horace is totally off-the-grid; a visit to Horace is like going to the Twilight Zone.

Karen: The crazy thing is that you can't get there by Google Maps. The street's not listed, so his wife gave us these weird directions over the phone: "Do this, then do that, then you ride the roller coaster." It was a rolly backwoods road. When we finally arrived, there was nothing but scrub brush, scraggly woods, and people living in double-wides.

Julie: I tell people, when you pull up to Horace's, be prepared. It's a bit of shock.

Karen: My first thought was, Oh-My-God.

Julie: Horace's house is completely handmade… from scraps, recycled windows, not a matching piece anywhere. Nothing is square. Even the driveway is bizarre. Nasty bits of indoor-outdoor carpet cover a dirt drive. When we went inside, the set-up for colonics was a colema board on a toilet, a bucket on the wall that he adds oxygen into, and a hose. I doubt that any of it is legal. Horace is in his eighties. He hooked me up and proceeded to give me this extremely aggressive lymphatic massage. He wrings you out like a corkscrew. Anybody who has any inhibitions about being lathered up with oil, then aggressively massaged on their breasts, and everywhere else, forget it. Don't see Horace.

Karen: You have to go with it.

Julie: It never felt inappropriate. He's definitely in a different world while he's working on you. He would sense this black, dark energy pushing through, then announce, "It's comin'," and sure enough this intense burning stuff came through. Thirty minutes into the colonic, I felt rocks coming through my gut, and I wondered, "Where the heck is this stuff coming from?"

Karen: I heard that he was trained by a Cherokee medicine man, Chief Two Trees. I think he's a true healer. He carries this confidence, this sense of knowing, but also deep humility. Energetically, you just feel it.

Julie: When I came out of the session, I felt this vivid clarity — almost high. Bruce, I don't think Horace would be your thing.

Karen laughed at the thought of Horace wringing me out.

By now, stacks of herbs, high-end supplements, and healing gadgets cluttered our kitchen counter. Karen also listened to a Walkman-sized BioAcoustics device that emitted custom-tailored healing frequencies that a healing genius deduced from a recording of Karen's voice.

I was not a big believer in Karen's throw-everything-at-it approach, but I admired her perseverance. Following every last crumb, Karen discovered Bernice, a leading practitioner of nutrigenomics — how foods interact with specific genes to increase the risk of diseases.

So, now you're with Bernice," I challenged, feeling a little snarky.

"Yeah, and so?" Karen countered.

"Didn't you encounter Bernice at the beginning, before you even started chemo?"

"That's right," Karen replied.

"So, why did you have to journey through Bernice, Catherine,

Zora, Bob, Horace, Elaine, coffee enemas, vegetarianism, BioAcoustics, and back to Bernice? Why not stay with Bernice?"

"That's not how a healing journey works," Karen countered. "You're supposed to be Mr. Octave. There are no straight lines in nature. Maybe, I wasn't ready."

I should mention that 60 years ago, my grandfather, Nathan Saltzman, an internist with a naturopathic bent, remarked that one day doctors would be able to scan your body, determine which chemical bits you need and prescribe the remedies. That day is here.

For ninety-nine dollars, Karen spit into a bottle and sent it off to 23andMe — the high tech/low-cost genotyping enterprise co-founded by the former wife of the Google founder, Sergey Brin.

A complete copy of an individual's DNA is called the genome. It contains all the information needed to create a you or me — more than 3 billion DNA base pairs. There are 10 million places in the genome where a single letter of the sequence can differ from one person to the next — less than one percent. Those spelling variations are known as SNPs, or single nucleotide polymorphisms. They form the basis for the genotyping used by 23andMe. A person who has a "C" at a particular spot, for example, might be more sensitive to bitter tastes than somebody with a "G" in that spot.

We have long known that some people are sensitive to alcohol, can't drink milk, digest gluten, or handle raw garlic. Our genetic variants explain these quirks. As you dig deeper, these genetic variants, or SNPs, impact the metabolic processes of the cell, including our ability to metabolize food, deliver energy, handle stresses, clear toxins, fight off disease, and more. Conventional cancer treatments don't address the vulnerabilities caused by genetic variants, so it comes as no surprise that cancer often returns after chemo-radiation-surgery.

Holistic strategies are often successful (avoid sugar, eat organic food, exercise, etc.), but since you don't know whether the genetic vulnerability is being addressed, success can be hit-or-miss. For example, alternative practitioners might recommend switching to soy milk or taking coffee enemas, but depending on your genotype, this might be the worst advice. In Karen's case, she learned that her genotype can't handle soy and coffee. Conversely, some smokers never get lung cancer. The world's oldest recorded living human, Jeanne Calment, smoked until age 117, an indication that she had the repair mechanisms in her genes to keep her lungs functioning until she finally passed at age 122.[10]

Karen's genetic report came back with Red, Yellow, and Green notations — red: something is missing, green: everything is in place, yellow: a mixed bag. Bernice, our genetic guru, studied the report and noticed that Karen was deficient in the neurotransmitter, GABA.

GABA (Gamma Aminobutyric Acid) is a natural occurring brain chemical or neurotransmitter. An important role of GABA is to provide a calming effect to the nervous system. Low levels of GABA can cause high anxiety and chronic insomnia.

As Karen explains: "When they removed the tumor, I was amazed that my ever-present anxiety was gone."

Yes, Karen's famous anxiety. For years, I wanted to throttle her: "Get a grip!" not realizing that her apparent "character weakness" was imprinted — a small glitch in her DNA. The tumor may have been the energetic expression of one of these genetic gaps. So, the goal of nutrigenomics is to support the deficiency and fill the gap.

I should add a note that the BioAcoustic practitioner discovered similar DNA gaps simply by listening to Karen's voice. Yowza.

Bernice suggested that Karen should eliminate soy and switch to bison. After the visit, we beelined it to Ted's Montana Grill where my beloved vegetarian devoured a bison ribeye like a high school quarterback.

And since we're quack-watching, Steven Novella, MD, a clinical neurologist at the Yale University School of Medicine, thinks nutrigenetics is nonsense:

10. "Jeanne Calment." 2016. Wikipedia, the Free Encyclopedia. https://en.wikipedia.org/w/index.php?title=Nicholas_Gonzalez_(physician)&oldid=684903885.

"There is no compelling evidence for... personalized nutritional treatment based on specific genetic types."[11]

Digging deeper, I discovered that Dr. Novella serves as president of the New England Skeptical Society. He's skeptical about nutrigenomics because there aren't any studies. Right. Good luck getting Big Pharma to plunk $40 million on a clinical trial studying green smoothies.

With 23andMe, Karen now had access to 600,000 genotype variations — the genetic hand she had been dealt in the game of life. She played her hand by remaining prayerfully alert, following the bread crumbs wherever they went, and acting in the moment.

Three months after the devastating news (the little lurker in the lung), Dr. Tien arranged for another scan. Our insurance wouldn't pay for another PET scan, so Karen received a cheaper CT scan (which, we learned, captures lung tissue more clearly).

I squeezed Karen's hand as Dr. Tien entered the room.

"That spot we were concerned about," Dr. Tien announced matter-of-factly, "upon further examination, the radiologists now feel it was nothing, just some left-over scarring from your radiation treatments."

I wanted to scream, "Fuck you radiologists and the scan machine you road in on." But, I also got to savor a delicious irony: Bob "Mr. No-Carrot" Gelder and his QXCI blinkity-box had gotten it right all along:

Not a speck of cancer.

11. Novella, Stephen. 2015. "Nutrigenomics – Not Ready for Prime Time «Science-Based Medicine." Science-Based Medicine. Accessed October 25. https://www.sciencebasedmedicine.org/nutrigenomics-not-ready-for-prime-time/.

18

Bruce 2.0

The work of the mature person is to carry grief in one hand
and gratitude in the other and to be stretched large by them.
Francis Weller

So, here we are — the fateful chapter.

My idea was to give Fortune a few months to work things out. Since I'm writing this book in real time, I planned to share my mishap upfront, pad the middle with back story, and finish by bringing the reader back into my mess — hopefully miraculously fixed through good Fortune. In music, it's called vamping — a way to keep the music moving until the star returns to the stage.

I was hoping to demonstrate that by noticing, trusting, and stepping through open doors, you too, can open to Fortune. Just let go, stay buoyant and let the miracle unfold. If Deepak and Oprah can reveal the secrets to prosperity, why not me?

Here's the problem. Writing a book about buoyancy while on a sinking raft doesn't leave much room for error. It's been a year since a fluke Georgia earthquake pulled me out of bed, and I have to admit, I'm frustrated.

Along the way, I've learned that Fortune and Misfortune are

inseparable. They are the twin agents of change — the push-pull engine that moves the story forward. And, if you're in it for the transformation, it's all about the story — not the payoff.

It's taken a year, but I have begun to embrace my crisis as an improbable gift. When you follow bread crumbs, you invite Hazard. And, if you stay with the journey, riding the Octave through the *Mi-Fa, Si-Do,* and beyond, real change is possible. This is the art of living.

> The story of my life can be defined in three words:
> I was raw, then cooked, and then burnt.
> –Rumi

Change is never comfortable, and that's why I'm pissed and frustrated. Money has been a blessing and a curse in my life — my money *blurse.* I like the word *blurse* (blessing/curse) instead of karma because *karma* implies that you (or someone in your family line) screwed up and now you must pay the price.

Our karmic tendencies only reveal themselves as life is lived. Others can see them, but for us, karma lurks in our blind spot. Anxiety plagued Karen, and now it seems that her niece has inherited the anxiety strands of the family genome — a karmic tendency that will likely drive her story going forward. Since the niece is getting married in two weeks, I'd like to diverge and offer her fiance a short didactic:

Dear Fiance: You are marrying a marvelous creature with some funky neurotransmitter pathways. This lovely person will require the following care:

1. *She needs you to remain buoyant and even-keeled. Morose states are not allowed.*
2. *She requires 15 minutes of caressing at bedtime, regardless of your physical state or disposition.*
3. *Despite the insurmountable challenge for a guy, you must master the use of emotionally-affirming language.*
4. *Baptist ministers often add a vow that the wife must submit to the*

*husband. Frankly, it's the other way around. You must trust her
intuitive guidance systems implicitly — even when she latches onto a
cockamamie mission.*

Okay, back to my *blurse*.

My dad, Ed Miller, was a creative visionary, but horrible with
making money. I don't think he cared about money, not a lick. He
started Sherwood Electronics in the 1950s and invented the modern
stereo receiver. When he acquired a partner to fund the business, he
neglected to claim much of an equity stake for his intellectual capital.
According to my mom, his competitors (Fisher, Harman Kardon,
Scott) copied his designs for the first solid state receiver, digital tuner,
and stereo FM. Those guys went on to create monuments in their
names (Avery Fisher Hall, Harman Family Foundation). Harman was
recently purchased by Samsung for $8 billion. In contrast, my dad
was more interested in gardening. He eventually moved to Malibu
where he could garden year-round and leave this world without a
penny to his name.

I pride my dad on a clean exit, but for me, the money *blurse* has
been more of a curse — a Dickens ghost that regularly visits to move
my story forward. I begrudgingly accept the blessing part — that self-
knowledge comes from living at your edge. But it gets a bit tiring
to keep raising the stakes, up-shifting to new and greater levels of
trust. There are people in this world who are never forced to trust.
They might have predictable jobs, or a comfortable trust fund, or a
rapacious drive that can't possibly fit through the eye of the needle.

So, here's where my *blurse* stood on the night of Karen's brain
surgery:

- Wife: Stage 4 metastatic cancer in the brain and lung.

- Design Coup, Inc.: Dissolved. No source of income.

- Magnatize, Inc.: Joint venture with AutoTrader.com relinquished.

- Karen's dream job: Starts in two days, minus part of her right occipital lobe.

- Overhead: Three mortgages, private education, looming medical bills.

- Savings: Consumed to pay off the business loan.

- Job prospects: Ha. Two years from retirement age.

- On the horizon: Bruce is about to become a full-time caregiver.

- Freelance: Am I too old to conduct business in coffee shops?

- Fortune: There's a whiff of blessing in all this, but not ready to go there.

Bottom line: Short of a burning bush or an alien abduction, I could see no way to make this kettle of fish work out.

So, at 4:00 a.m., the night of the surgery, heart crushed by despair, I beseeched the universe to guide me through my swirl of doomsday thoughts. What should I do? Be proactive, reactive, or non-active?

Joseph Campbell came to mind:

> If you do follow your bliss, you put yourself on a kind of track that has been there all the while, waiting for you, and the life that you ought to be living is the one you are living.[1]

Joseph Campbell, you can bliss my ass. I just want to pay the bills.

So, what to do? Since buoyancy worked for Karen, maybe I could also float to the surface. If God is writing the script, perhaps, like a Good Writer, He or She also sprinkles clues. So, I made an eternal vow:

> *I will remain mindful to every encounter, responsive to every seed thought, and focused on every breadcrumb that comes my way.*

That was my plan on the day of surgery. When my buddy, Jim,

---

1. Campbell, Joseph, and Bill Moyers. 1991. The Power of Myth. Anchor.

suggested I contact a fellow parent who worked in a local marketing firm, I felt vindicated. Fortune delivered Judi, my first breadcrumb.

Waking in a sweat at 4:00 a.m., I didn't procrastinate. I texted my friend, Connie, oblivious to the etiquette of messaging in the wee hours.

> Connie, do you have Judi's contact info? I need to keep pursuing ideas and leads to keep sane amid the crush of events.

Three hours later, my phone bleeped; I had Judi's number. Woohoo, my plan was working. There was light in the tunnel, and the breadcrumbs were forming a loaf. I immediately sent Judi a text:

> Hi, Judi. This is Bruce Miller. Karen and I have had some dramatic life events land in our lap, and Jim suggested you might be a person I should talk to. I would love to get on your official calendar to meet.

Ten days later we met (those breadcrumbs are annoyingly slow). Judi explained that her agency, "Fizz" did "word of mouth" marketing which was more like un-marketing than what I did. Judi offered to introduce me to her friend Pam who did traditional marketing. I waited several days for the intro, then received the inevitable text from Judi:

> Bruce, I misplaced your email address. Please send it to me again, and I will make the intro.

The crows were eating my breadcrumbs, but I vowed to stay buoyant and on track.

I finally arranged to meet Pam and her creative director. Being a lunch meeting, I ordered a chicken salad, so I could schmooze and sell without chewing and choking. Pam found my brand strategy piece interesting but had to rush off mid-lunch.

A few days later, I sent a follow-up and received the requisite rebuff:

> Hi Bruce, Thanks for the follow-up. I am swamped with client and new business meetings. Let's try to connect later in March or April — Pam

Did I mention that this was January? Alright, I'm staying buoyant, but God, please, throw me a bone!

Our accountant insisted that I drive a stake through the corporate heart of Design Coup and leave no trace. But, I ignored her and kept the Web site contact page up. The strategy worked. From the Design Coup contact form:

> We are a for-profit, social-purposed business in Chattanooga that offers outsourced call center services. We believe it is our God-given responsibility to use our time, talents, and resources to improve the lives of the suffering. Our passion is helping abandoned children and disenfranchised adults around the world.
>
> We provide a supportive workplace with chaplains, coaches, and co-workers who care for and love one another. We then use our profits to support widows and orphan ministries around the world.
>
> I'm looking to create a new brand platform from which we can build new websites, collateral, etc.
>
> Kurt
> Support Seven

Hmm? A God-directed call center business with co-workers who love each other, support abandoned children and need a brand platform.

My first thought was to question whether my "breadcrumb vow" was such a smart move. But, staying true to mission, I wrote back:

> Hi Kurt,
> Thanks for reaching out. I appreciate your branding challenge – to find the right balance between two elements of your brand identity — as a proven solution to the business community and your larger mission in ministry.

"Branding challenge" was an understatement. It would be easier to brand a mortuary-massage parlor than a Christian-themed call center. I set up a call to sell my branding skills.

Straight into it, Kurt pressed me: "So, what experience do you have branding a social-purpose business?"

Social-purpose business? I deftly queried Wikipedia: (*a business that maximizes improvements in human and environmental well-being, rather than maximizing profits*). I name-dropped Thrive Farmers Coffee, got over the hump, and sent off a proposal.

Then Kurt came back:

Bruce,
   Candidly, I've been struggling because another small agency in Nashville that I know is also deeply involved in the Social Enterprise Alliance. They have a staff of 5 people and offered a price of $2500 for the Brand Workshop. When I add up your Discovery, Brand Story Workshop, and Brand Platform (which I'm calling Phase I), the cost is $6850.
   How confident are you that we'll get the necessary depth, discovery, and rigor to get to the right place for Phase I.
   Kurt

I figured Kurt's other agency was a ruse, and I was determined not to let this fish get away. So, I lowered the price a smidge, pumped up my bravado, explained that my wife was a Presbyterian minister, name-dropped Chick-fil-A whose Corporate Purpose is to "Glorify God by being a faithful steward," and got the gig. Woohoo... The cranky gears of Fortune were turning in my favor!

At this point, Kurt and I started to bond, sharing buzzwords about "purpose-driven culture," "social enterprise," and how SupportSeven was responding to a higher calling. A few days later, the next shoe dropped:

Bruce,
   A question came up that I wanted to bounce off of you...
   As I've mentioned before, SupportSeven was originally set up to support the online payday lending activity for our owner. There has

been a lot of negative press in which SupportSeven has been mentioned relative to this activity; albeit mostly local. However, when one Googles "SupportSeven," there are a few articles that are negative in nature. I'm wondering if that might "spook" some potential new clients.

Kurt

Feeling "spooked" by this revelation, I bought a one-day subscription to the Times Free Press of Chattanooga to discover what was there. Ellis Smith, a courageous, local investigative reporter had written several articles about Carey Brown, SupportSeven's behind-the-scenes owner:

Letter Stymies Payday Empire of Chattanooga's Carey Brown

Carey V. Brown thought he was safe.

Since at least 2005, he's paid lawyers from Canada, Nevada, Georgia and Tennessee to craft an interlocking web of businesses that shielded his online payday loans from legal scrutiny, allowing him to charge interest rates in excess of the legal limit in many states, according to lawsuits filed across the United States.

Brown believed he was immune from state laws because he was operating from the nebulous world of the Internet... The 50 states, Brown was convinced, could do nothing to stop him.

Brown had the situation under control. He had all the angles covered. Except one.

Without warning, the business he had worked his life to build came crashing down. The legal and philanthropic walls he had built for himself were rendered impotent. Someone finally outsmarted the payday genius from Chattanooga.

Wow. Who was this modern-day Clark Kent who outwitted the untouchable Carey Brown? So, I read on:

It was a little-known New York official named Ben Lawsky, who rose through the ranks prosecuting terrorists and the mafia, who ultimately found a way to stop Brown.

Servers in Bermuda and on Indian reservations kept investigators guessing at the true scope and location of his businesses. Brown's legal team sued workers who talked to outsiders or violated non-compete agreements. His businesses were incorporated in Nevada, which has no usury laws. He paid third parties to maintain obscure post office box addresses for some of his companies, most of which were actually based in Chattanooga.

But that didn't matter on Aug. 6, when Brown's empire began to unravel.[2]

Whoa whoa whoa. My *terra* was losing its *firma*. My years-ago encounter with the greatest con man on earth was *deja vu-ing*.

I devoured everything I could find on Carey Brown — that he started his career in Rossville, Georgia, a dumpy little town across the border from Chattanooga and worked his way through college at Happy Motors, a used car lot that offered easy credit, car title loans, and check cashing. Brown was smart to realize that the future of high-risk finance would live on the Internet.

Brown started PayDayMax.com, MyCashNow.com, and DiscountAdvances.com to offer payday loans. If you needed a quick $100 to pay your power bill, payday lenders deposited the money into your checking account using electronic transfers (the ACH system) as an advance until your next paycheck came in. When payday came, the lender withdrew interest plus fees, but typically not the $100 loan. This was called *churn*. The original $100 continued to generate interest at usurious rates and quickly became $200. The scam is that the incoming paycheck does not settle the debt. The consumer must directly contact the payday lender to pay off the loan, thus, the need for an enormous call center.

The news article described how Brown scattered every functional piece of his business into untraceable parts using Indian tribes, off-shore Web servers, and overseas shell companies. The call center, ACH transactions, Web development, and other functions were broken into separate stand-alone businesses with contracts to handle the payday work.

2. Smith, Elllis. 2015. "Letter Stymies Payday Empire of Chattanooga's Carey Brown." Timesfreepress.com. Accessed October 25. http://www.timesfreepress.com/news/local/story/2013/aug/27/a-letter-stymies-payday-empire/117089/.

With an estimated $1 million to $2 million in daily revenues, scrutiny of Brown's empire heightened. Brown publicly announced that he planned to give $1 billion to charity, including millions to feed starving children around the world. He also gave to conservative causes like Focus on the Family and to Tennessee politicians.

But that didn't stop 43-year old Ben Lawsky, just two years into his job as New York's first Superintendent of Financial Services. He reasoned that if the states were unable to stop Carey Brown, he would cut off the oxygen Brown needed to operate — the ACH system that moves money electronically. Lawsky confronted the big banks with a veiled threat, telling them, "It is in your bank's long-term interest to take appropriate action to help ensure that it is not serving as a pipeline for illegal conduct." In essence, he asked them to choose sides: Carey Brown or The State of New York. The banks quickly pulled Carey Brown's plug from the ACH system.

Ten days later, Brown assembled a meeting of his workers. Effective immediately, seven companies closed and four hundred of his workers lost their jobs with no severance.

Wow, wow, wow — a few negative articles? Stunned, I called Kurt.

"Kurt, I'm troubled by this, the guy, his line of business, the whole thing," I explained.

"Yeah, it looks pretty bad," Kurt reasoned. "But, if you bounce a ten dollar check, what's that... thirty bucks in fees? That's usurious. We provide a lifeline to millions of people to avoid these onerous charges."

My mind reeled — less from the economics than the cultural crazy of the cult. And Focus on the Family? Wasn't that the Christian ayatollah, James Dobson, who claimed that the SpongeBob SquarePants was promoting homosexuality?

"Bruce," Kurt continued. "Here's the bottom line. Four hundred Chattanooga families are counting on you."

And with that, the misguided breadcrumbs entered my mind: "*I will remain mindful to every encounter, responsive to every seed thought, and focused on every breadcrumb that comes my way,* blah, blah blah." What if it's a crumb from a poisoned snickerdoodle!? Then what?

I see-sawed: Ethics versus flow, trust versus trouble. My mind raced in circles. Finally, I reasoned that every company I ever worked with was driven by corporate cult politics or the CEO's personal agenda.

"Okay, I'm on board," I conceded with a strained one-for-all spirit.

"Great," Kurt replied. "See you next week."

As I drove to Chattanooga, I reflected on a trip I took to the Soviet Union during the paranoid years of Reagan's "Evil Empire." At that time, my hope was to connect heart-to-heart with the "evil" Russians and stay grounded in our shared humanity. Instead, as I stepped off the plane in Moscow, I was shocked to discover that against the drab backdrop of the Soviet Union, I stuck out like a DayGlo Uncle Sam.

Would I stick out with these payday Christians? Would they spot me as a Jewish Sufi Whirling Dervish with a Mumbai guru espousing alien ideas in the heart of Carey Brown's cabal?

SupportSeven's parking lot had space for 200 cars. I pulled into an open spot which brought the car count up to six. The entrance resembled a minimum security prison. A security guard gave me a form and I slid it back through the bullet-resistant acrylic glass. He gave me my badge and buzzed the electronic lock to let me in.

Kurt greeted me, and together we walked past row upon row of empty cubicles. The vacant industrial space looked like any other defunct corporate setting, except for the walls. Floor-to-ceiling murals of starving children, desperate third-world suffering, and Christian-themed graphics sent a spooky chill up my spine.

"Toto, we're not in Kansas anymore," I murmured. Or maybe that was the point — this *was* Kansas.

For the next two days, I took Kurt's team through an in-depth brand strategy session. There was Kurt, plus two young uber–Christians, and two evangelical Costa Ricans who ran the overseas call operations. Kurt was the only person who knew anything about branding.

"Let us pray," Kurt began, bowing his head, "that this enterprise advances the Kingdom to grow and prosper..."

I snuck a peek to check everyone's level of conviction.

"...and, because we are commanded to love our neighbor as our self, we ask that our efforts serve the Kingdom and relieve pain and suffering for the least of these, in Jesus' name, amen."

I was struck by the irreconcilable irony of it all — that our efforts would actually *increase* suffering, that women would be denied family planning, that political power would skew to the wealthy, that young teens would struggle with self-loathing over their sexual orientation, that dogma would flourish, that minorities would be disenfranchised, and that Jesus' name would be co-opted to serve a purpose contrary to the life he lived.

Oh well. If there is a higher calling, it must certainly be to bond with your neighbor. I let my heart connect with the cabal and together, we discussed brand strategy as if it was Bible study. Our white board filled with ideas, about our "culture of service," our "servant heart" and our "mission to do good." Little by little I built a bridge between brand strategy and the Christian calling. Before long, business strategy was winning out over the pasty praise.

Every so often, the man himself, Carey Brown, would peek into our creative cauldron. Wow, the billionaire of payday lending, unstoppable by 50 states, checking us out. Carey Brown looked like he had just come off the lot, having sold a Chevy Vega to a single mother. Carey would stare at the white board, stare at us, register a quizzical look, then saunter out. I took this as a bad sign. It never goes well if the decision-maker doesn't participate in the process.

I was alone in the conference room unwrapping my sandwich when Carey wandered in during lunch. He didn't know what to do with me — me holding court in his elaborate high-tech conference room, the power center of his Kingdom.

"Do you know much about me?" Carey asked with a bit of Tennessee twang.

"Oh, hi," I responded. "No, just what I read in the paper" (shit, wrong answer).

"You always believe what you read in the paper?" Carey was trying to penetrate my game.

With a quick backpedal, I answered, "Uh, no… every paper has its ax to grind."

That seemed to be a good enough answer from someone who reads the New York Times in its entirety. The bad news: the outcome of our brand work was now suspect.

After lunch, we worked to rename SupportSeven into something less "spooky." With a stroke of Fortune, I remembered that the predecessor to CheckFree was a defunct Christian software company named Servantus. A quick domain search revealed that the name might be available for around $2000. "Servantus.com" would hit all the marks: dot com, single-word, techie-sounding, and most importantly — "Servant" was embedded into the name.

We worked on the brand position and tagline and came up with the following:

S E R V A N T U S

Mission-Driven Customer Engagement

It was a slam-dunk with high-fives all around. I headed home triumphant.

A few days later, I received a call from Kurt.

"Carey walked into the conference room after we met and saw one of the throwaway ideas on the board."

"Oh really, which one?" I asked.

"MISSION CONNECT,

Servant-Driven Customer Engagement,"

Kurt replied. "He loves it."

"We were just flipping the words around," I protested. "Can you tell him that 'servant-driven' sounds like 'Driving Miss Daisy' or maybe a coolie pulling a rickshaw?"

"I need you to work up a presentation explaining Servantus for tomorrow," Kurt replied. "I think I can sell this."

Kurt succeeded, (woohoo!) so a full year of work awaited. There would be two brands, two Web sites, collateral, sales tools, SEO, email marketing, trade shows, photography, and a trip to Costa Rica to film a video. I hired a designer, and we started work immediately.

Three weeks later, I received a call from Kurt:

"I need you to stop work on the project."

"Stop, meaning a change in direction?" I asked.

"No stop meaning it's over. The burn rate on the cash is killing us," Kurt explained. "In actuality, it's the Feds. They are starting to breathe down Carey's neck."

"Wow, I'm stunned."

"Yeah, me too," Kurt replied sounding defeated. "If you hear of anyone looking for a CEO or an SVP of marketing, I'll be out there looking, too."

Fortunately, I got paid. Unfortunately, my buoyancy project was taking on water, again. Two months later, I opened the New York Times:

New York Prosecutors Charge Payday Loan Firms With Usury:
A trail of money that began with triple-digit loans to troubled New Yorkers and wound through companies owned by a former used-car salesman in Tennessee led New York prosecutors on a yearlong hunt through the shadowy world of payday lending. On Monday, that investigation culminated with state prosecutors in Manhattan bringing criminal charges against a dozen companies and their owner, Carey Vaughn Brown... [3]

Okay, Mr. Fortune. My big Bruce 2.0 opportunity appears out of nowhere, then this. Open and close, open and close. What's going on?

J.G. Bennett observed the open-and-close phenomenon in the movement of pieces on the backgammon board. The dice roll randomly, moving the checkers to open points — two circular

---

3. Silver-Greenberg, Jessica. 2015. "New York Prosecutors Charge Payday Loan Firms With Usury." DealBook. Accessed October 25. http://dealbook.nytimes.com/2014/08/11/new-york-prosecutors-charge-payday-lenders-with-usury/.

movements, clockwise and counter-clockwise. Bennett recognized these openings and closings in the behavior of materials like ice, steel, and glass which when heated begin to distort and flow. He described the transition from solid glass to molten glass:

> "There are holes in the glass, and we know that these holes make it possible for one element of the material to enter into a hole and release a place for another one to enter… The melting of a piece of glass is really the same kind of process…as the game of backgammon. Someone, or something, is throwing the dice, and when the turn comes for the particular little aggregate of silicate to fall into a hole that is available, it will do so, and so the glass flows."[4]

I was now half way through my melt-down year, and my life was still in flux. I wanted to understand my molten life, but also desperately wanted something solid to hang onto. All I had was perplexity:

> The purpose of Divine Guidance is to bring us to a state of perplexity.
> -Ibn Arabi

Not much sympathy from Ibn Arabi, the 12th century Andalusian Sufi mystic. Soon, another hole opened:

> Subject: Available for a project?
> Bruce,
> We have an important project for Kimberly-Clark that I think you could help us with. If so, I would like to set up a briefing for Thursday a.m. of this week.
> Pam

Well, that's nice. Four months after my strategic chicken salad with Pam, the door finally opened. Pam set up a meeting, and I got the download from Nathan, her client-strategy guy in San Francisco. Five days later, I presented four designs for Kimberly-Clark's college recruiting campaign. They loved it.

---

4. Bennett, J.G. 1991. Hazard: The Risk of Realization. Revised edition. Santa Fe, N.M: Bennett Books.

Two hours later, I received an email from Pam:

Hello
  Just wanted to reiterate how pleased I was with your concepts. Very thorough and strategic. Thanks.
  I also wanted to have a different sort of conversation with you. Nathan is leaving the company which leaves a gap on our account team. I am looking for a senior consultant who can help build business and lead client strategy. Are you interested in talking about this?
  Pam

Hmmm. Nathan was job-searching in San Francisco. Maybe this project was actually an audition for his replacement. I wrote back:

Hi Pam,
  I'm just beginning to hit my stride as a freelancer, but I would love to meet and talk. What time is good for you?
  Bruce

And then, nothing.
  I sent another follow-up. Still nothing. What's going on?
  Around this time, I began to experience pronounced shifts in my sense of self — the process described as *fana* — the annihilation or dissolving of self. I've experienced periodic spurts of *fana* for decades; that's how we grow. But this time, the universe chose a remarkably inconvenient time to dissolve my inner bearings.
  Karen and I were enjoying a beautiful end-of-summer day at our tranquil mountain cabin. Part of Karen's regimen for lung cancer recovery was to swim across the little lake. Like tortoise and hare, Karen never broke from her frog-like breaststroke while I swam in spurts, changing strokes, resting, and sprinting.
  Halfway across the lake, I started feeling spacey. What is this? A panic attack? A medical event? Something esoteric?
  "Karen, I'm feeling funny... not sure what's going on," I puffed. Not a good time to create alarm, but the bottom of my being was

falling out. "Karen swim back and get the kayak. I'm going to continue across."

In a panic, I reached the dock and plopped down like an exhausted otter. Heart racing, anxiety through the roof, I took stock of my woo-woo situation. Was this garden-variety *fana*, some kind of nirvana, or something more serious?

Karen returned with the kayak and paddled me back. When we reached the cabin, Zora, an intuitive healer friend arrived to perform her healing magic.

"I think you're shedding some sort of spiritual skin," Zora reassured.

Karen was thinking, "terrible, horrible medical event." Whatever it was, it wasn't going away.

When I got home, not knowing where to turn, I called Bhagwan in Switzerland.

"Hi Bhagwan. Do you have a moment to talk?"

"Well, normally, you must make an appointment," he replied, "but we can talk."

"I'm a bit concerned. I was swimming; I felt spacey, panic, but also a weird feeling of disconnection from my body and mind. How do I know if an unexplained experience is spiritual or medical?

"Was it pleasurable?" Bhagwan asked.

"Uh, no, hardly."

"Hmm," he pondered. "I don't think there is any medical issue."

"Okay, that's good. But, I'm feeling unsteady. Something in my subconscious is dissolving. I feel like a polar bear who collapsed through a sheet of melting ice."

For the next twenty minutes, we breathed together over the transatlantic phone.

"It's okay to let go," Bhagwan reassured.

"Really. Just let go?"

"Yes. Let go of the struggle and just be yourself."

"What does that mean, be myself?"

"Stay in your center," Bhagwan instructed. "This feeling of disorientation is in the mind."

I was startled that I could feel Bhagwan's closeness despite the distance. I took a centering breath, adjusted to the new state, and began to feel composed. We were quiet together for some time.

"Bhagwan, can I ask a question?"

"Yes."

"It's a little off-topic."

"That's okay."

"It's been bedeviling me since you were with us in July, and now I'm writing this book..."

"Go ahead" Bhagwan replied.

"When we talked about synchronicity, you said that the entire universe is synchronous."

"Yes, every moment."

"So, what about when we're reacting, doing stupid stuff, making a mess in the world — is that included in *everything is synchronous?* Or just when we're harmonious?"

"Yes, that is also included," Bhagwan explained. "Something happens, then there's a reaction, then it gets worse, then there's a correction, then there's a war, then peace, then prosperity, civilizations rise, then collapse. Everything is synchronous."

"Hmm. Thanks."

I left it at that because the idea that everything is synchronous was unsettling. I've always placed a value on motive and mindfulness, but Bhagwan seemed to be dismissing it. Everything is synchronous.

Giovanni's dictum reappeared: *It doesn't matter what you do. It only matters that you do it.*

Well, the synchronous universe still had me out of work, which meant someone, somewhere was probably slammed.

You can imagine my excitement when the following email arrived:

Subject: "Partnering Possibility."

My friend Jim had developed benchmarking software that he

wanted to market. I wasn't remotely interested in benchmarking, but given my sinking sense of economic survival, I threw myself at his offer as if it was the next Facebook.

In the space of three weeks, I developed a multimedia business launch for our new business: Benchmark Genie. I leveraged connections, and we pitched NAPA Auto Parts corporate.

Soon after the NAPA pitch, through a web search, I discovered a direct competitor. Jim cleverly posed as a potential customer and took a tour of the competition. An hour later, Jim emailed me:

Subject: "We're Toast."

Another hole opened and closed.

I began to inquire into the zombie-like affliction of my despair. What is this constriction that has taken over my feeling body? Why doesn't it go away?

According to author/therapist, Francis Weller, depression and despair are natural functions. The psyche sounds a wake-up call to address an inner distress:

In depression the psyche says, "I'm not moving another step forward. I'm stopping right here until you pay attention to me."[5]

That's well and good, but I had been lavishing attention on my psyche for months, and now I desperately wanted to turn the page.

With despair, we're talking about the solar plexus — the largest nerve cluster in the body. This network of nerves and ganglia connects to the abdominal organs and radiates outward like the rays of the sun. In common parlance, it's the "pit" of your stomach. When fear and despair grip this plexus, it dims one's buoyancy like the moon eclipsing the sun.

Norman Cousins famously researched the biochemistry of human emotions. He lived with a life-threatening form of arthritis and

5. McKee, Tim. 2015. "The Geography Of Sorrow: Francis Weller On Navigating Our Losses." Sun Magazine, October.

survived on a regimen of vitamin C and Marx Brothers films. Somehow, he was able to kickstart his energy flow by laughing.[6]

My own negative vortex kept sucking me down big time, so I'm not sure watching Groucho and Chico would substitute for a paycheck. Juggling money to cover medical bills and three mortgages over the course of a year was fraying my nerves.

In traditional cultures people allowed a year or more to move through a significant loss, so maybe I had unrealistic expectations of where I was supposed to be at this point. Regardless, this was my emotional state when we traveled to Cincinnati to check out colleges for our son. What should have been a joyous rite of passage for our family was dampened by the chronic sense of doom that had seized my solar plexus.

I kept my game face on as we climbed the winding lane up to Alms Park, a century-old hilltop park overlooking the Ohio River. After strolling through the park, we started back down the steep curving street.

In a fit of help-me-god frustration, I kicked a black walnut. The rolling walnut careened toward the striped center line, then continued to roll down the street, curving left, curving right, all the way down the hill, never leaving the center line. Maybe the universe was synchronous after all.

"Did you see that?"

"See what?" Karen asked.

"The walnut." I pointed. "See it? It followed the yellow line all the way down the street."

"Really?"

"You know what?"

What?" Karen asked.

"I think we're going to be okay."

"I just want you to not be so morose," Karen complained. "I can't stand it when you're morose."

6. Cousins, Norman. 2005. Anatomy of an Illness: As Perceived by the Patient. Twentieth Anniversary Edition edition. New York: W. W. Norton & Company.

I don't think Karen believed in the cosmic enormity of my walnut.

The next morning, I awoke unsettled. It was 5:00 a.m. I laid in bed, still in the grip of my despair. Healing begins with recognition, so I placed my attention on the incessant rawness in my solar plexus — just pure awareness on the sensation. I breathed in and out, focusing on the gnawing sensation for an hour.

What the hell was that? Something shifted inside. Like an inner weather system moving from low pressure to high, maybe Bruce 2.0 was kicking *in utero*. I looked at my phone. It was 6:17 a.m.

I laid there for a few more minutes, and then *pzzong* — an email arrived on my phone at 6:25 a.m. It was from Adam, another prospective client who had fallen into the void. He was responding to a proposal I sent weeks earlier. The project was to re-brand his international parcel shipping company.

> Hi Bruce, thanks for your follow-up. Haven't forgotten about this. Can we plan to talk Tuesday morning about this?

For that brief moment, the universe proved to be synchronous — or at least Adam, my inbox, and the pit of my stomach were talking to each other.

Life is filled with seemingly random events: an email arrives, we feel down, the dog snuggles close, we feel up, we have a thought, we sneeze, we open the email, we have another thought, we take a walk, we remember the oven, we turn around, and so on.

This was Miriam's *noticing* — noticing the interconnectedness of seemingly unrelated events. As I laid in bed, I noticed the synchronicity between my energetic shift and Adam clicking "send." These events were talking to me, encouraging me to absorb Bhagwan's advice:

> "It's okay to let go. Let go of the struggle, and just be yourself."

But, suppose the universe *is* synchronous? Who's driving this bus? What does it mean to make an effort? What about free will and choice? Are we just puppets in God's hand to support a larger synchronous drama?

Adam and I met. I prepared for the branding project, but then he postponed a couple of times, presumably so a brand guy from InterContinental Hotels could join.

"Great," I thought, hanging to my hopes, "Now I can get my Brand Story process in front of a big-time corporate brand guy."

My brand strategy idea was to reposition Adam's shipping business from a post office alternative to a seamless e-channel connecting his clients with overseas markets.

The day before the workshop, I had everything ready to go. Then, I received the following email:

> Bruce, thanks for the follow-up. I want to table this project for now. I'll be in touch. Adam.

And that was that.

Fortunately, I could still keep groceries on the table by making periodic Web updates for an old healthcare client. One day, they asked me to update a career link. After making the change, I tested it. Indeed.com, a job site, appeared. The site asked me to enter *WHAT* and *WHERE*.

On a whim, I typed in *Marketing Strategy*, and *Atlanta*. Up came, "Marketing Strategy Consultant, Slalom Consulting."

Wow, a job. What a crazy idea. (I have to interject, that in my entire adult life, I've never had a job job. Always freelance, self-employed, or owning a company.) The universe was telling me that I needed a job. Yes, what a far-out concept. A job!

I put together a resume that obscured my age and lack of a conventional job record and submitted it online.

Two days later, I received a call — not from Slalom Consulting — but from my close friend, Amy.

"Bruce, I was thinking about your situation, and Jim Cope came to mind."

"Really?" My breadcrumbs went on high alert.

"Jim Cope's a dad in Jack's class. He had a marketing career just like you, that floundered…"

"Floundered?" I objected.

"He got a job as a consultant. I can't remember the name of the company."

"Was it Slalom Consulting?" (At this point, the *synchronous* thing was getting predictable.)

"YES, it was Slalom Consulting!" Amy blurted back, stunned by the magic of it all.

Jim Cope and I met at a local coffee shop and hit it off. He bypassed the slush pile and forwarded my resume directly to Slalom's managing director. A few days later, I received an email.

"Do you have a few minutes to talk about your experience tomorrow?"

Wow. That was fast. Amy coached me on how to interview, how to use consultant-speak, and prepped me to describe a project that made a big difference for a client — apparently the standard question.

When the big phone call came, the Slalom managing director asked about my career path and seemed impressed. Next, came the Big Question:

"Tell me about a project you are particularly proud of that made a big difference for your client," she asked.

I was on it. I explained how the Wing Zone chain was losing stores, how we repositioned their brand to focus on Flavor, and how their international sales took off. I also told her how we took a back-of-the-napkin idea for a coffee company and turned it into the new artisan coffee for Chick-Fil-A.

My pitch was pitch perfect. Then silence.

"That sounds like it was a lot of fun," she said breaking the pause. "You should expect a call from someone, soon."

Fun? I mean really? Fun? And that was the last I heard from Slalom Consulting.

Didn't matter, I was on a consulting tear. I received an out-of-the-blue call from another school dad. Rick was a former big time consultant at North Highland Consulting who had just gone freelance. Rick was creating a Web site and needed advice.

"Rick, I'll just build the site for you," I said. "Maybe you can share some connections to help me launch my brand strategy business."

"Absolutely," Rick replied. "Can I get you some nice wine, as well?"

Quid pro quo was the oxygen that Rick lived on. I built the site in a day; then we met at a coffee shop so I could hand over the keys to his brand new site. He was thrilled.

Rick opened up his email program and typed the following message:

> "Hi ____. I'd like to introduce you to Bruce Miller. He's done quite a bit of work in the areas of sales & marketing strategy, and I think some of his approaches would pair up well with the work you do."

Rick then copied and pasted the message into eight emails. Boom-boom-done. Eight prospective contacts handed-off in less than a minute.

One of the contacts resulted in an in-person interview, but I was over-qualified. Another, from a guy named Bo, resulted in an initial phone meeting scheduled for December. True to form, Bo postponed until January. When that date approached, Bo wrote again:

> "Hey, Bruce! We're in the middle of some unprecedented growth....I'll have to postpone our chat for a month or so. Sorry about that. For perspective, we had our biggest year ever last year and have gotten hired for roughly 80% of that number in the last month....lots to do!"

I wanted to respond, "Sorry you're too fucking busy to need help," but instead I wrote:

> "Bo — Excited to hear that you are on a roll. If I can support any of your projects – outsourced or part of the team — let me know. Bruce."

And Bo emailed his assistant, copying me:

"Darlene. Bruce comes highly recommended from Rick. Can you tag him in our Awesome Talent database?"

Cool cool cool. The Awesome Talent database — where aging creatives are sent out to pasture.

I began to accept that Bruce 2.0 was not going to be a corporate marketing dude. I decided to accelerate my writing and think about an agent.

In a bit of synchronicity, I contacted my yoga teacher, Mandy who had a great Fortune story.

"Mandy, I would like to interview you for a book I'm writing."

"You're writing a book? You need to talk to Bret."

"Who's Bret?" I asked.

As it turned out, Bret was the bearded guy on the adjacent yoga mat. He had eight New York Times bestsellers and 2.5 million books sold, including *Monuments Men*, a film with George Clooney and a host of A-list stars.

"Really? The bearded guy doing down dog next to me is a famous author? Mandy, can you set me up?"

Bret and I met after class to talk about pitching my book. I planned to follow the advice of 17,000 websites that strongly caution: "Don't submit anything other than a one-page query letter or you'll be instantly spotted as a rube."

"Here's what I do," Bret explained in contradiction. "Submit a three-page query that pulls the reader into the flow of the story. It needs to convey the style, the scope, and the drama of the book."

"That's great advice," I said. "I would like to submit to your agent. Can I use your name?"

"Sure, no problem," Bret offered. "Not sure if it will help. Instead of a hapless intern pulling it from the slush pile, you might get the lowest staff person to read your query."

"Thank you, so much."

I sent it off. The agent's site cautioned that I should anticipate up to eight weeks for a reply. After about 12 weeks, I relegated the whole exercise to my Awesome Rejection database — the first of countless non-responses to this book.

By now, you're probably wondering, "What happened to the Cincinnati rolling walnut? The transformational shift? The synchronous email?"

Unlike causal events, transformation happens on the inside first, then the outside follows — but not the way we expect. The walnut brought my buoyancy back. My circumstances didn't change, but they ceased to weigh on my emotions. So now, I was able to follow an odd bliss that was oblivious to my burdens.

I began to compare my plight to Tommy the Alcoholic Painter. By now, Tommy had drunk through all the money I gave him, lost his girlfriend, lost his teeth, lost his place to live, and had even lost some of his internal organs. I would see him passed out near the sidewalk or in the bushes. Tommy was now Exhibit A: Unemployable.

Tommy had a buddy, Rickie the Alcoholic Yard Guy. Rickie was still employable — barely, but only when he showed up 50 percent sober. Unlike Tommy, I made a point to keep Rickie going; I was his sole client. More importantly, we both shared the desire to keep hope alive.

One day, Rickie got thrown out of his Section 8 apartment for mouthing off at the apartment manager. This was a week after he lost his ID to a vindictive cop for public drunkenness. Rickie quickly found himself on the freezing winter streets for several weeks without food, ID, shelter, or money.

Rickie mirrored my vulnerability to fate, so I owed him a minimum of solidarity. Since I was still a "high-functioning" type of guy, maybe I could get him off the street and chalk up one success in our Fortune campaigns.

Rickie and I came up against roadblock after roadblock. The Alice-in-Government-Wonderland logic went: "Don't you know, said the Hatter? You need ID to replace ID, but you clearly haven't got ID!"

Eventually, Rickie went to the Legal Aid Society who helped get his eviction reversed by a judge. Rickie also needed to reinstate his rent, so I gave him a generous cash advance that I couldn't afford.

In a stroke of timely Fortune, Rickie reclaimed his heated apartment on the same day the temperature plummeted to 10 degrees. He left a voicemail:

> "Hey, Bruce. This is Rickie. I sure want to thank you for helping me out, man. It means a lot to me. It was a whole lot of trouble, but you stayed with me. Tell Karen I'm thinking about her too. Thanks again, man."

Rickie sounded a little drunk. True to form, I haven't heard from him, or the two hundred bucks since, but I did get him a temporary win on the board of Fortune.

So, there you go. The fateful chapter comes to an inconclusive end. Not with a bang, but a whimper. After twelve months of improbable headwinds from a beneficent God who is either 1) not so beneficent, or 2) a film buff who loves down-endings, I'm still stuck in Bruce 1.0.

§

Postscript:

Last night I finished this chapter around midnight, pounding out Rickie's finale at a furious pace.

"Bruce, please come to bed," Karen pleaded.

I ignored Karen and continued to hammer at my sorrowful plight — literally banging at the keyboard to prevent my despair from crystallizing into a pattern. Clickity, clickity, I seized my buoyancy before it could descend into a permanent state of funk.

Done, done, done. Thank you. Nothing to show for it, but I exorcised the demon of despair from my heart. And with that, I climbed into bed.

"Where have you been?" Karen murmured half asleep. "Give me some rubbies."

Eight hours later, the phone:

"Hello," I yawned.

"Hi, Bruce. It's Yvonne."

"Hi, Yvonne, great to hear from you."

Yvonne was a former client who got fired two months ago and was now consulting. I never met her in person, so I was startled that she thought to give me a call.

"What's your bandwidth for a sizable project?" Yvonne asked. "It's a new healthcare company that has come together from some acquisitions. They need an entire launch — brand messaging, identity, web, trade show, collateral, video, the whole thing. It's very fast track…"

"Bandwidth?" I replied. "Uh, yes, I have bandwidth… lots of bandwidth."

So, Yvonne and I bid on the project, and within 24 hours, we got the job. A nice $28,000 gig.

Within days, four other clients appeared: a printing company, a consulting firm, a technology developer, and a home health management company — all to be serviced out of my spare bedroom.

And just like that, Bruce 2.0 was launched.

19

Let Go and Be Yourself

Obey the nature of things (your own nature)
and you will walk freely and undisturbed.
The Third Patriarch of Zen
Hsin Hsin Ming by Seng-T'san

One day into Bruce 2.0, I picked up Bhagwan at the airport. He was visiting after an itinerary that included Mumbai, Dubai, and Zurich. Somehow, he was alert and engaging.

"So how are you doing, Bruce?" Bhagwan asked.

"It's been a difficult year, but I seem to have come through it."

"That's good," Bhagwan replied.

Stretches of silence intermingle in a Bhagwan conversation. After a minute, I started again.

"Bhagwan, remember how I called you after my episode swimming across the lake?"

"Yes. You were quite concerned that you were having a health issue."

"I felt like I was dissolving. Your presence, even long distance over the phone, was very grounding."

"Of course. Space and time are just in the mind," he explained. To Bhagwan, it was all matter-of-fact.

"I wanted to thank you."

The silence took root again, then I continued.

"Bhagwan, I've been writing a book about my life journey. I even tell the story of how you brought Karen and me back together."

"I brought you back together?" Bhagwan was amazed at the notion.

"The story of Radha and Rukmini — Krishna's two wives?"

Bhagwan still drew a blank. In fairness, it had been 20 years, so I continued.

"A couple of days ago, I completed a very painful chapter at midnight and the next morning I landed an enormous job.

"That's wonderful."

"What's important was the timing. I've been living on the edge."

"Of course," Bhagwan replied. "That's how it works."

Bhagwan's nonchalance was unnerving, but I continued.

"So, when I called you during my freak-out, you said it was okay to let go and just be myself. It seemed like a benign suggestion, but I was able to hear something deeper — to actually let go."

"At that moment, you were just ripe to let go," Bhagwan replied. "If I had said it earlier — and I might have said it many times earlier — it would not have had any effect. You may have been ripe just at the time."

"I was in crisis."

"You were in crisis. You had to let go. There was no other way. I said it in a benign way, 'let go and be yourself.' But it had a great effect because in a crisis when you let go, things get clear. It's the struggling that's making the crisis in the first place. There's misfortune, and you're struggling with it, and you're in crisis. It gets worse and worse until someone tells you, let go. Letting go of everything takes you to your self. In the self, there are no problems. In the self, everything is harmonious. Everything is fortunate. You're in trust."

We drove for awhile, again in silence. Bhagwan's not one to hash things out. Whatever the question, the answer is either you're in the mind or beyond the mind. So, I tried another tack.

"Bhagwan, during this past year, I kept knocking on doors that didn't open, or if they opened, they would miraculously close. Again and again, it was clear that I couldn't manipulate life. I was trying to make something happen — mainly out of fear."

Bhagwan remained quiet, so I continued.

"You're asking me to let go and trust, yet it seems so irresponsible.

"I'll tell you what's irresponsible," Bhagwan countered. "Trusting that things are going to happen the way you think. That's irresponsible, but trust itself is not irresponsible. True trust means trusting in whatever is happening. This is acceptance. That's not irresponsible because it's from moment to moment, trusting whatever is happening. Trusting the present, be in the present; that's trust. Not that I trust my child will pass the examination. What if he doesn't? Would I be disappointed? That's not trust. True trust would be that I trust that my child will pass the examination, but if he doesn't, I don't lose trust. I trust that that's the right thing."

"That sounds like acceptance, or even resignation," I replied.

"Talking about trust is difficult," Bhagwan continued. "Trust is really being yourself. Your true self is the infinite state. That's the state of trust."

"So, to truly trust requires a tremendous amount of allowing. Is that what you are saying?"

"That's right."

"That sounds like a precarious place to live."

"It is an insecure place. It is an open place. It is a vulnerable place. It's vulnerable because there is nothing definite there. Trust is not a doing. It is not a concept or belief. You can't say, 'I trust.' It is not a mental attitude. It is being yourself, accepting what happens, and not being affected by the result of anything that happens. It's an energetic state."

"So, where's the participant in all this acceptance?" I asked.

"There is no participant. You are an infinite state. Everything is happening in you when you discover yourself as consciousness. Everything in the universe is happening in that consciousness. That's the participant."

"So, I could become a doctor, a lawyer, make babies, have a fight, whatever. The story just unfolds on its own."

"If you are identified, you think you are doing it. If you are not identified, it is just happening. It is unfolding."

"Hmm, okay." I couldn't find much to chew on in this conversation, but I continued. "So, what's the upside of living this way?"

"Freedom."

Bhagwan made this sound as if it was the most obvious thing in the world. He continued.

"To be in the mind, there is no freedom because the mind traps you. The mind binds you. It limits you, and you've lost your freedom because the mind is always in conflict. Getting beyond mind through meditation gets you free of limitation, free of the trap of the mind. You are free of anything that happens in the world. You are unaffected by anything."

"Okay, I get it, sort of," I said. "Thinking gets in the way — thinking that I'm *doing*. But, don't we live in human experience where things do affect us, where events test us, and where circumstances create suffering and struggle? Shouldn't there be a purpose to our story?"

"The suffering is the purpose," Bhagwan replied. "Why? Because the suffering brings to your notice that you are identified. If you were not identified, you wouldn't suffer. So suffering brings to your awareness the fact that you are identified. And when the suffering becomes too much, you have no other option except to inquire: What is this all about? Why am I suffering? You eventually come to understand that it's identification that's causing suffering."

"Maybe I'm suffering because something happened in my

childhood," I added. "But you're saying that if I inquire more deeply, I would recognize that suffering results from identification itself."

"Identification is the cause of suffering. With meditation, you are not disturbed by difficult situations or situations of success or failure or any misfortune. You are not affected by them. You retain your equanimity and harmony. If you are not identified, then there is no suffering. It's just something that's happening."

I couldn't digest any more, so we continued on in silence. According to Bhagwan, answers only come through the silence. Still, I didn't like the idea that life's big, purposeful events are "just something that's happening." If life's highest pursuit is to search for meaning, I wasn't ready to accept that things are "just happening."

We pulled up to the little carriage house where Bhagwan stayed, and I dragged his enormous suitcase up the stairs — a curious load for someone who spends his time meditating. Bhagwan's visits are not very social. I drop off meals, exchange a couple of words, and we sit in silence during the seminar. For this reason, the trips to and from the airport offered rare opportunities to question him about Fortune.

The challenge from these conversations was that my ideas about Fortune would get undermined in the process. I had been painting a picture where an awakened human being participates in Fortune — in making "good things happen." But Bhagwan seemed to relegate my actor to the sidelines. Life was like watching a movie where the protagonist watches as well.

Sensing a potential hole in my cosmology, I asked Bhagwan if I could interview him at length with the camera rolling.

"Of course. Ask me anything," he agreed.

Four days later, this is how it went:

> **Bruce:** Thank you, Bhagwan. We just finished a meditation seminar, and now I'd like to explore how the practice of meditation plays out in the world. First, for people who have not worked with you, could you summarize the practice of meditation?

Bhagwan: Sure. The first point is that it's not important to know how to meditate.

Bruce: Really? We just spent the weekend learning...

Bhagwan laughs.

Bhagwan: The focus of meditation should be on the question of "who's meditating" — not to do something, but to be in this question. You sit quietly; you try to be effortless in the sense that you're not doing something. You're not doing anything, but you need to be alert — alert and effortless. These are the two key words that define meditation. In that state of alert effortlessness, you can inquire into who's meditating. Who am I? That's meditation. That inquiry is meditation. Discovering who the meditator is — is meditation.

Bruce: So, it's a process of discovery through being alert and without effort.

Bhagwan: Yes. It's also important to know what's not meditation. If you're in your thoughts or your feelings or your imagination, that's not meditation. People call it meditation. For example, guided meditation. They talk you into something, into a story with a river and waterfalls, and landscapes. If you start imagining any of this, that's not meditation. That's mind. Any mental activity is not meditation. Meditation is getting beyond the mind. To get beyond the mind, you can't have any mental activity. This means you can't be engaged in your thoughts or feelings or issues or sensations. You can't be struggling.

Bruce: Again, this word "discovery."

Bhagwan: You have to discover this because you think of yourself as this body and mind. The person that you are in reality has to be discovered.

Bruce: Is it an energetic kind of discovery?

Bhagwan: Yes, it's an energetic discovery because as you inquire, the mind quietens. When the mind is quiet, there's clarity. Things are easily understood. Difficult situations are easily understood. What action needs to be taken is also easily understood. There's no conflict. There's no struggle. There's no effort. Because of the clarity, what needs to be done is easily understood. Not only is it understood, but the energy to perform that action becomes available because you're not wasting energy with turmoil and effort and struggle.

Bruce: How do we find our way forward when we're blocked? During my entire last year, no matter how hard I tried, I kept coming up against this blockage. My trust was shaken because what I expected to happen never happened. I'd been meditating, doing all the right things, yet I couldn't find a way through.

Bhagwan: In this difficult situation you were in, you were not in a quiet mind. You say you had done all this meditation, but still, there was this expectation. You see? If you have an expectation, you're in the mind again.

Bruce: So, if I say *I trust*, I'm holding out a little caveat — that I expect things to go in my favor.

Bhagwan: That's right. To be in trust means no expectation. If there's expectation, where's the trust? To be in trust means to be in surrender — to not have any expectation. You have to trust that whatever is happening is for the best. That's trust and not, "I trust it's going to happen the way I want." That is not trust. You can't put a condition on trust. It's unconditional. Whatever happens in this moment, I accept. It's a fact because it's happened. It's the reality of the situation, so I trust it.

Bruce: But at the moment of crisis, there's also fear. There's a battle between my mind — which sees everything going to hell — and this clarity that sees everything unfolding perfectly.

Bhagwan: Meditation takes you into this state of clarity where there's no fear, and there's trust.

Bruce: But can't this trust take you places that you're not prepared to go?

Bhagwan: In what way do you mean?

Bruce: You say to stay calm and centered, but what if my life has been turned inside out, upside down?

Bhagwan: To be in acceptance means there's no struggle with it. There's no doubt or mistrust of it. Out of that acceptance, an action may happen.

Bruce: I don't like this expression, "an action may happen." We are wired as human beings to act in the face of crisis, to choose, to solve, to turn over a new leaf, to take a big step. I'm writing a whole book just about these junctures, but you're saying it just happens.

Bhagwan: Yes. You're choosing, and you're deciding. That's a problem. You're in the mind. Instead of you choosing and deciding with your mind, meditation would quieten the mind and bring a state of clarity. Clarity is far more intelligent than a decision made in the mind because the mind is not clear. The mind is turbid. In clarity, the turbidity is gone. You see things easily. In clarity, you don't have to decide. It's already decided. It's clear.

Bruce: You're saying that there's an inherent intelligence in this clarity.

Bhagwan: The intelligence is in seeing which way to go. That's the intelligence.

Bruce: How is that different from knowing which way to go based on experience? I've seen this situation before; I know what to do.

Bhagwan: There's nothing original in that. It's just a repetition of a pattern from past experience. If you put the mind aside, this moment has never existed before. There's a freshness to it. You're living in that freshness, in that spontaneity and creativity. An action from that state would be far superior to using past experience to take an action.

Bruce: You're saying that we can trust spontaneous action?

Bhagwan: Of course.

Bruce: So, in spontaneity, we don't know what's going to happen. But are you're saying that there is an inherent intelligence which is guiding the story?

Bhagwan: That's right.

Bruce: Are you saying that there is a creative force which is writing the story?

Bhagwan: No, the creative force has already written the story, but this creative force is guiding you in your role. If you're in the mind, your role must still play out, because the role is already written. You play the role in struggle. If you're in clarity, the role is also played out, but you're in tune with your role. You're in harmony with yourself and your role and the universe.

Bruce: So, the story unfolds. But if we're in the mind, we're going to struggle. We won't be able to act in the moment, act in spontaneity, and respond to what's calling us.

Bhagwan: That's right. You're not in tune with the story. Because there's inherent conflict in the mind, you're playing a role, but in confusion.

Bruce: So why wouldn't we gladly give ourselves to this harmonious story? Why do we resist it and resist where it wants to take us?

Bhagwan: You wouldn't resist the story if you're in clarity.

Bruce: I get that. But why do I resist it when I'm not in clarity?

Bhagwan: You resist the story because you have doubts. With doubt there's resistance.

Bruce: Is it because the story is taking us to places the mind doesn't want to go?

Bhagwan: The story is written, but the mind doesn't know what the story is. It doesn't know how to deal with it.

Bruce: It's more than the mind can process?

Bhagwan: Yes.

Bruce: So, I tell this story in my book about my neighbor's daughter, Julia. She breaks up with her boyfriend in Boston.

Soon after, her mom comes to help her move. They walk to a restaurant, and she bumps into her best friend's sister from Atlanta — a chance encounter. The sister invites Julia to a party, where she meets a guy; they hit it off, moves to Prague, gets engaged and married — boom, boom, boom, all from that fluke encounter.

Bhagwan: Okay.

Bruce: But suppose she was tired and said instead, "Mom, let's stay in and get some pizza delivered?"

Bhagwan: But it was also written that she was not tired, and so they went out. Everything is written.

Bruce: Everything is written?

Bhagwan: Yes, every detail.

Bruce: Every detail?

I take a sip of water.

Bhagwan: That you drink this glass of water at six in the evening before it is dark, that's written. Do you want me to prove that?

Bruce: You have the book in your pocket?

Bhagwan laughs.

Bhagwan: Maybe I can explain it, not prove it. It starts with this feeling that you can do. You tell this story about Julia and the idea that it could have happened the way it did or some other way. There's also the feeling that I can drink this water if I want, or I can stand up or sit down whenever I want. That's the feeling — that you can *do*. Now, if you meditate and inquire into yourself and come into silence, you'll eventually discover that there is no "I." If there's no I, how can I do? It's an illusion. If the I is an illusion, then the thought, the notion that you can do must also be an illusion. There's nothing you can do. It's all written. It's all happening.

Bruce: It's a powerful illusion.

Bhagwan: Yes, and the cause of a lot of problems.

Bruce: So, I have my problems. I face the problem, surmount the problem, and feel good. Soon I have a new problem and feel bad. Are you saying that we are given this melodrama, this up and down, not to become more skilled at navigating life, but to see through the illusion?

Bhagwan: The thought that you can do is an illusion because the "I" is an illusion. The I, through the mind, creates the illusion of the world and the illusion that you have choices to make in the world. This is the root cause of all misery.

Bruce: Yet, life without doing seems passive.

Bhagwan: It's not a lethargic state or a state of resignation. It's a state of alertness. In clarity, you can do much more at a faster speed. The resistance of the mind is not there. Things move very smoothly in a flow.

Bruce: So, when you say that the entire universe is synchronous, is this the flow?

Bhagwan: Everything is of a certain order, but if you're in the mind, you're not in tune with the order. You're not enjoying the state. But, if you're in the state of clarity, you can feel the synchronicity of everything. You can feel exactly in each moment that this is how it's supposed to happen.

Bruce: What about when we're creating trouble and grief and disharmony and making a mess of things — is this also synchronous?"

Bhagwan: Aren't the planets and galaxies synchronous? If the whole universe is moving in a synchronous manner, why wouldn't our earth and the actions of the people in our little world also be synchronous? You don't realize the synchronicity because you have the feeling that you can do.

Bruce: In my book, I tell a story about driving down a mountain in my VW bus, watching every action and decision, yet being unattached to all of it. The driving happened on its own accord. I attributed it to organic mescaline, but now it raises questions. If we can drive the bus without being identified, something in us must know what to do.

Bhagwan: This silence or this pure consciousness has intelligence. It is intelligent. It's what gives the mind intelligence. It is the source of the intelligence of the mind. If the mind has the intelligence to drive a bus, this pure consciousness would have even more intelligence because it is the source of intelligence. Consciousness is intelligent.

Bruce: Is knowing where to go, what to do, when to do, not coming from the mind?

Bhagwan: Consciousness won't know what to do, but consciousness functions through the mind without identification. Consciousness uses the mind and acts through the mind. The mind knows the maps and the routes and knows where to go. In consciousness, the mind is now a tool which can be used without identifying. Hitherto you identified as the bus driver and thought you were driving the bus. In clarity, there is an awareness that drives the bus, that uses the mind to find the route, but there is no identification with the mind. You are using the mind.

Bruce: So, at that point, who is driving the bus?

Bhagwan: Who is driving the bus? The bus is just being driven. Who is moving the planets? Who is making the sun rise and set? There is a lot going on without you doing it — without the driver doing it. A lot within your body is going on. The circulation, the breathing, the digestion, cell repairs, growth, destruction in your body is going on. Who is doing it?

Bruce: If I have great plans and great dreams, where do they fit in with all this orchestration?

Bhagwan: You can have great dreams and plans without identification. Yet, there's nothing you can do. But a lot of activity can happen through you. You understand the situation, and the action happens. Clear cut, precise, a perfect action producing no reaction.

Bruce: What does that mean, a perfect action produces no reaction?

Bhagwan: When you act from the mind, there's always a reaction because every thought or feeling has its opposite. There will always be a reaction to any action that you "do." You have to bear the consequence of the reaction because it's yours. It's called karma. A perfect action produces no karma. There's no residue.

Bruce: Karma is the residue from imperfect action?

Bhagwan: Yes, the residue and the consequences.

Bruce: So, an action may carry a charge and create ripples?

Bhagwan: Yes. In fact, it carries on and on. The effects come back to you — the effect of karma. This goes on and on throughout your life. When you die, you still have the karma you built up. All the consequences of your actions, you have to bear. When you die, they're not over. They're carried on to your next life if you can believe in that.

Bruce: When you observe people as they age, they appear to be carrying the weight of their world, the weight of their lives. Is that the residual karma?

Bhagwan: Yes, the more karma you carry, the more burden you carry. And with more burden, you're susceptible to diseases, aging, and death. Not only death but rebirth. Rebirth is like a punishment. You have to go through the whole process again. You have to go through it again by getting born again.

Bruce: I see myself as a creative person. Creative people act from inspiration. I might be meditating and think, "Oh, I should do this. I should try that." When these inspiring ideas arise, are they from the mind or do they reflect the creative force seeking to manifest?

Bhagwan: Inspiration is not of the mind. Inspiration comes from a deeper place. If you can remain in the place of inspiration and work from there and not from your mind, that would produce a different quality of creation.

Bruce: When we talk about thinking, could it be that what's coming through our thoughts is actually communication from a deeper place?

Bhagwan: The challenge is to not lose that deeper place and get lost in your thoughts. Silence is the creative space. You want your creative actions to come from that place.

Bruce: So when we talk about creativity, are we describing spontaneity arising from this deeper place?

Bhagwan: From that deeper place you're in harmony with the whole story, and you're enjoying the whole story, even if there are trauma and misfortune and all that. It's not affecting you because you see the whole.

Bruce: Maybe this is the place to bring up my story of woe, how I discovered that every misfortune carries the seed of Fortune, that the two seem inseparable.

Bhagwan: Let me share an example. A client of mine moved from India to Dubai to start a business importing electronics. The business was successful at first, but then after a few years, it failed. He was forced to go back home to India and start over. I told him, "Look, in misfortune, there's always something fortunate in it. Even if you can't see it now, you'll see it later. Be in trust." He went back to India and his business started booming again. He realized that in Dubai, he had been wasting his time. It was a place without a soul, without culture, just a desert with buildings. But, he couldn't make the decision to go back to India on his own. He had to fail first. Destiny had to push and take him out of Dubai, bring misfortune to him so that he could proceed to India and find Fortune.

Bruce: So what made the difference? How did he find the path of Fortune again?

Bhagwan: It wasn't easy for him to get unstuck from the situation. When you're identified, it's hard to get unstuck. The mind can't get you unstuck; the mind is what put you there. But when you access your self, this releases you from identification.

The business problem may still be there, but you're not identified with it, so things start flowing. A new situation, a new opinion comes, and things get resolved. It may not be in the way you think. Whether or not you're able to pay your bills ceases to be the problem. Something else may happen, in which case that problem becomes irrelevant.

Bruce: And this is what it means to let go and be yourself.

Bhagwan: Yes. When you let go, there's flow. Things start moving. In clarity there's creativity, there's flow, there's abundance. Whether it's new opportunities or new situations arising, it's all taken care of. In this awareness, there's a trust. Not a trust that things will go according to how you think, but trust in whichever way they go. That trust itself is an energy — an energy that prevents you from going into the situation that is causing the suffering.

Bruce: This has been a lot to absorb. And, I'm going to try not to think about it.

Bhagwan laughs.

Bruce: Let's leave it on that note — on letting go and being yourself. Can we do it again next time?

Bhagwan: We can do it every time.

20

Garden Variety Miracles

Miracles do not, in fact, break the laws of nature.
C.S. Lewis

I've never been a fan of magical thinking or seeing God's hand in an open parking space. But after my convoluted career reboot, the world of cause-and-effect seemed increasingly suspect. But what about synchronicity? My conversation with Bhagwan put it in a different light.

According to Bhagwan, *it's all just happening.* No magic; no personal god who thinks you're special; just one big intelligent, synchronous universe chugging along. It's the mind that thinks it's special. But, if we're all an expression of one big conscious intelligence, what about *me?*

I began to experience the *me* as an illusory correlation: perceiving a relationship between variables where no such relationship exists.

The feeling that *I am drinking a glass of water* is woven from a compelling mix of variables. All those thoughts, feelings, and sensations, hard-coded over a lifetime, create the unshakable feeling of *me*. But, if it's an illusory correlation, why can't we see through the illusion? Well, for one thing, the alternative — *no me* — is terrifying.

The mind creates illusory correlations from associations. My favorite example was the woman invited by our Georgia Legislature to testify against forced implantation of subcutaneous microchips by the Federal Government.

> "Microchips," the woman began, "are like little beepers. Just imagine, if you will, having a beeper in your rectum or genital area, the most sensitive area of your body. And your beeper numbers are displayed on billboards throughout the city. All done without your permission."
>
> "Ma'am, did you say you have a microchip?" asked state Rep. Tom Weldon (R-Ringgold).
>
> "Yes, I do. This microchip was put in my vaginal-rectum area," she replied.[1]

Before you say, aha, the correlation is illusory, the Legislature is paranoiac, and the woman is crazy, the woman had unshakable proof: all those digital billboards clearly change as she drives on the freeway — an illusory correlation.

The Muppets' Bert and Ernie provide a better analogy. Imagine Ernie singing to his rubber ducky. Ernie never falls out of character to acknowledge the great and powerful Oz running the show — that would be Frank Oz with a hand in Ernie's mouth and a pole under his arms. Ernie's fully convinced he's Ernie — the unshakable feeling of *me*.

I asked Bhagwan if there was a time when we were not so identified with the I-thought and our melodramatic stories.

"Yes, I think when you are born, you are not identified," Bhagwan replied. "A baby doesn't have this I-thought or this I-feeling. The infant is in harmony with everything around. A young child, a six-month baby, would go to anyone — to a stranger, a terrorist, to anyone. The baby will just go. There is no resistance."

---

1. Lach, Eric. 2010. "GA Woman To State Judiciary Committee: DoD Implanted A Microchip Inside Me." TPM. April 20. http://talkingpointsmemo.com/news/ga-woman-to-state-judiciary-committee-dod-implanted-a-microchip-inside-me.

"So, when does this change?" I asked.

"Perhaps at the age of two," Bhagwan replied. "The I-thought comes, and then the child begins to say, 'My ball, that's mine, this belongs to me' and starts quarreling over things he wants to possess. That's probably the start of the I-thought."

"So, the I-thought begins at a young age?" I added.

"Yes. Your family trains you and encourages you to be identified, to develop yourself, to have an identity, to be ambitious, and so on. You start growing up in the educational process in the way that your family and society encourages — to be strong and be an individual. You only begin to unbind from this when you realize that this identification is causing problems."

I could see how identification invites life's problems. Psychotherapists, yoga teachers, and Zoloft wouldn't exist if we didn't need to unbind from identification. But "unbinding" carries its own dangers. The conviction that "it's all God's will" can make you feel special, smug, spacey, disengaged, and passive.

The author and spiritual prankster, E.J. Gold once explained that religious people were the least likely to know God. A plumber, not being afraid to look at the shit in life, had a better chance. A theoretical physicist probably holds the most accurate picture of what's going on. When he puts the world under the electron microscope, he finds mostly nothing there — nothing but the attraction and repulsion of sub-atomic particles.

And that's how I felt in the weeks following my lake swimming experience. When I put the microscope of awareness on my sense of identity, the I-thought had evaporated; the solidity of my subconscious armor had collapsed.

I asked Bhagwan to describe the process.

"The cause of identification is the I-thought and when that's dissolved, you experience the world without separation," he explained. "Dissolving the I-thought is the dissolving of your identity, and that's fearful, that's fearsome."

"That describes the panic and despair of my fearsome year," I replied.

"It's the fear of death," Bhagwan continued. "It's worse than physical death. It is extinction, total extinction. Physical death is not your extinction because your mind is still there. Your thoughts are still hovering around and may be reborn and so on. But with the dissolution of the I-thought, they are gone forever."

"Whoa…" I blurted with a double-take. "Are you saying our mental experience continues? After death?"

"After physical death?"

"Yes," I said.

"When you have not resolved your mind, and you have not discovered consciousness, and you just die like everyone else, the body dies," Bhagwan explained. "Why should your thoughts die? Thoughts are not physical."

"Yeah, that makes sense. Sorta. I guess."

The blunt obviousness of the statement startled me.

"So, Bhagwan, how do you experience the world?" I asked.

"The forms are still there," Bhagwan continued. "You still see different forms; it's not that you just see a blur. You see the forms clearly, but you don't experience them as separate from yourself. It's as though they're all in your consciousness; they're all you. Everything that you experience is yourself."

That was a lot to digest, but I had read the literature. I had studied Attar's epic poem, *Conference of the Birds,* where thirty birds on a spiritual quest pass through the seven valleys of quest, love, understanding, detachment, unity, astonishment, and finally nothingness. In this seventh valley, they become lost in the sea of God's existence. I had no idea what valley I had stumbled into, but as Bhagwan explained, when this happens, "it's neither wanted, nor expected."

"Bruce, the whole world experience is yourself," Bhagwan explained. "It's not other than yourself because it's all in your consciousness. And when you are established in that state of consciousness, everything is in you. That's how you experience it. And because of this, you can't help but experience love."

This love bit was more satisfying. What we experience as love could be a co-mingling of consciousness, a little tickle of shared awareness, an opening to the sameness that underlies our separateness.

My curiosity about "it's all in your consciousness" was now on high alert. Bhagwan's insistence that "it is just happening" and "you can't do," and "it is written" raised the stakes of my question. Does all this *synchronicity* and good Fortune reflect a bigger story that is playing out at a higher level?

According to Bhagwan, you can only answer this question through your own experience — by remaining *effortless* and *alert*. "Efforts, even spiritual efforts," he explained, "are in the mind."

I could see how effortlessness requires letting go, releasing expectation, and finding ease in the moment. I also began to see how alertness was a form of self-awareness. Mental activity and emotional struggle create a friction that disturbs self-awareness, drains energy, and blocks the flow. In this way, mental friction gets in the way of a creative, productive, and authentic life. Rather than fully inhabiting our life, the cultivation of being is suppressed through distraction and busyness.

To test this out, I chose to become a consciousness guinea pig, staying watchful and alert amid daily life. I maintained a clean slate to observe if *it's just happening*. In this way, I identified five tiers:

First, I paid attention to my little nervous actions — scratching, adjusting, sighing, tapping, picking the skin, shifting in the chair, crossing legs, stroking the chin. We don't give much importance to our fidgeting, but these unconscious movements present a little version of *it's just happening* — a symphony of random noise in the nervous system. No big deal. But, if it's automatic, who's doing this? Presumably, no one.

The second tier of *it's just happening* includes functional automatic actions, like swerving to avoid an accident, lurching when a baby is about to fall, or reflexively hitting the brakes while fiddling with the phone.

Sitting at the computer, I would marvel at the "intelligence" that bolted me out of my chair to attend to the oven. I'd be deep in my work, not thinking about baked chicken, then ka-voomp, an impulse "knew" the chicken was done. Who's doing that? As multi-taskers, we do this all the time, but we don't consider the implications.

Consider a recent Florida news story: *"Boy's Amazing Reflexes Help Him Catch Plummeting Baby Brother."* The nine-year-old boy's mother was distracted by other children when her baby rolled over the edge of the changing table and plunged three feet toward the hard floor below. A video monitor captured the action as the sibling felt an unexplained force push him across the room to catch his 30-pound brother inches from injury.

"I would have never caught him," the youngster told Fox 21 News. "I can't run that fast, so I felt like something just came and pushed me forward, and when it happened, I just ran and caught him."[2]

The third tier of *it's just happening* includes life's synchronicities — bumping serendipitously into people or sensing that things will happen before they unfold.

For example, today Karen and I went out for lunch, but we finished too soon to head straight to her 1:30 p.m. hair appointment.

"I guess we'll go back home," I reasoned.

"No, let's pull into CVS," Karen blurted as we drove past the store. I groaned in defiance, dutifully making a u-turn.

Karen searched for a seven-day pill box to manage her massive supplement regimen. As we debated the seven-day capacity of the 2XL version, my old buddy, Daniel unexpectedly appeared in the adjacent aisle.

"Remember when we were younger and wondered who bought all this stuff," Daniel teased with a wink.

2. Moran, L. (n.d.). Boy's Amazing Reflexes Help Him Catch Plummeting Baby Brother. Retrieved November 18, 2016, from http://www.huffingtonpost.com/entry/boy-reflexes-video-changing-table_us_582ee05ce4b058ce7aaa856f

Karen looked up startled, then laughed.

"Isn't today Reshad's birthday?" Daniel asked.

Daniel and I met in Boulder in the 1970s when we were both studying with Reshad.

"How old do you think he is?" Daniel wondered.

"Eighty-one," I replied. "Reshad's birthday was yesterday."

"Let's take a picture and send it to him," Daniel suggested.

And with that, we went outside the store to get Daniel's wife from the car. We assembled into a group shot on the sidewalk.

"I don't think we can take a group selfie," I remarked. "It's an oxymoron."

I scanned the parking lot looking for a photographer, but no dice. "Hey, Karen…"

I turned around to see Todd, an old friend of Karen's, approach from behind. After hugs and hellos, Todd graciously snapped the pic which I later emailed to Reshad while Karen got her haircut. Again, no big deal, but I enjoyed feeling the synchronous universe at work, masquerading as everyday life.

The fourth tier of *it's just happening* comes from trusting the flow. In the flow, knots untie on their own. Yesterday, four important events conflicted on today's calendar: a phone consultation with Karen's doctor, a parent meeting to plan my son's graduation, a client meeting, and an unexpected early-afternoon departure for a funeral. Like a log jam of necessity, something needed to give. And, sure enough, the client called, asking to move the meeting to Monday. Clickity-clack, an invisible Control Tower seemed to be slotting the events into place.

Obviously, our lives are not always so effortless. The logjams stay stuck, over-thinking blocks the flow, and expectations go awry. We are conditioned to think of blockage as a sign of failure, unworthiness, or a dysfunctional world. But, if you see Fortune's flow like a river, blockages don't stop the river from reaching the sea. They change the course and character of the flow. Jagged rocks turn a gentle stream into turbulent rapids the same way that mental boulders create inner turmoil. How boring it would be if our lives were devoid of whitewater.

Philip Shepherd shared a remarkable "following the flow" story from his childhood. One day at school, a schoolmate named Jack suddenly bolted from his desk and ran out of the classroom. Not only did Jack leave the room without asking permission, but he also ran down the hall, out the front door, down the street, and sprinted all the way home without stopping. When he arrived, he found his mother collapsed on the kitchen floor, hemorrhaging in a pool of blood.

"Jack, I was praying and praying for you to come," his mother gasped with dwindling strength.

The moral of Jack's story might seem to be about the power of prayer, but Jack wasn't praying. He was learning algebra while simultaneously staying connected to his instincts. Jack's actions bypassed thinking, permissions, decorum, and considering. He wasn't a world famous psychic either. He was a child — a child still young enough to respond to his subtle senses before his "executive function" matured enough to get in the way.[3]

Karen shared a similar story:

"When I first became a chaplain at Emory University Hospital, my plan was to wear a clerical collar so that people in need could seek me out," Karen recollected. "But then I had a realization. I didn't need care-seekers to recognize me; I could recognize them.

"One afternoon while I was writing a paper in my closet-sized office, a feeling came over me that I should get up and head to the elevators. The paper was important, so I tried to ignore the impulse, but next thing, I was out of my chair, out the door, and heading toward the elevators. Of the six elevators, the one right in front of me opened. Out stepped the mother of one of my young cancer patients. She was clearly distraught. I attended to her with pastoral care and importantly, I learned to listen to my intuition."

Science is begrudgingly acknowledging intuition and

3. Shepherd, Philip, and Andrew Harvey. 2010. New Self, New World: Recovering Our Senses in the Twenty-First Century. Original edition. Berkeley, Calif: North Atlantic Books.

incorporating it into its world view. Some scientists see intuition as the rapid recognition of subtle patterns — an instantaneous blink-of-the-eye computation, processed by the more primitive and nimble reptilian and limbic brains.[4]

According to this theory, a doctor might form an intuitive diagnosis by sensing how the symptoms fit together. But rapid pattern processing can't explain how Jack and Karen bolted from their chairs unprovoked and without patterns to process.

In a famous, but controversial experiment by Benjamin Libet in 1983, subjects were asked to choose a random moment to flick their wrist while watching a precision timer. Scientists recorded the brain's electrical activity of the wrist flick. The researchers discovered brain activity occurring several hundred milliseconds *before* the subject became aware of the urge to move. In other words, the action happened *before* the subject *chose* to act. The implication? Our so-called decisions may not be prompting our *doing*. And, if that's the case, who or what is causing the flicking of wrists and bolting from chairs?[5]

In another experiment, researcher, Charles Limb, gave a group of jazz musicians a piece of music to memorize. Using a functional MRI, he saw the lateral prefrontal cortex of the musicians activate whenever they played the melody. This part of the brain focuses on executive function and goal-directed behavior.

When the musicians shifted into pure improvisation, the lateral prefontal cortex would go dark and the medial prefrontal cortex would light up as they spontaneously responded to the other players. Dr. Limb explains:

> To be creative, you should have this weird dissociation in your frontal
> lobe. One area turns on, and a big area shuts off, so that you're not inhibited,

4. Popova, Maria. 2015. "The Science of 'Intuition.'" Brain Pickings. Accessed October 25. https://www.brainpickings.org/2012/11/08/the-science-of-intuition-answers-for-aristotle/.
5. Sinnott-Armstrong, Walter, and Lynn Nadel. 2010. Conscious Will and Responsibility: A Tribute to Benjamin Libet. Oxford University Press.

you're willing to make mistakes, so that you're not constantly shutting down all of these new generative impulses."[6]

This image of the frontal brain shutting down to let rogue impulses rush past our mental security gate thrilled my imagination. Finally, the proof I needed: Jazz musicians, mystics, and children are all on the same page.

But, during a recent dinner with Karen and Bhagwan, he cautioned against seeking answers with MRI scans of the brain.

"The brain is physical," Bhagwan explained. "What we're working with is beyond the brain, beyond the mind. This story about Karen and the patient and Jack and his mother — why did they leap up? For one thing, Jack felt close to his mother; Karen felt connected to that patient."

"Yes, I felt very close to that mother," Karen remembered. "She was very much in my heart and my thoughts."

"It's because of the connection that you were drawn to act," Bhagwan reiterated. "The whole universe is synchronous. It's all just happening."

The next day, while driving Bhagwan back to the airport, I asked for his reaction to a statement from one of the most important physicists of the 20th century, David Bohm:

In relativity, we have the notion of the universal field which is dynamic, flowing... So, we have an unbroken universe which is in constant flow, dynamically, and even the very notions of space and time have become relative, which were previously absolute.[7]

"That's fine," Bhagwan challenged, "but it's just theoretical. You have to prove it in yourself, know it in yourself."

And with that, we hugged goodbye and I watched my mentor of

6. Charles Limb: "Your Brain on Improv, TED: Ideas worth spreading, November 2010, accessed November 26, 2016, https://www.ted.com/talks/charles_limb_your_brain_on_improv.
7. Interview With David Bohm At The Nils Bohr Institute – Copenhagen, 1989. (2009). Retrieved December 05, 2016, from https://polynomial.me.uk/2009/12/01/interview-with-david-bohm-at-the-nils-bohr-institute-copenhagen-1989

twenty years wheel his bag into the terminal while I pondered the quantum mechanics of my experience.

Is there a fifth tier of *it's just happening*? Gurdjieff describes an all-encompassing view of life that is very much at home with the Theory of Relativity and quantum physics. In Gurdjieff's view, called the Ray of Creation, all of the creation functions as an interconnected series of worlds — from the highest vibration to the lowest, from the most expansive to the most dense, and from pure intelligence to inert. The highest is the Absolute (the all-embracing God) and the lowest is symbolized by the cold and lifeless moon. Life on earth exists within this grand cosmic scheme.

In Gurdjieff's view, our thoughts, feelings, and deeds are not separate from nature. They are natural reactions to stimuli that are not separate from the cosmos.[8] From the vantage of the Ray of Creation, human beings are part of organic life on earth — governed by natural forces no different than the forces that move bees from flower to flower.

> "I believe in Spinoza's God, who reveals himself in the harmony of all that exists."
> — Albert Einstein

We are inseparable from the cosmos, yet we aren't aware of the sweeping energies passing through us. We know from science that high-energy cosmic rays bombard us all the time, but we fail to recognize how higher impulses might play a direct role in "driving the bus."

In Gurdjieff's view, since we exist within this sliding scale of energies, the Ray of Creation is the Really Big Octave. Using Gurdjieff's symbology, the biggest picture of the universe begins with the Absolute (God) and materializes downward in scale and density through all worlds, all suns, our Sun, the planets, the Earth, and finally the Moon. As the Really Big Octave, the Ray of Creation

8. Needleman, Jacob. 2015. "G. I. Gurdjieff and His School." Gurdjieff International Review. Accessed October 28. http://www.gurdjieff.org/needleman2.htm.

manifests up and down: The higher energies descend to infuse our world. Conversely, our inner work transforms the emotional density of worldly experience into the Light.

If our lives are inseparable from the cosmos, I wanted to prove my thesis — that Fortune unfolds through a choreography of forces that play out through the Octave and the Law of Three. Is there evidence that within a synchronous universe, our lives unfold "as written?"

"This thing of *it's written*," Bhagwan cautioned, "one has to be very careful about that."

"How so," I asked?

"I had a client in Switzerland who didn't want to take responsibility," Bhagwan explained, "so I reminded her of the story of the man who wanted to prove his complete trust in God."

I knew where this one was heading.

"To prove his trust," Bhagwan continued, "the man lay in the road. A passerby shouted, 'Get up. Get up. There's an elephant coming.' 'No, no,' the man replied. 'I trust in God. I have complete trust in God. God will save me.' The elephant stamped on him and killed him. The man went to Heaven and met God. The man said, 'God, I had full trust in you, and see what you did!' And God replied, 'I came down and shouted, *move out the way,* but you didn't move!'"

"Yes, it is written," Bhagwan explained. "But it's also written that someone yells to move. It is written, but you can't live your life by that. You can't use it as a mental belief. If you're in the awareness of yourself, you will see that's it's all written. Yes, there's a cosmic energy moving the planets and moving all your actions and the wars and rioting and storms and volcanoes. And, if you're in the awareness of yourself, you will see that it happens in a perfect way. You're aware of yourself as a person with a role to play. It doesn't mean you don't play your role. You play your role without identification, and then you're part of this whole happening. You're in harmony with it. You're not struggling with any situation."

I thought about Julia and the effortlessness of her chance encounter on a Boston sidewalk. In her words, *"Why do you make a choice? It's because of the state you are in and how open you are to a scenario."* The key is *"how open you are."* If the entire synchronous universe from sub-atomic particles to love affairs is written, it must also operate according to natural laws — the laws of attraction and repulsion working through our mental, emotional, and physical openness.

To run my experiment, I chose to be on the lookout for people like Julia who were at critical cusps in their lives. I wanted to observe if life's knots untie at these junctures — at the *Mi-Fa's* of life — and see if openness to grand adventure allows Fortune to unfold.

I chose to call these junctures "garden variety miracles." I also wanted to observe how these miracles work through human connections — octaves intersecting with octaves, one cusp colliding with another, or in common parlance, "networking."

I didn't have to look far for my first subject. I started a yoga practice to strengthen my back but ultimately used it to manage my despair. My once-a-week practice became twice a week, and soon, almost every day. The physical concentration needed to hold a Crow pose kept my emotional demons at bay.

I fell in love with Form Yoga, a fledgling little studio that opened around the corner. I was attracted to Form because its struggles mirrored my own. A graphic designer friend, Michele Dehaven, launched the studio in an unused half of her office space. Business struggles along the way challenged the new business and ultimately forced a change of hands. I asked the studio's new owner, Mandy Roberts, to share the improbable story of how she became the owner of a very successful business.

Bruce: Mandy, thanks for sharing your journey. Over the past year, yoga has kept me from falling apart — physically and emotionally — and I understand your story is similar.

Mandy: Very much so. I was married for fifteen years and for much of it, yoga was my escape. I practiced seven days a week, sometimes twice a day. My marriage was crumbling and the more it crumbled, the better I got at yoga. That was my release. When my husband and I decided to split, we had become two very different people, two different outlooks, and two different paths on how to get what we wanted in life. From the outside, it looked like we had a picture-perfect marriage, but we had our shit.

Bruce: So what did you do?

Mandy: My friends would ask, "How are you going to support yourself as a single mom?" And my answer was always, "I don't know." And they would ask, "So what are you gonna do, be a yoga teacher?" And my answer was always, "No, yoga teachers don't make any money. I can't support my family on that." After being pressed and pressed, I conceded, "I guess I'll be a yoga teacher." I still thought I would be able to fix my marriage.

Bruce: So what happened next?

Mandy: I finally realized I couldn't fix my marriage. It was my birthday when I decided, okay, I'm going to yoga teacher training. I got on the Internet and found a teacher training starting the very next weekend. I had never heard of the studio, never heard of the teacher, but wrote down the name. I asked around, "Ever hear of this guy?" And people replied, "Oh my God, he's amazing."

Bruce: So, after the training, you started teaching?

Mandy: Not exactly. The owner of the studio I attended wouldn't give me a class to teach because I wasn't a seasoned teacher. She only hired teachers who could bring students with them. She'd only let me substitute. Interestingly, a very prominent teacher in town, Cheryl Crawford, happened to take my class — the very first class I subbed! As it turned out, Cheryl was helping a graphic designer, Michele, start a new studio, Form Yoga.

Interjecting here, I located Cheryl on Facebook and asked her what she remembered of Mandy's first class. Cheryl wrote back immediately:

"Hi, Bruce! I took Mandy's very first class and knew right away she had what it takes to be an incredible teacher. I suppose you can call that instinct or an inner knowing. Most teachers are not in their authentic voice for many years. The big studio in town wouldn't hire Mandy, so I told Michele to hire her."

A big clue jumped out of Cheryl's story: *recognition* — what Cheryl called "inner knowing." By recognizing Mandy's potential, Cheryl provided the outside force that shifted Mandy's fortunes and allowed the Mandy Octave to unfold.

Back to the interview:

Bruce: So, Mandy, when did this breakthrough come?

Mandy: I had been subbing for a couple of months when, with this stroke of Fortune, I was hired for the new studio — without even having to teach for Michele! That was wild, to say the least. She just trusted Cheryl.

I contacted Michele for her memory:

"Even though Mandy was a new teacher, she embraced the energy and flow of what Form Yoga was all about," Michele remembered. "Plus, she had incredible music lists! Her playfulness and willingness to always try something new began to build a community."

More reflection: Mandy didn't try to impress Michele to get the gig. Michele *recognized* Mandy's playfulness and the energy she brought to the studio. Mandy's energy provided the outside shock that the Form Yoga Octave needed — a shock that Michele was receptive to receive. Back to the interview:

Bruce: So, describe your first classes.

Mandy: I'm very shy, not that you'd know. I would get so nervous before every class that I would get butterflies in my stomach, and sweaty palms, dry mouth, the whole shebang. Oh God, I was so afraid of speaking in front of people. I'm very much an introvert and teaching yoga was the hardest thing I've ever done, other than my divorce and giving birth.

Bruce: But you managed to pull it off.

Mandy: My teacher, Mitchel, told me, "Just fake it. Pretend that you're on a stage, and this is your production. You're putting on a show." As un-yogic as that sounds, that's how I was able to show up day after day and teach because I looked at it as a production instead of me leading other people, which was terrifying.

Bruce: But now your new career was on a roll.

Mandy: Yes, but all of a sudden, there's bad news. The classes weren't growing. The studio was losing money every month.

Michele remembers: "The yoga studio was becoming a distraction from our design business and there weren't enough students for it to be self-sufficient. It was so hard for me to let people down who had been so supportive. I had put in the time and energy that I could, but the yoga studio needed more love."

Mandy: I happened to be in Jamaica when Michele made the decision to close the studio. When I landed in Atlanta, I turned my cell phone on, and there was a voicemail from Michele. "Mandy, I respect you and love you so much. I'm sorry, and I know you're on vacation. Know that I tried. I did everything that I could. I adore you, and I'm here to help you. However, you need to move on."

Bruce: That must have been a terrible shock coming back from paradise.

Mandy: Exactly. I was a single mom. I was going through a divorce. My child came with me to teach because I was homeschooling him at the time. I felt stuck. My head was thinking, "Oh great, how am I going to make this happen? What other studio is going to let me drag my kid to work?"

Bruce: Let me interject my role in the story, my role as an intersecting octave. At the time, I was thinking about this book, about Fortune and the doors of opportunity. I was asking: How do they open? How do they close? When Michele announced that the studio was closing, I was concerned for you. And I thought, how can we turn Mandy into a marketable business? I was impressed with your stage presence and the way you worked with music.

Mandy: My stage presence?

Bruce: Yes. I saw this opportunity for you, a yoga TV channel: "Mandy in the Morning," the Internet's first wake-up yoga DJ. In my mind, I worked out the whole production scenario — YouTube, music licensing, canned modules, fresh intros, subscriptions, revenue projections... My brain was going tickety, tickety, tickety. I saw the whole thing. I was also holding the philosophical question of the book, "How do the doors of opportunity open?" My thesis at the time was: Forget about luck, forget about God, opportunity comes through another human being as a manifestation of the One.

Mandy: Yeah, yeah.

Bruce: But then I said to myself, "I'm not going to push this river; I'm not going to taint the experiment and push this idea on you. I'll wait for an opening. If it's meant to be, it's meant to be." And so I waited. I was amazed that during that dark period when Form Yoga was about to die, I would wait until the end of the every class to spring my idea on you. But, you always had to go, tend to other business, gather up your child. The opening never came. "This is curious," I thought. "My super-duper idea is not taking root." So, I took that as some sort of sign. Go ahead; finish your story.

Mandy: With the studio closing, I was understandably busy. The other teachers had other gigs, but I had nothing. I had no other options. So, I emailed Michele explaining, "Michele, I've given this some thought. I have figured out a way to keep the studio open, to restructure it where you guys will not lose money. We'll change the classes, change the teachers, change the pay structure, add a monthly membership, and I'll manage it for you. I'll take a dollar a head for people who walk into the space every month as a management fee. I think this could work."

Bruce: So, you were hoping to manage the business full time and make one dollar per student? That's not enough to live on.

Mandy: I just wanted to keep the doors open. But what happened next is important. Michele read my email and replied, "Okay, this sounds like a great idea. Why don't you take it and run with it."

Bruce: Sounds reasonable.

Mandy: I thought the same thing; she's interested. And then she sends out an email to the community: "We've got some good news. We might be able to keep the studio going after all. If you have questions, send them to Mandy." So, I started working furiously — working the numbers, considering different scenarios, teachers, classes, researching other studios. Crazy, like crazy. My ears were perked. I'm going to make this happen. I'm going to be the manager. I might even get more money now because I'm managing. This is good. This is good.

Bruce: I sense the hand of Fortune.

Mandy: So, at one point, a business question came up, and I emailed Michele. "Hey Michele, I need to know how to do something or other." And she replied, "Mandy, what don't you get? It's yours. The studio is yours. I'm done."

Bruce: Just like that, from newbie teacher to studio owner.

Mandy: Yeah.

I was curious why Michele *gave* Mandy her business, so I asked Michele, and she replied:

"Mandy was at a time of change and evolution in her life, so I wanted her to take it and run with it," Michele replied. "She had the energy and entrepreneurial approach to do it. Unlike the other teachers, Mandy always took charge of things when she saw an opportunity — even if it scared her a bit. So, I thought, what's there to lose?"

I considered Michele's impulse: "What's there to lose?" and her willingness to trust Fortune.

The interview continued:

Bruce: So, here's my memory of the big announcement when Michele gave you the studio. It was a total shock to my expectations; I must have been invested in the YouTube idea. I saw how all these possibilities hovered in latency. The course of events could have gone in a different direction. The studio could have closed, and you could have become a YouTube star. But, in one sense, it wouldn't make any difference. A path emerged, and you took it.

Mandy: Just go. Just go.

Bruce: It doesn't make any difference.

Mandy: Yeah, just go, just move.

Bruce: The stream took you where you needed to go. I was holding this possibility for you. But so were all these other people — looking out for you, on one level. On another level, you could say your soul was watching out for you.

Mandy: When I realized that I was being given the studio, it was magical. I knew that this was going to happen one day. Not Form Yoga, not Michele, but I knew I would own a studio. My teacher gifted me an astrological reading at graduation. He knew why I went to teacher training. He knew what I was suffering from. We connected on a very deep level.

I asked Mandy's teacher, Mitchel Bleier why he felt moved to gift Mandy with an astrology reading:

"Mandy and I got close during training," Mitchel explained. "I was aware of her life changes. I wanted to support that."

"But why Mandy? I pressed further. "You probably have oodles of students."

"The moment of attraction is a mystery," Mitchel continued. "And, it's in the force of being together that you understand why things are. But, why something comes into being in a particular moment? That's the mystery."

My conversation with Mandy continued:

Mandy: The astrologer predicted that I would own a studio. I believed it. I was so afraid of standing on my own two feet and taking charge because I was afraid of screwing everything up. But, I knew it was going to happen. The astrologer said it's my *dharma*. She said, "The rose is always going to smell like a rose. It's never going to smell like a gardenia. This is already in the stars for you. It doesn't matter if you sit on your couch." She said these words. I've got it recorded. I can play it for you. "It doesn't matter if you sit on your couch, or if you go out there and work your ass off every day. It's going to happen." I'm more inclined to get out there and work my ass off every day because I like to push the river.

Bruce: Even when the river's pushing you.

Mandy: So, when I heard the news, it was an affirmation of what I already believed – that everything was going to be okay. I was a divorced mom, thirty-four years old, and had never been out on my own. I had never even lived alone. And here I was, being catapulted into the role of business owner in a profession I just started doing. All these people now depended on me, all these teachers and students. It was affirming. My outlook shifted when I learned my marriage was falling apart. I always believed in something – chance or will or divine intervention – but I never had proof. And now I had the proof.

Yoga teachers are a special breed. They must cobble a living out of a spiritual quest. For this reason, they are the perfect canaries to sniff out Fortune. When Maria Cadena, a beloved yoga teacher announced to our class that she was moving unexpectedly to Nashville, my canaries went on high alert. Another cusp.

Maria taught like a trapeze artist without a net. There was always this sense with Maria, "I'm going over the cliff, so come on, follow me." Like an inspired artist who makes it up as she goes along, Maria was my kind of teacher.

Maria was from Guatemala. At the time, more than 47,000 unaccompanied minors seeking asylum from Central America had massed at the southern border, so I was intrigued by her story. How did Maria even get here and why the sudden move to Nashville? I invited Maria to join me for arepas at a local Venezuelan restaurant:

Bruce: So, Maria. Thanks for taking this time. I've always been curious. How did you get here from Guatemala?

Maria: I come from a family of well-known attorneys, so ever since I was little, I thought I'm going to be a bad-ass attorney. I went to law school and studied four and a half of the six years to become a lawyer, but I had to pull out when my parents divorced. It was pretty bad. My dad said, "You need to move out of the house." The house belonged to him, so my mom, my younger sister, and I were kicked out.

Bruce: So, what did you do?

Maria: In Guatemala everyone knows everybody, and as it turns out, my mom was friends with the First Lady. She learned that there was an opening to be the vice consulate in Houston. The job was offered, and my mom took it.

Bruce: So you joined her?

Maria: I couldn't live with my dad, and I couldn't afford law school, so I went with my mom to help her transition for a year, then I would move back to Guatemala. My passion had always been law school. I thought maybe my dad would reconsider and I would get the money to finish school.

Bruce: Is that what happened?

Maria: No. Things get worse. We got to Houston; I'm working in the office of a painting company, and my mom gets a promotion. She's offered the highest position in Miami. I realize that I can't go back to my dad, so I go to Miami hoping to go to school there. But, I never really understood how the system worked. No one could explain it to me. With four and a half years of law school, I expect to transfer some of it. But they transferred nothing. I fought the system for a year trying to get my transcripts sent. Then I discover that my dad didn't pay for the last year and a half of school. They won't release the transcripts until it's paid.

Bruce: That sucks.

Maria: And it sends me down a not very good path — a lot of drinking, a lot of drugs. It was tough seeing all my friends graduate, going down the path that I thought was my path — and I was nowhere near it. Finally, I got a paralegal certificate at the University of Miami. Then my mom got transferred again, this time to Atlanta.

Bruce: Another move.

Maria: We came to Atlanta, and I realized that I have to start from the beginning and study undergraduate political science. My mom couldn't afford it, and I couldn't work because of our legal status. Diplomats have full immunity, but you cannot work. So, I worked at a law firm without getting paid, but they would pay for my school, and I would study at night. I did that for four and a half years.

Bruce: Wow. So, now you're back where you started, but nine years later.

Maria: All this time, I'm doing yoga — first on the physical level, and it felt good. Then I began to understand the other layers. I start yoga teacher training. The training also brought me a lot of depth into my stuff that I didn't fully understand about addictions, eating disorders, and other things. I am still going to law school, but something was telling me it wasn't my path.

Bruce: You were still at the law firm?

Maria: Yes, for over four years. I remember feeling very fake every time I would walk into the office. Like the type of shoes I was wearing. Why should I wear high heels when they are so uncomfortable, and they're killing my legs? Little things like that I would keep thinking.

Bruce: So, was there a breaking point?

Maria: I felt this anxiety — like I either need to get out and do something, or continue with this anxiety. I felt like I was coming out of my skin. I don't even know how to explain it. It was like all this noise, and I just walked into the bathroom. I stayed there for some time. I stepped out, and I said I couldn't work there anymore, and I quit.

Bruce: Boom, you pulled the plug on law. How did you manage?

Maria: I had a little money. They paid for my books, but I would take the money to buy cheaper books and save some money. The important thing, I knew I cannot keep moving in a direction that was against what I need to be doing. I don't know what I need to do, but I know it's not that. Everyone would be telling me what I need to do. What I knew is if you get the urge and ignore it, you just learn to ignore it for the rest of your life.

Bruce: So you started feeling the urge?

Maria: Yes. This time, I got on my computer. I don't know what I was looking for — maybe a potential attorney I could email. And there was an email from Scoutmob announcing a new yoga studio two blocks from where I live. I clicked on the email and was drawn to it.

Bruce: I feel the hand of Fortune entering the story.

Maria: Yes. I planned to go to the new studio on a Tuesday, but then for some reason, I couldn't. I end up going to the studio on a Wednesday. I walk in, and there's just one student in the class, some guy sitting there cross-legged. I look at the guy and smile. I say hi and he doesn't even respond. So, I set my mat next to him. It was a very different class. The teacher had long hair down to his butt, even longer. All of sudden I'm thinking what is this? You recognize something is going on, but you don't know how to label it.

Bruce: Like a moth drawn to the flame.

Maria: Yes. Long story short, I started learning pranic healing from this teacher and two months later, I started teaching yoga there — one class, then two, then five. More important, I started to date the guy who sat next to me at that first class — Adam. He was six years younger than me.

Bruce: So what happened next?

Maria: Yoga doesn't pay a lot of money, and my mom wanted me to go back to law. I remember not sleeping for the entire December trying to figure this out. But then the next big thing happened.

Bruce: Which is?

Maria: A new government comes in, and my mom loses her position. This means going back to Guatemala. We ask for a visa extension to get a little more time. I send out my resume and get a call from an attorney. It's seven in the morning; I'm putting a suit on, I look at myself in the mirror and know that I'm cheating myself if I go to that interview. So, I take the suit off and jump back in bed.

Bruce: You dump your career a second time, plus you're facing deportation.

Maria: Yes. I go to a yoga conference and bump into another person opening a studio. He says, "Hey, I've taken some of your classes would you be interested?" I'm like, oh yeah. Three months after not taking that law interview, I'm teaching 2 or 3 times a day, and I'm making a living. Everything is good. My relationship with Adam is going well. Then, my mom gets a letter. The visa request is declined. We have one month to pack our stuff and return to Guatemala. My mom is devastated. I spent ten years of my life in this country and now this. How can I go back? It's scary.

Bruce: What about Adam?

Maria: I remember Adam telling me this is a blessing. I say to him, "What do you mean this is a blessing?" I'm crying. What am I going to do? I can't teach yoga back in Guatemala, and I don't want to go to law school. I'm trying to figure it out in a very negative way. Adam just looks at me and says this is a blessing. And, I'm like, what? And he says, "I was thinking of proposing to you in the fall. Let's get married right now." So, we go to one of our favorite cabins in the Smoky Mountains. We go to the courthouse, and we got married.

Bruce: That's beautiful. But why the sudden move to Nashville?

Maria: The full story is that when Adam was a freshman at Emory University, he met these two guys in music theory class, and they clicked. They entered the Emory arts competition with a song they had written for class — but they did not get picked to perform. They came in 11th place for the ten performing slots.

Bruce: Bummer.

Maria: But, the judges accidentally sent an email to Adam inviting him to come to the performance meeting. The email was only supposed to go to the ten finalists. So, when Adam's group showed up at the meeting, the organizers said, "Okay, we made a mistake; I guess we have to let you perform." So, Adam and his two friends performed in the competition."

Bruce: That's very cool.

Maria: But, there's more. They ended up winning first place!

Bruce: Wow.

Maria: They became The Shadowboxers and started playing shows around Atlanta.

Bruce: Talk about Fortune. So, what about Nashville?

Maria: Adam got this idea to record a cover on the first Tuesday of every month and just put it out there on YouTube. They might record it in a hotel bathroom, wherever. They are thinking, "What song should we cover? Let's cover Justin Timberlake's, 'Pusher Love Girl.'" And, they do. On a whim, Adam sends the track to Justin Timberlake: "Hey Justin, check out what we did." Adam didn't expect any response — 'cuz he's Justin Timberlake!! But, big surprise, Justin listens to it, loves it, tweets about it, and then flew to Atlanta to hear them.

I searched Twitter and found the infamous Justin Timberlake tweet — the outside force and moment of *recognition* — which reads:

@jtimberlake: "Every once in a while, you come across something... This is GREAT, fellas. Took it and made your own. I'm humbled."[9]

Bruce: So why are you moving to Nashville?

Maria: Long story short, Justin Timberlake signed The Shadowboxers for his new label. He's going to produce their record next year.

Bruce: Wow.

Maria: Yeah that's...

Bruce: Very cool.

Maria: Yeah. Yeah. We flew up to meet Justin Timberlake in New York, went to a club with him, paparazzi, the whole thing. It was pretty amazing.

Bruce: So what were you saying earlier about following your path?

Maria: For me, it is kind of sad to leave Atlanta. But if there is a path we need to follow, it is just going to happen once. And, if we don't take it, then it won't happen again. It may keep presenting itself in different forms and different shapes, and you might notice it in the background, but you might not be ready. Your path will fade away or reappear in a different way until you notice it, are open to it, grab it, and go with it.

Bruce: Is that what happened in the law firm bathroom? Was it your path calling?

Maria: Maybe. The more I think about it, it was about being brave. I finally had the guts to say, "This isn't for me!" I stepped out of this idea that was planned for me since I was five years old. I like that version better.

Karen and I went to see The Shadowboxers at their last Atlanta show before Maria moved to Nashville. We hung out in the balcony with the drummer's parents — the only people in the audience remotely our age. It was after midnight — too late for old hippies — but fun to watch the sea of affection from the standing room crowd. I spotted Maria downstairs at the bar, so I pushed my way through.

9. account, Justin Timberlake Verified. 2013. "Every Once in a While, You Come across Something..." http://youtu.be/BLHkDBrlUIs." Microblog. @jtimberlake. December 6. https://twitter.com/jtimberlake/status/408851735982010368.

"Maria… Maria!" I screamed over the din. Maria turned and smiled. My yoga girl from Guatemala was now queen of the night with her vampy make-up, sparkly shimmer, and sexy top.

"Hi, Bruce. I'm so glad you came."

"The band is great," I screamed. "I just wanted to wish you the best in the next chapter of your life."

"Oh, thank you."

"I'll be rooting for you. Stay grounded."

Maria smiled again. We hugged. I was afraid that the forces of fame and Fortune might gobble up Maria's free spirit — but hey, she signed up with enthusiasm for the E ticket ride.

New Year's Eve was now just around the corner — the one-year anniversary our double demise. We had postponed plans to celebrate for as long as possible because Bruce 2.0 hadn't hatched and money was desperately tight. At the last possible moment, we said screw it, and with a week's notice, the invite went out:

IT'S NEW YEAR'S EVE

And the plan is not to spend it at Piedmont Hospital.

Instead, we are gathering for a Gratitude Party and you are invited.

The night before the party, I set a very long table for thirty guests while Karen marinated ten pounds of Chicken Marbella. We didn't buy Champagne given Karen's strict (but always evolving) health regimen. I was hooking up AV equipment for a karaoke sing-along of "I Give Myself Away" when the phone rang. It was Dr. Tien. During a recent exam, Dr. Tien found something in a lymph node.

"Karen, the results came back from the biopsy," Dr. Tien shared. "The cells in the lymph node show some cancer."

My only thought was, "You gotta be shitting me. This is either one fucked up synchronous universe, or one with a dark sense of comedic timing."

I held Karen. The Gratitude Party suddenly looked obscene.

After the shock had subsided, we made a plan. It's a Gratitude

Party, not the Erasure-of-Every-bit-of-Cancerous-Flotsam-from-my-Body Party.

At first, we first rationalized: "It's likely old flotsam, not new flotsam," which morphed into, "Hey, there are no straight lines in healing journeys." Any way we looked at it, our buoyancy was bashed. We considered canceling the Gratitude Party, but that would alarm our friends. So, we decided to go forward, but keep mum on the news. Nobody wants a detailed medical explanation with their Champagne. But for us, it was a Humility Party.

We managed to shift our emotional gears, hosted New Year's 2.0, and savored connections with our friends — connections made richer by our newfound humility and our gratitude to have made it through the year.

Arm-in-arm, the room full of friends swayed and sang:

Take my heart
Take my life
As a living sacrifice
All my dreams all my plans
Lord I place them in your hands[10]

---

10. McDowell, William. "I Give Myself Away." Lyrics. Delivery Room Publishing, 2008.

21

Don't Worry, Be Happy

There is no free will.
Everything is in accordance with the
working out of one's own sanskaras,
and even this depends on the preordained plan
set in execution with the emergence of
the original whim of God.
Meher Baba

Our windshield wipers could not keep up with the deluge of
Ana, the earliest tropical storm on record to hit the East Coast. The
Weather Channel lady positioned landfall "near the Tanger Outlet
Mall," which for you synchronicity folks, was about a hundred yards
from our destination: What I affectionately call "Baba Beach."

Twelve months ago to this day, the radiologist misread Karen's
lung, sunk our emotional buoyancy, and led us to Baba. This time,
our bigger concern was to keep our tires grounded amid horizontal
blasts of rain.

The New Year's lymph node was now behind us. In the spirit
of bread crumbs, Karen hooked up with a famous San Francisco
surfer who also happened to be a leading-edge cancer researcher. "It's

nothing new," Dr. Renneker assured. "That lymph node was there from the beginning."

I clasped Karen's hand feeling a swell of gratitude as we drove past Dolly Parton's thirty enormous billboards promising "Fun, Feast, and Adventure."

I didn't care about Dolly's landmarks, nor Ana's full force blow. Karen and I were happy in ourselves as we sang full force with Stevie Wonder on the car stereo. Stevie was closing the show in front of 100,000 people at the Glastonbury 2010 festival.[1]

Stevie's Glastonbury performance of *Free* captured the pure expression of the Octave — the flamenco acoustic opening, lifting through key changes, vocalists joining in at the *Mi-Fa*, a rousing burst of percussion taking us higher, all the while building and swirling like a dervish turning freely until the chorus bursts the heart open to the *Si-Do* and beyond.

Yes, my old friend, the Octave — the ancient knowledge I gleaned from Reshad, who incorporated it from Gurdjieff, who got it from who knows where? Prehistoric Egypt? Central Asia, Assyrians, Babylonians, Sufis? When asked, Gurdjieff replied, "Maybe I stole it."[2]

The Octave describes how everything in life is either growing or dying, evolving or dissolving, ascending or descending, up and down the vibrational ladder. The Octave also predicts the energetic barriers that impede Fortune, divert development, and constrain one's world. Forty years ago, this secret science of alchemical transformation provided my original impetus to write a book one day about Fortune.

But then I met up with Hazard, the force of uncertainty that adds suspense to the plot. Hazard co-mingles with the creative force to introduce risk at every significant juncture. Doors of opportunity inexplicably open — and close. The potter shapes beauty to the brink of collapse. The lover risks rejection by opening her heart. A chance

---

1. Stevie Wonder Glastonbury 2010 Free. (2012, June 6). Retrieved November 24, 2016, from https://www.youtube.com/watch?v=qQY6QBEZ924
2. Mouravieff, Boris. 1997. Gurdjieff, Ouspensky and Fragments. Praxis Research Institute.

sperm out of 100 million makes its way to fallopian fulfillment. A young inventor proposes to his date at Disney's Pirates of the Caribbean — not marriage — but the idea for the name of an electric car company. "How about Tesla Motors?" he asks. "Perfect!" she replies. And by the way, they get married, too.[3]

My inquiry finally brought me to Bhagwan who threw a wrench in all of my theories about Fortune:

"It's all written," he explained. "There is nothing you can actually do."

Yeah, thanks.

For now, the freak appearance of Ana kept me enmeshed with Hazard. The unpredictable forces of warm waters and high evaporation conspired with just the right amount of low pressure and rotational forces to provide the opening for this, the last chapter. And just as auspicious, the clouds opened, and the rain subsided as we pulled through the gate of the Meher Center.

We dutifully acknowledged Meher Baba's directives at the gate office ("No divining cards, Ouija Boards or I Ching). Cleared of any divination desires, we drove slowly down the primeval path, under dripping moss, to our cabin on the lake.

To set the record, I am not a card-carrying "Baba Lover." This is easy to admit because Meher Baba insisted that there would be no cards to carry, nor any rituals to observe, nor religious structure left behind as his legacy. Baba Lovers follow a path of inner devotion.

Coming from a Jewish background, I'm not hard-wired for lordship, guru worship, deities, avatars or saviors. But, I'm also not put off by the "God incarnate" certitude of Baba's followers that Meher Baba was an avatar — or present tense, is the avatar. Yes, avatar, like that other Really Big Religion that believes God incarnated in human form.

I asked Bhagwan about the avatar thing.

"Did Meher Baba claim to be an avatar," Bhagwan asked?

---

3. Baer, Drake. 2015. "Tesla: The Origin Story - Business Insider." Accessed October 25. http://www.businessinsider.com/tesla-the-origin-story-2014-10#ixzz3a7jOBKYr.

"Oh yes," I replied. "The last and the greatest."[4]

"A true avatar would never claim to be one," Bhagwan countered. "To a realized being, everything is realized. How can an avatar claim to be something different?"

I conceded the point; we're all God incarnate to various degrees.

"Maybe people needed an avatar back in the 1940s," I reasoned, "and Meher Baba was obliged to play the role."

Bhagwan wasn't impressed, and I don't know why I was defending Meher Baba.

But now we were at Baba Beach. At this point, I had let life answer my queries about Fortune. Real or imagined, I had imbued Baba Beach with mystical significance and decided to let Baba answer my question.

Fifteen months after a freak Georgia earthquake kicked me out of bed to start this book, a freak tropical storm was adding the final punctuation mark. More importantly, being the last chapter, Meher Baba reemerged to solve the riddle that started it all: *What is this mysterious, guiding force behind Fortune?*

Karen and I settled into our cabin amid palmetto palms and hanging moss. Getting into the spirit of the place, I started a conversation with Meher Baba.

"Okay, Baba. I don't know much about you, but since Fortune brought me to you twice, a double-dip, please illuminate my question: 'Somewhere in the nexus of noble effort, sweet surrender, and shit happening by chance, is there a sweet spot? A waypoint to set life's compass? Does Fortune unfold by God's effortless decree or by hacking one's way through life? And, let's not forget dumb luck, either. Baba, I like this idea of floating along life's river, but don't we need to give it an occasional push?'"

Being around a bunch of Baba Lovers might not be the best setting for this critical discernment to take place. That's because at Baba Beach, all good Fortune springs from Baba. Yes, another example of

4. Statement to Meher Baba's women mandali, December 1942, as quoted in *Gift of God* (1996) by Arnavaz Dadachanji, p. 72.

magical thinking — the belief in mystical forces, deities, and dogma outside of direct experience. In my estimation, magical thinking simply clouds the mind. I asked my Baba Lover friend Julie about this.

"It makes no difference," Julie explained. "The delineation between magical thinking and so-called critical thinking doesn't really exist."

Okay, I conceded the point. Thinking is thinking. True clarity comes from not thinking at all. And with that, I let myself slide the slippery slope into Baba's embrace. Some people feel that the bhakti path of pure devotion is the most direct path to enlightenment. Devotion concentrates the emotional energy of love through the illusion and toward God — which is the self. Lord Krishna makes this point in the Bhagavad Gita:

"Those who worship me and meditate on me constantly without any other thought, I will provide for all their needs." (9.22)

Yeah. If I had followed Krishna's advice, I could have spared myself a year of money worries — maybe. But, since I also treasure my innate Chicago cynicism, the bhakti thing probably would not have worked. All those Chicago hot dogs protect me from too much spiritual Kool-Aid. Yet, at Baba Beach, even cynical Chicagoans like me can raise prayer hands when greeting a Lover on the path, "Jai Baba." And why not? Beats "Howzit goin'?"

This is Baba's land and his spirit pervades. Case in point: This morning, we encountered a baby deer who remained eye-to-eye relaxed as we approached. I kept thinking, "Okay, deer you're gonna bolt right now… uh, how 'bout now? Oh, really? What kind of deer are you? Something wrong with your reptilian brain?"

It's that kind of place.

Later that morning, we walked the raked paths to the abode — the 1950s brick bungalow where Baba stayed during his two visits to Myrtle Beach. Inside, I was drawn to the small dining room where two artifacts in a glass case caught my eye — a pressed flower in a

Bible and a blood-stained pillow. After a little research, here's what I learned:

The flower belonged to a prominent Baba devotee, Elizabeth Patterson. Uncharacteristic for a woman of the 1920s, Elizabeth was a Wall Street insurance executive who came from a distinguished family. She had also been an ambulance driver for the Red Cross in France during World War I.

In 1931, Elizabeth joined a scientific expedition aboard a Soviet icebreaker traveling near the North Pole. That same year, she met Meher Baba. Fortune double-dipped six months later when Elizabeth met Baba again. This time along the Hudson in upstate New York. She described the May 1932 meeting:

> Vividly I remember the beautiful late spring morning of May 24 when Norina and Anita and I motored 35 miles from New York to join Baba's party for a day in the country… Baba greeted us with a warm embrace and we found a number had gathered there already.
>
> Baba led us outside to the stone terrace and then along a path to a field with wild flowers. Some went here and there picking the flowers, but I stayed close to Baba. He quietly picked a small pink flower and handed it to me…Baba spelled out slowly that I should always keep the flower and should write down the date, that some day I would know the meaning.[5]

Elizabeth pressed the flower into her Bible, packed it into a trunk, and forgot about it.

I studied Elizabeth's small wood-covered Bible through the glass. More than eighty years had passed, yet Baba's tiny pink flower was still intact, lovingly affixed inside the Bible's cover. In penciled letters, Elizabeth wrote: "BABA, May 24, 1932."

In the years that followed, Elizabeth fulfilled Baba's request to find land that could be "given from the heart" and helped establish the Meher Spiritual Center in Myrtle Beach.

And what about the blood-stained pillow? Meher Baba prophesied

5. Davy, Kitty. 2001. Love Alone Prevails: A Story of Life with Meher Baba. South Carolina: Sheriar Foundation.

that he would spill his blood on American soil. In 1951, a year before his first visit to Myrtle Beach, he announced that soon he would "be facing physical annihilation."

In 1952, Meher Baba came to Myrtle Beach. Afterward, a small entourage of cars assembled to drive Baba across the country to California. Elizabeth, with her superior driving experience, would drive the lead car. Before they left, Baba insisted, "Where are your insurance papers?" Elizabeth went back to get the documents and packed them into her case.

They drove for several days and then on May 24, 1952, the caravan of cars reached Oklahoma. After breakfast, the group waited for Baba's signal to get into the cars. But Baba delayed the start, standing for a long time at his motel doorstep. Kitty Davy who was part of Baba's inner circle remembers, "He was sad, withdrawn and unusually still." Finally, after a long ten minutes, Baba walked to the car with his female travel companions and they were off.[6]

While Elizabeth drove toward the crest of a hill, a paraplegic driver using modified driving controls approached from the other direction. A mail truck blocked the lane, the driver swerved and forced a head-on collision. Baba was thrown clear of the car and landed on his back in a muddy ditch. Elizabeth was crushed, against the steering wheel and most of her ribs and both arms were broken. Her shoulder was dangerously cut. The others were critically hurt as well. Delia De Leon, an English actress and close follower of Baba ran to the crash site from another car. She placed her pillow under Baba's head — the sacred pillow now in the glass case. It was Delia in her later years who was instrumental in guiding Pete Townsend of The Who to Meher Baba.[7]

Elizabeth was likely distraught about her role in the accident. Yet, the flower Baba picked transmuted the tragedy into grace, as she later wrote:

6. "God Rides – In A Ford | Rosamondpress." 2015. Accessed October 25. http://rosamondpress.com/2013/07/03/god-rides-in-a-ford/.
7. Wilkerson, Mark, and Eddie Vedder. 2008. Who Are You: The Life of Pete Townshend. London; New York; New York: Omnibus Press.

Not until many years after… did I discover again the New Testament among my effects. Opening the cover, there were the words, "Baba — May 24, 1932." In a flash another date, May 24, 1952, came to my mind, the date the accident had occurred in Oklahoma when I was driving Baba and four of His close disciples. It had been a catastrophic occurrence, yet, despite serious injuries, all eventually recovered.

I do not know fully the meaning and deeper significance of the accident which happened twenty years later to the day, May 24, but I do know that Baba knew then and now…

The gift of the little flower was grace from the Master to be treasured in the heart.[8]

Looking at the pillow and the flower, I flashed to our miraculous misfortune — Karen's collapse, the brain surgery, the nurses, the community of helpers, and here we were again at Baba Beach, a year to the day. I remembered marveling at the scripted perfection of it all — a telling choreography that allowed me to embrace the crisis with trust.

During moments of crisis, the curtain briefly lifts to reveal life's purpose. Meher Baba seemed privy to the divine drama long before the parts were played.

A year ago, Baba Beach provided spiritual buoyancy for our Fortune journey. This time, another terrible shock hit.

Julian, our friend Renee's son and a classmate of our son, was discovered dead from a heroin overdose at his girlfriend's college dorm. While we walked back from Baba's abode after getting the news, Karen shared her thoughts:

"I went into Baba's room and knelt down at his bed, and a feeling of peace and love and letting go came over me. It was lovely to be back, a sense of returning home. Yet, it feels different this time. I feel a lot clearer without having to carry the uncertainty of my diagnosis. But, this time, I am weighed down by my concerns about Julian.

"I was asked to cut our visit short to officiate at Julian's funeral. This

8. Davy, Kitty. 1968. "Baba's First World Tour – Part 2." The Awakener. http://www.theawakenermagazine.org/avol12/avol12n03/av12n03p06.htm.

put me into a bit of a tailspin. Was this going to be a distraction during this sacred time?

"When I entered Baba's bedroom, I held Julian with me. I had the realization that we are all interconnected. I don't have to have an experience here that's separate from everything going on in the world. And with that, a palpable peace washed over me. This time, I can be myself and come in touch with who I am."

All of this swirled in my consciousness — the sense of prophecy around Baba's flower, the automobile crash, Julian's untimely death, and the torch of grieving passing to Renee, Julian's mom. For a moment, the veils felt tantalizingly close to revealing their mysteries.

"Okay, Baba, you have my attention," I thought to myself.

I felt close to Julian, too. I saw him carrying his dog-eared copy of *Man's Search for Meaning*, where Viktor Frankl concludes, after imprisonment at Auschwitz, that the meaning of life is found in every moment of living.

Julian wanted to peel back the veils. He cavorted with the subtle worlds like an old soul. I was always struck by Julian's self-awareness, especially when he described his solo camping trip:

"My solo trip allowed me to think about the effect that noise has on me… and how I think differently when I'm around people versus when I'm alone. Other people have a huge influence on the way we feel and think. I hadn't realized the power of that until I spent three days by myself."

Yes, Julian could hear the *silence*. Not many people can. Our thoughts obscure this entry point to the Self.

I went to Julian's Facebook page and discovered a string of cryptic koans he posted during his final weeks at college:

• "Is it better to endlessly contemplate the possible answers to a question you don't want to ask, and accept that you'll never know for sure; or ask the question and risk getting an answer you don't want?"

- "Your body is not a temple; it's an amusement park."

- "When what is desired is impossible, and what is possible is undesirable — what then?"

- "In the end, I just feel defeated."

Three days before his death, Julian posted a prophetic story from the Hungarian writer Útmutató a Léleknek. In a lively dialog, two unborn twins in their mother's womb argue the existence (or not) of a world outside of Mother, forming a parable of life after death. The story ends with the second twin explaining to the first:

> "Sometimes, when you're in silence and you focus and you really listen, you can perceive Her presence, and you can hear Her loving voice, calling down from above." [9]

And with that, poof, Julian was gone from this world.

Julian's death forced me to question, why do we come into this world and why do we leave?

In Baba's view, the soul is on a journey of realization — a journey which encompasses countless lifetimes. On each successive incarnation, the soul plunges into human experience to absorb life's lessons and pay its karmic dues.

I thought of Julian and how his promising life was cut short. Did Julian choose to leave the stage to fulfill a karmic imperative? Or was it just a bad flip of the heroin coin — a trip laced with the opiate fentanyl?

I couldn't answer this question, but Meher Baba's view of karmic compulsion offered a clue. From a karmic perspective, we plunge into birth like an actor taking on a role. We perform page after page of conflict and resolution and then leave the stage for intermission, or more accurately, to return for the sequel.

Baba compares the law of karma to the law of cause and effect.

9. "Útmutató a Léleknek Quotes." 2016. Goodreads. Accessed January 12, 2016. https://www.goodreads.com/author/quotes/13931986._tmutat_a_L_leknek.

Physical cause and effect describe how the physical universe operates. Karmic law describes how the moral universe operates. In a lifetime, we accumulate moral debts to pay and experiences to redeem. At the same time, our good works build a storehouse of goodwill to reap. In and out, pay and reap, residue and reward, the karmic ledger is maintained.

In the simplest analogy, karma consists of binding and unbinding. The yogic terms are *pravritti* and *nivritti*. *Pravritti* describes the gravitational pull of identification, the pull of the world for position, carnal pleasure, and possessions. *Nivritti* is the unbinding — turning away from these compulsions through meditation, contemplation, and a spiritual life.

As I reflected on my own binding and unbinding, the sculptures of George Segal came to mind. Segal was an American sculptor whose work profoundly impacted me as a youth in the 1960s. Segal wrapped his models with gauze strips dipped in wet plaster, binding the person like an orthopedic cast. After the plaster bindings set, he would cut away the sections and reassemble the life-size figures into eerie ghost-like scenes from everyday life — a bus driver at the wheel, a pedestrian waiting for the light to change, a man shaving, a customer getting a cup of coffee.

Segal found mystery in the mundane. The frozen earthly moments he captured raised questions: Why are we here? What is this world? Is this prison or paradise?

Segal's plaster-wrapped models appeared rigidly bound by karmic law. Neither fairy godmother nor magical thinking was going to remove their bindings. Why? Karma demands an energetic payment.

Baba compares the law of karma to the law of conservation of energy which states that energy remains constant, is neither created nor destroyed, and can only be transformed. Similarly, once Karma comes into existence, it persists until it bears its own fruit or is transformed. Karma operates like the spin on a racquetball. The ball's trajectory looks predictable until it hits the wall and reacts according to the mix of forces and physical laws hidden in its spin.

When Bhagwan said, "It's all just happening," he was talking about these laws. We live in a world set into motion by natural laws. Our karma emerges when we hit the wall.

Imagine the karmic forces compelling John Wayne's character to throw a punch in the saloon. His narrative arc follows the octave of the hero's journey. He wrestles with his karmic imperative, confronts the villains, and kisses Marlene Dietrich in the end. When the lights come up, we see the projectionist in the booth holding a 35mm spool of narrative conflict, aka *it's just happening,*" to be projected by the Light.

All of creation *is just happening.* It's a cosmic game of hide-and-seek where God ultimately comes to know Him or Herself through creation itself. In the cosmic dance of creation, life takes an evolutionary journey from unity, to individuation, to inanimate existence, to rudimentary sensing, to instinctive behavior, and finally to self-awareness:

> I died as a mineral and became a plant,
> I died as plant and rose to animal,
> I died as animal and I was Man.
> — Rumi

Darwin discovered this chain of unfoldment, but he missed the bigger picture — and that is the "I" in Rumi's poem. The "I" is the Absolute's urge to know Itself or what Meher Baba called "the whim:"

> It is the original infinite whim which is responsible for giving Cause to the latent-all...
> — Meher Baba[10]

Like a sound creating an echo, this original whim emerged from the infinite and created the first vibration and the first finite impression.

10. Baba, Meher, *God Speaks*, Dodd Mead; Reprint edition (1997)

We cannot see ourselves without a mirror, nor can the Absolute know itself without the world.

And so, the Cosmic Whim becomes a wave — a surfing wave carrying all manner of individual journeys through their individual lifetimes. Living life would be so much easier if we sensed The Whim propelling our story. If we could trust this wave throughout the entire drama of our life, like Stevie Wonder, we could live free like "a river flowing through infinity."

I began to consider how this wave — our karmic imperative — directs our stories. It explains why, like the karmic spin on a racquetball hitting the wall, my spin veers left while someone else's spin veers right. I knew I was onto something when I discovered the following statement from Meher Baba:

> "The very foundation of all my explanations is *sanskaras*, which no religion has explained."[11]

Really? The foundation of it all? Will *sanskaras* reveal the mystery of Fortune?

And with this, I sought out Fortune's riddle through the lens of *sanskara*. As I walked the raked paths, nodding "Jai Baba" to the lovers, I kept my inner focus on this one word, *sanskara*. Meher Baba describes *sanskaras* as mental impressions. The word *sanskara* (or *samskara*) comes from the Sanskrit *sam* (joined together) and *kara* (action, cause, or doing). The Chicago definition would be: "Life sticks when you're doing stuff."

I like to think of *sanskaras* as the ongoing mental process of "own-making" or identifying. It explains how the ego edifice, the "I-thought," is built one impression at a time. It's analogous to the chemical process of electroplating where a metal cathode (the "I thought") is placed in an aqueous bath of chrome ions (impressions) and charged with electric current (identifying), which attracts the

---

11. Kalchuri, Bhau. Lord Meher. Vol. 2. Manifestations, Inc.

metallic deposits to become a chrome plated bumper (*sanskara*) — a shiny little *me*.

When the child says, "my ball, that's mine, this belongs to me," *sanskaras* are being formed. After a few decades, the *sanskaras* become, "my Jaguar, my dream home, my Château Lafite Rothschild, as well as my sadness, my backache, my loss… they all belong to me."

Sanskaras describe how the sausage of self is made. Merriam-Webster describes *sanskara* as "a latent karmic tendency shaping one's present life." They are latent because the mind cannot see, touch or feel a *sanskara* because that would be like looking at your nose. The "I" cannot sense itself except by quieting the mind.

According to Meher Baba, *sanskaras* are both created and removed. They are released by the usual methods: renunciation, solitude, fasting, penance, sublimation of desire, asceticism, meditation, selfless service, love, devotion, and the intervention of the perfect master. Bhagwan adds that this release is neither expected nor desired during the process.

Let me give an example. During a recent visit to Dr. Tien, Karen experienced what could have been a *sanskara* in the making. We had been anxiously awaiting Karen's CT scan results to learn how the little lymph node was faring, the one that bummed our Gratitude Party six months earlier. Because of the lymph node, Karen added an integrative doctor from Chicago to her support team in addition to Mark, her San Francisco doctor-researcher-surfer.

We flew to Chicago where Karen gave twenty-nine vials of blood for twenty-nine off-label tests. Based on the tests, Karen started taking a long list of exotic supplements.

"So Mark," Karen asked her surfer doctor during a phone session. "How do I explain all these blood tests and supplements to my Atlanta oncologist? She's very mainstream and conservative."

"You should tell her everything," Mark replied. "She needs to be exposed to the bigger world."

As we headed up the elevator to visit the oncologist, I asked Karen if she planned to rock the world of mainstream medicine.

"Absolutely," she replied with 2.0 conviction.

Karen handed thirty pages of blood tests and supplements to the nurse who dutifully entered it all into the Piedmont Hospital system.

A few minutes later, Karen's beloved Dr. Tien entered the room looking flustered. She dumped the stack of pages on the exam table like Exhibit A in the case of *Piedmont v. Miller*.

"I can't do anything with this," she announced with an unexpected sense of distance.

Karen got up on the exam table, Dr. Tien listened to her lungs and then added a prized bit of information:

"The lymph node, the tiny spot on the liver, and the one on the hip — they did not show up on the scan."

This joyful news came off more like a lunch order than a triumphal moment.

"Come back in four weeks and meet with Stephanie. Have you met with her before?"

"Not really," Karen replied. "I've only met with you."

With that, the appointment was over.

As we headed down the elevator, I asked Karen, "So, how was that for you?"

"Strange."

"You realize, that was a potential *sanskara* in the making."

"I think you're right."

"If Dr. Tien had made you feel strange or bad, that would have added a big *sanskara* to your emotional body."

"I was surprised, but Dr. Tien's response didn't affect me," Karen said with a smile. "I got my entire off-label regimen into my official medical record."

I loved watching my Tennessee girl stick it to the system.

"Isn't this the moment that we've been hoping for?"

"It is," Karen replied.

So, we kissed to celebrate the lymph node — our Gratitude Party Redux — right there in the elevator, and without any *sanskaric* residue.

Just to clarify, *sanskaras* may have earned a bad rap, but impressions are vital to our functioning.

Gurdjieff posited that there are three types of food, each fueling a metabolic process: the food we eat, the air we breathe, and lastly, the impressions we receive.

The first two foods are readily understood: We eat physical food, and it gets digested, metabolized, and excreted — nourishing the physical body.

We inhale the second type of food — oxygen enters the bloodstream, and carbon dioxide and water are released.

The calories from physical food nourish the physical. The *prana* from breathing fuels the metabolism, nourishes the subtle body and produces the marvelous buzz you feel after exercise. In-out, in-out, the human body functions as a metabolic machine.

But how are impressions a type of food?

Consider our sensory impressions (skin sensations, temperature, balance, vision, sound, etc.) We couldn't survive without a sensual context to our existence. These impressions anchor and orient the self in the vast sea of consciousness.

How about the caress of a lover, listening to Beethoven, or holding a baby? These impressions are also a type of food. They feed the soul and awaken higher energies. Conversely, slasher movies, death metal bands, and lying politicians are a type of junk food. They can leave a *sanskaric* residue.

We know that poor digestion can cause weight gain. But if impressions are a type of food, the incomplete metabolism of impressions — *sanskaras* — contribute to "egoic" weight gain.

To help metabolize impressions, Reshad taught the Clearing Exercise. When I lay in bed, right before sleep, I sense my body, starting at the toes and slowly sweeping to the head, allowing the impressions from the day to bubble up as feelings or images. In the exercise, you acknowledge these lingering impressions without judging or interpreting them. This effectively clears the impressions and releases the bind of the *sanskaras*.

According to Meher Baba:

The accumulated *sanskaras* determine each experience and action of the limited self. Just as several feet of film have to pass in a cinema to show a brief action on the screen, many *sanskaras* are often involved in determining a single action of the limited self.[12]

As I write this, the doorbell rings.

It was Rickie. He showed up with a wild tale that explained his disappearance after I gave him the $200. Rickie had been picked up by the police in Butts County, Georgia and arrested for public drunkenness. Rickie made the mistake of telling the cop he'd like to beat his ass, then kicked the squad car in anger. Rickie's outburst led to a string of charges that included "making terroristic threats" and "destroying government property."

Now a terrorist, bail was set high, but Rickie managed to post it. Rickie missed his first court date because the guy he had lined up to drive to Butts County had an alternator problem. Rickie phoned the D.A. who suggested turning himself in. Rickie saw this as a ploy and a quick trip to five months in jail while awaiting trial, so he didn't take the bait. Bounty hunters were now after him for jumping the $16,000 bail. Rickie moved to an unsafe part of town to hide out, but couldn't hack it and was now back in the neighborhood.

I listened to Rickie's story and saw Meher Baba's description of *sanskaras* played out like frames of film. In Rickie's five-second outburst, imagine 120 frames of film, a string of *sanskaras* playing out from alcoholism, violence in the family, quickness to anger, his sense of injustice, a gallbladder problem, and his penchant for unreliable friendships.

Society might say that Rickie made bad choices. From a *sanskaric* point of view, no choices were made. Rickie's karmic footage simply unspooled.

I let Rickie mow the lawn at my still-unsold *sanskaric* office

12. Meher Baba. 1987. Discourses. 7th edition. Myrtle Beach, S.C., U.S.A.: Sheriar Foundation.

building and gave him twenty bucks. When I drove over to check on him, I discovered Rickie drinking two big malt liquors. But, I didn't fire him on the spot. At this point, our karmic waves had *karassed* (using the Vonnegut sense of the word).[13]

Back to the chapter:

My plan was to take my Fortune question to Meher Baba. And since it was tea time at the Meher Center, I sought out Steve Klein who was visiting. Steve is a writer, poet and long-time Baba Lover who spent some years living in India in the 1970s and 80s. Steve also helped some of Baba's closest disciples write books about Meher Baba. I poured my tea and introduced myself.

"Hi, Steve, Bruce Miller. Remember me? I lent you the flashlight last night."

"Oh, yeah. Hi, Bruce."

"Steve, I'm intrigued by Meher Baba, particularly his views on karma and predestination. Can I ask you a question?"

"I'm not the authority," Steve replied, "but shoot."

"From Baba's teaching, is it all God's will," I asked? "Is it pointless to think we can do? Or do we need to make efforts?"

"It's one of those paradoxes," Steve explained. "Both seem to be true. Everything's predetermined, but you also feel like you have to do something. As long as you feel that, you have to do it. If you can't honestly accept that whatever happens is God's will and you think you're the one making efforts, then you have to take responsibility for your efforts."

"Sounds like we get to choose," I added.

"It's not easy to accept that it's all God's will," Steve continued, "because immediately you want to change some things. You know it's all God's will… but you hesitate — like maybe He made a mistake!"

We laughed at that, but the paradox, that doing and not doing both seem to be true, caught my interest.

---

13. Vonnegut, Kurt. *"karass. n. A network or group of people that unknown to them, are somehow affiliated or linked, specifically to fulfill the will of God."* From *Cat's Cradle.*

By definition, a paradox is self-contradictory. Doing is an illusion, but you must also make efforts. If you step back, a paradox always expresses an underlying truth. In this way, I began to view Fortune as a double-tier system: Effort versus effortlessness, self-identified versus self-aware, and *sanskara* versus freedom. Fortune is a breath mint and a candy mint. Your perception is not separate from reality.

Taking this further, I began to consider Fortune as a three-tier system — the Law of Three. Somewhere between effort and effortlessness, doing and not doing, we recognize synchronicity at play — the grace we experience as the universe flowing in our favor. The reconciling force of grace is the third force. In the truest sense of the word, effortlessness is the self-realized state. It is the witness — the stillness of mind amid the synchronous activity of life. It is a place of deep trust, surrender, and acceptance.

As Fortune would have it, Bill Le Page was visiting the Meher Center again from Australia. Bill is one of the few people still alive who knew Meher Baba as an adult. This might be my last chance to collar Meher Baba with my question — even if second-hand.

We gathered in the library to listen to Bill share memories from his time with Baba sixty years ago. I was struck by how Bill's brief moments with Baba formed the seed of his life journey. Bill cherished those moments. As he told the stories, I could sense the Baba lovers in the room longing to touch Baba through the hazy fragments of Bill's memory.

"Bill, what do you consider to be Baba's central message?" I asked. I was hoping Bill could pick out a clear signpost to Fortune's path.

"Of all the things," Bill replied, "I think if we were going to count up all the words that Baba used in various messages, the one he used most often was, 'Don't worry' — how important that is. At the bottom of his letters to us, he would emphasize, 'Don't worry.'"

"Don't worry? That's the big idea, don't worry?" I protested to myself, feeling short-changed by Baba's Alfred E. Neuman insight.

"The emphasis was so strongly on don't worry," Bill continued. "It's so clear that the real challenge we have is the agitated mind. The mind automatically worries about this or that. At every point, the mind is actively worrying about what was in the past."

"But worrying is so central to modern existence," I interjected. "Is Baba giving us permission to not worry?"

"Exactly."

"It's a radical notion to live without worry," I insisted.

"The challenge," Bill explained, "is that worry is a feature of a feverish mind. Do our worries feed the activeness of the mind? Or the feeling side and the love for God?"

"Okay," I continued. "More than just the activity of the mind, is Baba saying that our worries aren't legitimate?"

"No," Bill replied. "What he's saying is, 'Don't worry, turn to Me each time. Whatever is upon you, leave it to Me.' This is the extreme. The ideal would be that we live in such thought of God, that nothing else matters to us. But to get to that point, we have billions of impressions within us, not only within our consciousness but in the unconscious, impressions we've accumulated during the process of becoming humankind."

Bill paused for a moment and then shared, "There's a lovely saying from the Upanishads where it says, 'Everything that lives is full of the Lord. Enjoy, but do not covet.' You see, there's nothing wrong with enjoying. 'But do not covet.' Don't take it into yourself and identify yourself with that. 'And then hope for a hundred years of prayer and penance, so strong is one's pride in being Man.'"

Perhaps Bill — or Baba — was telling me: You can't outwit, unlock, or decode Fortune. Your pride will always get in the way.

And with that, our time at Baba Beach had come to an end. I can't say that I felt content with how Fortune's riddle played out. Amid the parade of Harleys snorting down the highway, Bobby McFerrin's happy-go-lucky pop song looped endlessly in my head.

"This can't be it," I complained. "There has to be a greater truth to life than a silly jingle! What about the Octave, the Law of Karma, Hazard, Law of Three and Seven, and *Sanskaras*? What about my all-compelling question: Does personal will, random chance, or divine destiny move the ball down the field? There has to be more!"

I located Bobby McFerrin's song on my device and plugged it into the sound system:

> Here's a little song I wrote,
> You might want to sing it note for note,
> Don't worry. Be happy.

Bobby McFerrin once saw a poster of Meher Baba and thought "Don't worry. Be happy" was a "pretty neat philosophy in four words." More than "pretty neat," I now saw those four words as the spiritual challenge to humankind:

> In every life we have some trouble,
> When you worry, you make it double.
> Don't worry. Be happy.[14]

Like a distant storm sending a gentle wave to my shore, I let the song wash over me. The entire year came back into focus: New Year's in the ER, Bhagwan encouraging Karen, "Tell her all will be OK," our refusal to be defined by the "C word," our secret word: *buoyancy*, the total financial wipe-out that never happened, my *sanskaras* dissolving in the middle of the lake, and synchronicity's unceasing attempts to penetrate my thick skull.

Finally, I have been humbly checkmated to recognize that Life does its thing perfectly.

We had finished our year of living precariously, but now the baton was being passed to Renee. As we pulled away from Baba Beach, Renee was at the pulpit in Emory University's Cannon Chapel for Julian's "Celebration of Life." I had sent my son to film the event and when we arrived home the video of Renee's eulogy was waiting. I watched Renee open her soul as she spoke to the standing-room crowd of mourners:

14. Bobby McFerrin "Bobby McFerrin – Don't Worry Be Happy". EMI-Manhattan Records 1988.

I got a real gift yesterday. Because we found out that Julian had died on Mother's Day, I didn't expect a Mother's Day card. Julian didn't have time for that crazy crap. He didn't think sending a card was important. But, I thought I would talk to him. And, it dawned on me: Wow, I didn't get a card; I didn't get a call, and this is my last Mother's Day with him.

Yesterday, [nearly a week after Julian's death] I was leaving the house. The mail had come, and I popped open the flap. I didn't really want to get the mail, but I just wanted to look. I saw this little glimpse. I could see Julian's name. I thought wow, that's a Mother's Day card. I'm not going to look at it right now. I'm going to keep it there. I'm going to savor this for a little bit. I don't think he wrote it, anyway. I bet his girlfriend, Kat, did it because she would do that.

I got home and my husband Jay had already arrived. He had the envelope on the table, and he said, "Renee, there's a card for you." I said, "I know." And I opened it. We opened it together. The cover showed two cats. There was a mama cat and a baby cat. The mama cat had her arm around the baby cat. The mom's saying, "I'm not mad. I'm just disappointed... AND MAD!"

I opened the card, and Julian wrote, "Mommy." Julian didn't say Mommy very often, even from a young age. It was probably Mother. The card says, "Happy Mother's Day from your Little Troublemaker."

Of course, I'm analyzing the whole time. Is this his handwriting? Is this really from him? He changes pens in the middle of it. They're the wrong ink; they don't match. It's him.

He wrote, "I love you so much. Thank you for being the greatest mom ever and always helping me through stuff. Love, Julian."

What's really miraculous: it's postmarked May 12, which was Tuesday. He died on the previous Saturday.

Kat was worried; she knew he'd sent it to me. She didn't ask him to buy the card. I don't know how he even had stamps.

Kat told me, "I thought that he probably put it in the post box and it didn't have stamps on it because he just wasn't worldly like that." But it did arrive, and he put two stamps on it instead of one just to make sure. They're Forever stamps, so they were definitely the right postage.

There are a lot of gifts in all of this. Julian is here, and I'm grateful for the connection and for his love.

I listened to Renee's words several times, but what touched me more were Julian's words, possibly composed in the final hours before he passed:

> "Mommy… I love you so much. Thank you for being the greatest mom ever and always helping me through stuff."

And there it was: Fortune. Like Meher Baba offering a prophetic flower outside of time, Julian's knowing soul shepherded his passage between the worlds. Fortune ensured that Julian's love for his "Mommy" would be sealed and sent before he passed and that his consoling words would somehow arrive on the eve of the celebration.

Our soul takes care of us, all through our lives. Eighteen months ago, our Unexpected Guest hand-delivered these comforting words to Karen and me in the ER. They provided the critical buoyancy, the sense of being guided, and the basis for a trust that would carry us through. I also know that our soul plays a mean game of hardball; the stakes are that high.

But now I know: When we let the stream of Fortune carry us toward the sea, we don't have to worry. In a crazy, subversive, and irresponsible way, it's okay to be happy.

It's okay to be happy because the script is written — and we get to make it up as we go along.

Epilogue

In the spiritual world, it is the unpredictable,
the unexpected that happens.
It is the realm of freedom.
It is spontaneity.
J.G. Bennett

I love movies based on real life, especially the "where are they now?" credits that play at the end. For this reason, I want to tie up some loose ends, especially after Jay, a psychotherapist in my neighborhood kindly offered to read my manuscript and shared, "Every time Reshad appeared in a scene, I wanted to yell at you, get out of there! Get away! Get away while you can!"

It's hard for people today to appreciate the heartfelt, mostly sentimental, spiritual phenomenon that characterized the dawn of the New Age. Beginning in 1973, practically to the day the Vietnam War ended, a mass inner migration sent millions of twenty-somethings in search of the spiritual antidote to Nixon, Watergate, and the untimely slaughter of 60,000 young Americans. The stars were pulling for a generational change.

I'm not cynical about my spiritual search. When the curtain pulled back at Reyes Peak, I had no choice. Reshad came into my life, and my unenviable task was to integrate the dark side of Reshad's school with the blazing spiritual brilliance of its moon.

I made a bargain with myself: "As long as I'm getting knowledge not offered elsewhere, I'll find a way both to keep my wits and stay in the fire." For the next 25 years, I stayed in that cauldron, a perseverance that built the inner foundation that forms the spine of this book.

But like all hero's journeys, the prodigal son's time with his teacher must come to an end, and my exit went down like this:

I was the leader of Reshad's school in the States during the summer of 1999, so I accepted the task of hosting his International Summer School. With Johanneshof gone, the torch was being passed back to the Americans after a decade in Europe. With just a few months to organize, and with Reshad and the Swiss not interested in the event, I plowed forward with my decision. I booked Shambhala Ranch, an off-the-grid retreat center in Mendocino, California.

The retreat invited Hazard at every level. My friend Sherill experienced a mild heart attack; Nick carried on with his usual swagger while suffering from undiagnosed lung cancer, and my friend, Joell arrived showing early signs of the schizophrenia that would later cause her demise. Unaccustomed to working in the cauldron, our food shopper mutinied (she had the thankless task of driving a winding 40 miles each day to the store). We also wrangled small children, skinny-dipped in a bullfrog pond, disco-danced during study sessions, hosted a clinically-depressed performance artist from the Netherlands, and whirled like Dervishes. The biggest jolt was Karen's out-of-the-blue announcement that she was planning to go to seminary and become a Presbyterian minister. Oy. Somehow, I managed to steer the ship through the storms and expand the tent for Reshad's school.

A couple months later, I wasn't surprised when Reshad came to Decatur and dissed the entire enterprise. He invited me to lunch, unfolded a napkin in the restaurant, pulled out a pen, and drew a dot.

"See this dot? This represents the center," Reshad explained.

Then he placed a second dot next to the first.

"This is another center."

"Okay," I replied not getting the drift.

"You can't have two centers."

At that moment, the 25 years came to an end. Not because Reshad was putting me in my place. It was his school, and I was the second dot. Maybe, he didn't need his protege messing with his turf — and I was okay with that. The relationship came to an end because I felt my solar plexus twitch — a counter-clockwise twitch to be exact. In all those years, even in the midst of mind-bending, outrageous excess, there was one constant — and that was the expansion of the heart.

Feeling my gut reverse and my heart tighten signaled that my learning and growing with Reshad was done.

A year later, I joined Reshad one last time. He invited me to introduce his talk at the Open Center in New York City. One unexpected bit of misfortune: Two weeks before the talk, the World Trade Center towers came crashing down. The routine lecture was now weighted with significance, aka Hazard. We were in SoHo, a few blocks from the carnage, and the air was still acrid with toxins and shock. Flowers, pleas, and prayers adorned impromptu fire house shrines in the neighborhood.

The New Yorkers wanted a message, some knowledge, a little hope, anything to salve their collective shock and fill it with meaning. Reshad and I sat in the green room, waiting to begin. I hadn't planned my remarks; I was more concerned with this new side to my spiritual teacher — he was nervous. Was the master showman out of his depth, not knowing how to connect with trauma so raw? Or maybe, his standard Sufi message would be off-pitch after a perceived Islamic attack.

We stumbled through the talk, but my heart was no longer in it. Afterward, I emailed the flock goodbye, euphemistically calling my exit a sabbatical.

Nick died right after the New York City talk. Years later, I pulled Nick's script out of the drawer. Hoping to salvage my Giovanni investment, I took my creative ax and chopped the script to the bone in search of the story's spine. Renaming it *Confidence Man*, I printed it out and prepared for a good read.

To my disappointment, Mort's Frankenstein still haunted the script. Nick never went through his hero's journey. He never tapped into the pain and alchemy needed to transform his dark experience into gold.

Miriam suggested that I retell the story from Nick's son, Mitchell's perspective. Mitchell came into the world while Nick and Giovanni toasted in a North Beach bar. In the new telling, Mitchell was now a young man.

The story would begin with the twenty-one-year-old Mitchell surrounded, Fellini-style, by the women in Nick's life. We see Nick's mistresses, girlfriends, patrons and benefactors standing cliff-side in Big Sur, tossing Nick's ashes into the Pacific. Casey, one of Nick's friends (who also lost all his money to Giovanni) reads the passage from Attar that Nick presciently shared during the final weeks of his life:

"There was a man, mad from the love of God. The mystical prophet, Khidr, said to the mad man: 'O perfect man, will you be my friend?'"

"The mad man replied: 'You and I are not compatible, for you have drunk long draughts of the water of immortality so that you will always exist, and I wish to give up my life. I am without friends and do not know even how to support myself. Whilst you are busy preserving your life, I sacrifice mine every day. It is better that I leave you, as birds escape the snare, so, goodbye.'"[1]

And like that, Nick escaped the snare of life.

After the cliff-side ceremony, in my new telling, Casey drives Mitchell back to Los Angeles. Along the way, Casey hands Mitchell a box of his dad's belongings. At the bottom of the box, Mitchell discovers the toxic screenplay.

Mitchell is shaken by the story and seeks out the same church pew in Santa Monica that started dad's journey with the greatest con man

---

1. Attar, Farid ud-Din, and Nott, C.S. 2000. The Conference of the Birds. Continuum.

on earth. Mitchell is already a party boy with an uncertain future. Sobbing in the pew, Mitchell realizes that he carries his dad's legacy. He sets out to complete the redemptive journey that foiled his father.

This new story angle excited me. Maybe, I could redeem the Frankenstein, but first I needed to find out more about Giovanni Mazza. Who was this man? Thanks to the invention of Google, I discovered the following op-ed in the New York Times. The article was published twenty years after my time with Giovanni.

GIOVANNI'S GIFT
By CHRISTOPHER MATTHEWS
The man who called himself Giovanni Mazza had, in Conrad's phrase, an air of having been wallowing all day, fully dressed, on an unmade bed.

Bald, overweight and sweating like he had Dengue fever, he stumbled into my restaurant well before noon and, with what might have been his last breath, implored me for glass of water. He collapsed onto a banquette without waiting for a reply.

I brought him a bottle of green-label Nepi. It turned out that Conrad wasn't far wrong: Giovanni had slept all night, fully dressed, on a park bench.

This was his story. While on a business trip from Los Angeles, where he produced movies, his wife's divorce lawyers had blocked his bank accounts and credit cards.

His cash had run out and now he was down and out in Rome — but he couldn't turn to his friends for help.

What a producer crucially depends on, Giovanni explained, is not so much his money but his ability to raise money. What counts is his credibility.

There wouldn't be a shred of that left if word got out that his Rome address was no longer the Hotel de Russie but Doria Pamphili park.

Maybe Giovanni named the films he'd produced, but if he did, they weren't ones I'd ever heard of.

He did have one claim to fame, however, and that was that he'd once paid $27,000 to rebuild the 45-foot-tall first "O" in the "Hollywood" sign above Los Angeles. Other sponsors included Hugh Hefner (Y), Gene Autry (L) and Alice Cooper (O).

In choosing my restaurant, Giovanni had come to the right place.

Some people react to being brutalized by calling at their workplace or school with an AK-47, selecting "automatic" and opening fire.

Instead, I'd opened a restaurant. I proposed to make people feel happier. This was my way of showing the Creator of the Universe there were better, kinder ways of treating people than what He or She had done to the woman I loved.

Not much of a business model, I know.

So I invited Giovanni to eat with us after we'd finished serving lunch. His troubles had left his appetite intact. In fact, he came back for dinner. And lunch the next day.

Fate, and his wife's lawyers, had been particularly cruel to him, he revealed forking a mouthful of Chef Angela's memorable honey-glazed coniglio.

When the rat-trap snapped on him he had been about to close the deal of his lifetime. He had a script any studio would do genocide for and George Clooney and Jennifer Lopez were anxious to sign up. If only he could get back to Los Angeles.

I naturally assumed Giovanni was a con man, and by the look of him not a very successful one. So it was shocking to discover that the green-bound manuscript he carried under his arm was brilliant.

It could have been written by Dan Brown. Jesus Christ (Clooney) returns to earth as promised. Like the first time round, his arrival is greeted with general skepticism but a few miracles are enough to enlist some followers, including Mariah Madeleine (Lopez) as the romantic interest.

With zillion-dollar corporate holdings at stake, the Vatican tries every dirty trick to stop the Messiah. Nothing doing. The pope then orders a concrete jacket for the Son of God.

I didn't mind that Giovanni was a con. For whatever his real intentions, he was clearly a partner, an accomplice in disaster, another human being whose life had at some point suffered a direct meteorite hit.

Losers owe each other a minimum of solidarity. I gave him a bed in a flat being renovated, and occasionally slipped him a €50 bill.

I suspect he knew I knew. But whatever the reason, although he sometimes verged on making what would be his usual pitch — a loan for the plane ticket to Los Angeles, plus hotel and limo expenses, in return for a cut of the profits on the film deal — he never did.

Instead, three weeks later he arrived for lunch with the news that he had found the money to go home. Maybe he sensed he was overstaying his welcome. Or he was getting tired of the food. At any rate, he left with this parting gift.

"I can't pay you back now," he said, "but one night a long black limousine will stop outside your restaurant, and George and J. Lo will, I promise, be inside. They will dine at your restaurant because Giovanni Mazza sent them."

For days after he left, I replayed the scene in my mind — the shining limo, the uniformed chauffeur opening the door, the glamorous movie stars stepping out.

It made my eyes shine like the mother scene in the movie classic when the faux Father Christmas turns out to be the real Santa after all because grown-ups have it wrong and reindeer do fly and Father Christmas is alive and living on the North Pole.

At the cinema, that's when you reach for the tissues because you suspended your normal disbelief in such claptrap an hour ago.

Similarly, in accepting Giovanni's gift I defiantly chose to disbelieve that the grim rules governing human affairs invariably preclude the occurrence of the whackily, outrageously impossible.

Sometimes, if you close your eyes, there's light at the end of the tunnel.

* * *

After three years the restaurant went belly up. One morning they cut off the electricity because I hadn't paid the bill for months and, worse, had run out of credit. Mafiosi from Naples have now taken over. They charge €200 a plate and presumably recycle narco-euros.

These days shiny black limousines stop outside all the time. One night Georgeous and J. Lo might be in one of them.

The irony isn't wasted on me. But what do I care? I'm waiting for The Second Coming (Part I) to hit the screen.

Christopher Matthews opened a restaurant in Rome after his wife died. He returned to his usual business of selling words when it folded. [2]

2. Matthews, Christopher. 2009. "Giovanni's Gift - The New York Times." October 8. http://www.nytimes.com/2009/10/09/opinion/09iht-edmatthews.html.

Giovanni's gift, Nick's gift, Mory's gift, Dede's gift, Reshad's gift, Bhagwan's gift, Meher Baba's gift, Julian's gift, and all of the hidden teachers' gifts — thank you and bless your hearts.

Who else belongs in this epilogue?

I'd like to give a shout-out to single-mom Mandy. She just returned from Italy and took off yesterday to lead a yoga retreat in Mexico. She has another one coming up in Maui. Her Form Yoga business is booming, and she just signed a lease for a larger studio across town.

And what about my business? For the two years I worked on this book, my former office sat unsold and empty — guzzling $2500 per month out of our business bank account until it hit zip.

One month after we put the building on the market, Jason Carter, Jimmy Carter's grandson, sought a short-term rental for his campaign office. Carter offered $1500 per month, which would pull the listing off the market for ten months and hit us with a $10,000 loss. My basic business sense declined the offer. Plus, Matthew was a staunch Republican.

Ten months later (the day Jason Carter would have been moving out), a young couple approached wanting to start a dog-training school. They offered $2800 per month for a year with a contract to purchase for $500,000 after 12 months — our top dollar price. I was eager, but Matthew declined because he didn't want to tie up the property for another year and he didn't want dog smell in the building. A little later, we got three low-ball offers of $400k. Like a Vegas loser in too deep, we couldn't bear to leave $100k on the table.

We finally sold the building 12 months later (the day the dog school deal would have closed at $500,000), but to a job placement firm for $420,000. Adding it up, if we had followed Fortune's flow without questioning, we'd be $125,000 richer. Yes, the knots finally untied, and the river reached the sea, but with expensive whitewater along the way.

Speaking of whitewater, the past year brought some challenging passages to my friends. Remember Sarah? And how she put her list into the New Year's fire and bumped into Joe at a dance? Sarah and Joe had a sexually fulfilling, yet emotionally difficult fifteen-year relationship — even buying an unmarried house together. Sarah loved Joe — that is until his eyes began to seek out other women at the dance events they enjoyed together.

The dance events led to tantra events, and then to something called a "play party." When Joe announced that he wanted a "polyamorous" relationship, Sarah put her foot down. Despite her valiant efforts to salvage the relationship, including, at her therapist's suggestion, attending a play party to demonstrate her willingness-to-stretch, Joe left her. The pain was overwhelming. Sarah went through all five of Kubler-Ross's stages of grief — especially, full-blown anger.

I tell the story because Sarah is in her late 60s. The sinking sense that she may never have another lover hit her hard. As she remarked, "The pubic hairs are getting gray."

Somehow, Sarah rode the waves of grief all the way to the other side. "Acceptance" was the tough one, but she did it. Seven months later (the Octave thing) three men simultaneously seek her affection.

"Isn't that the ultimate irony?" she remarked. "Joe wanted polyamory, and here I am trying to figure out how to juggle relationships with three men when all I wanted was one."

And Polyamorous Joe? Going off-script, he quickly got married.

On a happy note, Miriam's flirtation with the Lottery has blossomed. She is now a full-fledged Lotto savant. "A thought comes to me," Miriam explained, "'Blue ticket at the Publix.' I do my best to ignore the impulse until it becomes impossible to avoid. I made $317 in the last three days."

Maybe, the universe is compensating Miriam for her tireless work as the Unexpected Guest, holding hands in the hospital and reading fortuitous passages for friends in need.

On a sad note, Julie, our Baba lover friend, discovered that she has early onset Parkinson's disease. She shared the news during a visit while she was traveling to Alabama to see her dad who was dying of cancer.

"When I found out I had Parkinson's, I felt strangely buoyant about it," Julie confided during a long walk with me. The leaden swing in Julie's arm gave it away. Understandably, Julie's instinct was to reboot her life.

"I'd like to quit my job and go to Meherabad in India to work in Baba's clinic as a nurse practitioner," she confided.

Over the next couple months, Julie began to work with several practitioners to support her healing journey. The next time we talked, her vision had shifted.

"I plan to become a Parkinson's coach and help others find a path through the disease," Julie shared.

And then, last week, we got a call from Alabama. Julie was with her dad during his final hours. And with the loss came an opening.

"It was amazing," Julie shared beaming. "This man, Clint, was helping my dad's cancer with a Rife machine that he is developing. He's been able to come the closest to generating Rife's frequencies."

A Rife machine is based on the work of Royal Raymond Rife, an American inventor in the 1920s who developed a method of beaming precise electromagnetic frequencies (like sound waves) to treat diseases. Rife observed bacteria and cancer cells under a high-powered microscope while applying different combinations of frequencies. Rife's results have never been successfully repeated (and his machine lives on the list of official quacks), but Clint's machine appears to be showing results.

As Julie shared her story, I sensed Fortune making a big entrance.

"My brother offered to purchase one of Clint's machines to see if it would help with my Parkinson's," she explained. "So, I visited Clint to get started and…"

Julie paused to take a big breath.

"And! We fell in love!" Julie beamed. "Totally in love. Clint and I are going to work together. Who would have expected that with my dad passing, this other door would open?"

The next time Julie visited, I asked how her Parkinson's was going.

"What's giving the best results," I asked, "the L-dopa therapy, Rock Steady Boxing, or having a lover to cuddle with in bed?"

Julie paused to consider.

"To be honest, none of these," Julie replied. "Working on my attitude is making the biggest difference."

Chalk one up for buoyancy.

And then there's Tommy, the alcoholic painter and Rickie his alcoholic buddy. Rickie, being stronger and more often sober, was always concerned about Tommy's precarious health. Recently, we learned that Rickie died suddenly from a massive hemorrhage. Fortune's capricious ways never cease to surprise.

Today marks the two-year mark since Karen's initial diagnosis and the one-year mark since the ill-fated "Gratitude Party." As we worked in the kitchen preparing for New Year's "Third Time's the Charm" party, the phone rang with an ominous sense of doctor déjà vu. Blessedly, it was Dr. Mark Renneker, our San Francisco surfer-oncologist.

Karen and Mark discussed her medical progress; then Mark asked the question:

"Karen, when you talk to Dr. Tien, how does she characterize where you're at?"

"Well, she's very encouraging and pleased that the CT scans are stable."

"Stable implies that you have active disease that is not progressing," Mark explained. "That's not what we have here. How do you think of yourself?"

"I feel very positive that I'm doing so well," Karen replied.

"Karen, You... Are... Cancer... Free," Mark pronounced stressing each word.

Karen and I absorbed the significance of Mark's pronouncement while he continued.

"You have a lot to be proud of. You have a life-affirming attitude, and it's inspiring to watch you take it one rung at a time, but you haven't stopped. You are in a great place. I'm proud of you."

After reading this book, you might be trying to piece together Karen's regimen. How did she go from stage 4 lung cancer with a brain metastasis, to becoming healthier than before? I've described her health journey as following the "breadcrumbs," with a mix of conventional and alternative therapies, and bolstered by continuous soul work. At its core, the success of Karen 2.0 was a life reboot, a stop-start-change that broke the pattern of the past.

There was a similar story in the news of Mark Pischea, a 42-year-old sufferer of Crohn's disease who was told his only remaining options were a sixth surgery or the removal of his stomach. Feeling ready to die, Pischea opted for a Hail Mary trip to the Amazon. It was his wife's suggestion, but he scored points for following her intuition. The Peruvian shamans induced vomiting several times a day with plant medicinals and prescribed the hallucinogen ayahuasca and the venom of a rain forest tree frog. The goal, a total reboot of his immune system. Four months later, Pischea was free of Crohn's symptoms and the debilitating depression that came with the sickness.[3]

Rebooting is rarely a pleasant affair. A few months after Karen's chemo and radiation, and while deep into her alternative journey, Karen developed a debilitating case of shingles. Mark surmised that the shingles might have rebooted her compromised immune system back into high gear.

And just to blow your mind: Moye, the husband of our beloved Bosnian housekeeper, was suffering from lung cancer at the same time as Karen. With impassioned gestures and halting English, Moye shared a cancer remedy he learned from a friend. You get a large piece of smoked pork and eat one slice per day for thirty days. The pork regimen, plus a large dose of buoyancy, (and let's not forget chemo and radiation), did the trick. Moye is on the mend.

One other story: A few weeks ago, Karen called from Charleston, SC where she was serving on three committees for professional

3. Gregoire, Carolyn. "Scientists Put Shamanic Medicine Under The Microscope." The Huffington Post. N.p., 16 Oct. 2015. Web. 7 Oct. 2016.

certification. That's right; she now sits on the other side of the hot seat in the evil Committee, now passing judgment on shit-scared candidates.

"Bruce, I had a whole different experience about the Committee now that I'm on the other side of it," Karen shared. "I saw how hard the Committee members work, that they have to read all the student's materials, write reports, and invest themselves in the process — and it is completely volunteered. I could also see myself in the student's position. I was rooting for them, 'Don't get stuck, express yourself; show up as who you are.'"

There's one other person who belongs in the epilogue — me. If you're reading this book, then I will have pulled off a coup, turning my psycho-emotional-financial disaster into Fortune, not measured in dollars, but into a body of work that gives meaning and context to my life.

The "swimming across the lake" experience continues to deepen. Is it "pleasurable?" Let's just say it's "curious" to watch this fellow Bruce. He says the right words and performs the right actions without much effort. Maybe, it's all just happening!

Best of all, the synchronous universe still has a sense of humor. Last week, I received an unsolicited email from Christine, a friend I hadn't seen in a year:

Subject: Angel Visit
Dear Bruce,
The time of your Angel visit will be this Friday night at 10:30pm!
Some pretty wonderful things happened while they were here, so I am sending them to you with great expectations for some cool things to happen.
Please let me know what happens!
XXXOOOO
Christine

So, Gabriel, Michael, Raphael, Uriel, and Metatron get to have the last word.

Gotta cut this short. I'm rushing out for a Seven-Day candle, white flower, and apple. I don't have any expectations, but my door is always open for cool things to happen.

Acknowledgements

I would like to thank all my teachers for priming my journey of self-discovery.

Mory Berman demonstrated how writing your opus, no matter how humble, provides a frame to recognize the story of your life.

Thanks to Philip Shepherd for landing at our doorstep, belly brain fully awakened, just when Karen and I began to collide with Fortune.

I humbly acknowledge Reshad Feild who guided me to the esoteric path and the Sufi embrace of unity. As an Octave magician, Reshad inspired my life question around Fortune. As a prolific author, he demonstrated the style that I would later adopt — blending memoir and philosophy so that each reinforces the other.

And I am deeply grateful to Dr. Bhagwan Awatramani who demolished my philosophies and guided me to the self. He continues to show me how, in the stillness of mind, Fortune unfolds without effort.

Parts of this book started from a CaringBridge blog launched during Karen's hospitalization. I would like to thank Karen's many friends who suggested putting my ramblings into a book.

Thanks to my steadfast friends who kept me going as the chapters emerged, including Richard Rozsa, Amy Lighthill, Eleanor Hand, Subhana Ansari, Jeff Black, and our ever-present angel, Miriam. Writing a first book raises a host of doubts. Your encouragement propelled me across the finish line.

I would also like to thank the contributors who shared their most intimate journeys, including Mandy Roberts, Maria Cadena Hoffman, Renee Hall-George, Julie Andrews, Nancy Verre, Lynden Harris, and so many others. Also to Nicoli Bailey for her astrology insight, Jill Hendrix for our back cover photo, and to Richard Webb for sharing the blow-by-blow that Karen and I mercifully missed at our wedding.

Special thanks to Sallie Anderson, who starting at age 14, embarked on an unexpected transformation from typical teen to virtuoso opera singer. Unfortunately, the chapter's length forced me to cut her *Garden Variety Miracle*. Sallie demonstrated how when you you let life inform you, miracles unfold from within.

My scoundrel-in-arms, Nick Saxton, may he rest in peace, also gets special acknowledgment. In addition to dragging me into a heap of misfortune, Nick pushed me artistically, even from the other side, to plant my passion into each page so that this book would grow.

I want to thank my two sons, Jacob and Nathaniel, for not freaking out while I invested countless hours into the uncertainties of writing while our financial ship was sinking. A special thanks to my RISD student, Jacob for dissing my attempts at cover design and visualizing the yin yang design at the final hour.

Finally, this book only exists through the love and courage of my beautiful wife, Karen. Thank you for taking a bullet by sharing your most intimate thoughts and feelings so that others might discover the wisdom of their own healing journeys.

— Bruce Miller

A Message from the Author

Dear Reader,

Thank you for taking the plunge with a self-published book from a first-time author.

I rely 100 percent on referrals and reviews from people like you to reach new readers. Please take a moment to write a few words on the retail site where you purchased this book.

If you would like to connect with me regarding the ideas in the book, please visit www.ithou.com. You may also be interested in my professional work at: www.milleremedia.com

Best Regards,

Bruce Miller